Global Masculinities

Series Editors
Michael Kimmel
Dept of Sociology
Stony Brook University
Stony Brook, NY, USA

Judith Kegan Gardiner
University of Illinois at Chicago
Chicago, IL, USA

The dramatic success of Gender Studies has rested on three developments: (1) making women's lives visible, which has also come to mean making all genders more visible; (2) insisting on intersectionality and so complicating the category of gender; (3) analyzing the tensions among global and local iterations of gender. Through textual analyses and humanities-based studies of cultural representations, as well as cultural studies of attitudes and behaviors, we have come to see the centrality of gender in the structure of modern life. This series embraces these advances in scholarship, and applies them to men's lives: gendering men's lives, exploring the rich diversity of men's lives - globally and locally, textually and practically - as well as the differences among men by class, race, sexuality, and age.

More information about this series at
http://www.palgrave.com/gp/series/15013

Ashwiny O. Kistnareddy

Migrant Masculinities in Women's Writing

(In)Hospitality, Community, Vulnerability

Ashwiny O. Kistnareddy
University of Cambridge
Cambridge, UK

Global Masculinities
ISBN 978-3-030-82578-2   ISBN 978-3-030-82576-8   (eBook)
https://doi.org/10.1007/978-3-030-82576-8

This Palgrave Macmillan imprint is published by the registered company Springer Nature Switzerland AG.
The registered company address is: Gewerbestrasse 11, 6330 Cham, Switzerland

Migration is an expression of the human aspiration for dignity, safety and a better future. It is part of the social fabric, part of our very make-up as a human family.

—Ban Ki-Moon

For my parents and my brother.

ACKNOWLEDGEMENTS

This book draws its breath from my own personal experiences and those of the people around me. As I began to formulate my ideas, Hughes Azérad was the first guiding hand on my path, from the proposal to the first draft. Hugo has been a source of inspiration, boundless references and a great buffer for all the initial ideas. Ian James has provided the spur I needed in the second chapter. His useful comments, and his own writing, inform my work in the third chapter, and so it is that I owe him for different reasons. Emma Wilson has been wonderful and inspiring. Her comments have allowed me to think beyond but also curtail my writing. For the guidance, the camaraderie and the beautiful way you treat us all, thank you so much. Many thanks to Amaleena Damlé and Sura Qadiri for their thoughts on parts of an earlier version of this manuscript. My gratitude also goes to Martin Crowley and Françoise Lionnet, whose advice and suggestions have also informed this book. Many thanks to Laura McMahon who has been very supportive and encouraged me in every possible way since I have met her.

I would not have been able to complete this project without the support of the French section of the MMLL faculty and Lucy Cavendish College, Cambridge. I was awarded the Evelyn Povey Award (2017–2020), and several grants and awards funded some of the trips to conferences. I was also awarded the Ruth Tomlinson Award. Other conference trips were funded by the Odette de Mourgues Award from the French section, which I benefitted from in 2018 and 2019. SFS and ASMCF funded the French conference I co-organized in 2019. Magdalene College, Trinity College and the Mellon fund provided funding for the other symposia I organized in 2018 and 2019. I conducted research at the BNF in Paris in July 2019, supported by the Santander Mobility Grant and the MMLL Faculty field-work funding.

My gratitude also to Annette Mahon at Lucy Cavendish College who made sure I had the support I needed to complete the initial draft of this book. The College librarians at both Lucy Cavendish College and Gonville & Caius College will always have a special place in my heart for their kindness and their flexibility. Since I won the Contemporary Women's Writing Essay Prize in 2019 and a Special Commendation in 2020, I was able to access resources and was gifted books from OUP, for which the CWWA has my heartfelt gratitude.

A much-edited version of part of Chap. 2 has been published in Québec Studies under the title 'Elsewhere Home: Hospitality, Affect and Language in Ying Chen's *Les lettres chinoises* and Kim Thúy's *Vi*' (Vol. 71, 2021).

Of course thanks will never be complete without a special message to those friends old and new who know who they are, and who have my respect, loyalty and love always.

My biggest debt of gratitude, as ever, is towards my parents and my brother. Their continued support and guidance accompany me in all my endeavours. This project, as with anything I undertake, carries their indelible mark. Merci pour tout.

CONTENTS

About the Author

Ashwiny O. Kistnareddy is Bye-Fellow and Director of Studies in Modern and Medieval Languages at Lucy Cavendish College, University of Cambridge. She lectures and teaches for the Faculty of Medieval, Modern Languages and Linguistics at the University of Cambridge. She completed her PhD in French at the University of Cambridge. Her first monograph, *Locating Hybridity: Creole, Identities and Body Politics in the Novels of Ananda Devi*, was published in 2015. She has published a number of articles on Ananda Devi, Kim Thúy, Léonora Miano, Fatou Diome, Maryse Condé, Nathacha Appanah and Malika Mokeddem. She won the *Contemporary Women's Writing Prize* in 2019 and won a Special Commendation for the same prize in 2020. She has co-edited a volume with Alice Roullière, *Catching Up with Time: Belatedness and Anachronies in Francophone Literature and Culture* (2021). Forthcoming are *Refugee Afterlives: Contemporary Diasporic Vietnamese Narratives* (2022), *Refugee Childhoods* and *Refuge*.

ABBREVIATIONS

In this book, I will be using the following shortened titles:

Léonora Miano

Afropean Soul et autres histoires (2008a)	*Afropean*
Tels des astres éteints (2008b)	*Tels*
Marianne et le garçon noir (2017a)	*Marianne*
Crépuscule du tourment 2 (2017b)	*Crépuscule 2*

Fatou Diome

Le Ventre de l'Atlantique (2003)	*Ventre*

Assia Djebar

Ces Voix qui m'assiègent (1999)	*Ces Voix*
Nulle part dans la maison de mon père (2007)	*Nulle part*

Ananda Devi

Les Hommes qui me parlent (2011)	*Les Hommes*

Ying Chen

Les Lettres chinoises (1993)	*Lettres chinoises*
La Lenteur des montagnes (2014)	*Lenteur*

Shorter titles, such as Kim Thúy's *Ru* (2010), *Mãn* (2013) *Vi* (2016) and *Em* (2020) and Malika Mokeddem's *Mes Hommes* (2005), remain unchanged.

CHAPTER 1

Introduction

Tu as été élevé ainsi, conditionné ainsi. […]
tu es prisonnier de ta nature d'homme.
—*Devi, Les Hommes*

My first thoughts on masculinities were ineludibly linked to my family and
the changes which I could see occurring within the family unit as we
moved to the UK. As we negotiated life in a host society with new values
and different positions be they in the family or in society, I grew aware of
the alterations within my family as shifts occurred through work, through
education and as each member had to readjust to new challenges and a
range of experiences, including gender hierarchies. The ways in which
masculinities are affected by these paradigmatic changes became central to
my reflections after I published a critical analysis of the notion of hybridity
in Ananda Devi's novels,[1] at the end of which I wanted to reflect on what
my conclusions had generated in terms of further avenues for study. In my
reading of Devi's novels, the sensitivity with which she writes about men
and masculinities in *Les Hommes* opened up possibilities for thinking about
men, not necessarily as oppressors, but as individuals who are sometimes
victims of the laws of patriarchy and petrified definitions of masculinities.

[1] Kistnareddy (2015a).

I found this notion compelling as I began to examine the work of other immigrant women writers foregrounding the full range of experiences of migration and its effects on migrants, who often were men, and, later, as they settle and become immigrants, on their offspring.[2] Their portrayal of masculinities,[3] not only as a means of explicating their own trajectories as women who have emigrated from non-Western countries, into France and Canada, and their reassessment of the positionality of men, were particularly inspiring. While they look to patriarchy ineluctably as establishing modes of constructing masculinities, they do not emphasize themselves as victims but as agents of change. The present study stems from my interest in immigrant women writers' conceptualization of men as equally vulnerable human beings subject to the complexities of migration, which destabilize their own notion of masculinities. Migration and masculinities become interconnected in this analysis as I contend that it is precisely the process of migration and its attendant losses and gains that are conducive to the reshaping of the concept of masculinities.

Migration itself is a complex notion as an overview of recent discussions makes abundantly clear. David Coleman claims that 'many of the events driving it [are] unpredictable' (2015: 376). Coleman examines both the demographic migration entails, and the economic ramifications on host countries in Europe. According to Fatima El-Tayeb, for a long time, the discourse has centred on 'migrants and their contested ability to adapt to European societies' (2011a), 'but paradoxically, these debates have seen little change over the last five decades—their focus often is still on the moment of arrival and "what if" scenarios: namely, what happens to Europe if these people stay' (2011b: xii). El-Tayeb points out that 'the face of Europe has changed accordingly' (2011b: xii). Karen O'Reilly asserts that 'international migration is now a *normal* feature of

---

[2] The Migration Observatory at the University of Oxford notes that although the dictionary distinguishes between migrants (entering a country for a short term) and immigrants (long-term stay and settling down), often these terms are used 'interchangeably in public debate and even among research specialists [...] No two definitions of migrant are equivalent, and their effects on our understanding of migration and its impact are significant' (Migration Observatory 2020). For the purpose of this study, I use the dictionary distinctions to differentiate between the two categories. The authors are referred to as 'immigrant' women and the protagonists are referred to as migrants or immigrants, depending on the circumstances at hand, or (im)migrants when both categories apply.

[3] I use 'masculinities' in keeping with the notion that each society defines masculinity in different ways, and it is shaped and reshaped in diverse situations.

contemporary societies; a global phenomenon of flows and counter-flows; geographical fluidity rather than population shifts' (2015: 25). Nonetheless, her statement regarding the relative normalcy associated with global mobility in the contemporary world must be nuanced: mobilities can occur within the same country, within the same continent, from the Global South to the Global South,[4] as well as from the East to the West, or the Global South to the Global North and vice versa. Imbricated in the notion of migration are complex questions of borders and power dynamics.[5] With the upsurge in the number of refugees and asylum seekers moving across borders, often in grim and precarious circumstances, Deirdre Hughes et al. (2019) remind us that we must distinguish between migrants and refugees since they have distinct legal statuses as per Amnesty International.[6] In addition, they underscore the fact that there is a human aspect to displacement which is shared by both categories, insofar as it involves 'addressing trauma, displacement, mental health, transitional readjustment' (2019: 2). It is precisely this human, individual, affective experience of migration which interests me in this book.

Mobility often generates new paradigms that are lived differently by each individual. As Emma Bond suggests in her introduction to her analysis of migrant bodies, 'identity and self-imaginings are affected by the often multiple shifts afforded by migration' (2018: 2). Migrants might be impelled to re-evaluate their gendered roles and preconceived ideas about what a man's or a woman's role might be in the new space they come to inhabit. Indeed, they might interrogate gender binaries and hetero-patriarchies. Nevertheless, there are instances where individuals cling on to their home societies' values and culture, thereby complicating the process of integration and negotiating life in the host society, as I argue in this analysis. In particular, I consider the extent to which divergent experiences of (im)migration from different geographical spaces ultimately generate similar feelings and have consonant effects on those who migrate by their own volition or by force. The writers whose texts I examine provide

[4] For Dados and Connell, 'The phrase "Global South" refers broadly to the regions of Latin America, Asia, Africa, and Oceania. It is one of a family of terms, including "Third World" and "Periphery," that denote regions outside Europe and North America, mostly (though not all) low-income and often politically or culturally marginalized' (2012: 12).

[5] See Song (2018).

[6] Migrants have definite or indefinite leave to remain depending on their situation. Refugees are allowed to stay as per human rights conventions. See Amnesty International (2018).

valuable insights into lived experiences of migration, into the events unfolding or imagined through creative processes. Through their texts, alternative means of conceptualizing the home, race, language, relationships, family, gender and, in particular, for this study, masculinities as transformed through migration are garnered. The intersection between masculinities and migration has been explored by Michael Kimmel in a chapter on global masculinities in *Misframing Men: The Politics of Contemporary Masculinities* (2010). The chapter informs the premise that for a long time, men migrated first, and the rest of the family either followed later or remained in situ in the country of origin. Providing for the family while grappling with a new society can also be a part of a new form of trauma which is induced by societal pressures and values. Ideals of masculinity and the models instilled by the home society at times fail.[7] These (im)migrant men discover new ways of understanding their new circumstances, adapting their version of masculinities and readjusting it to the new situation they are experiencing, or sometimes fail to do so.[8] The destabilization encountered can also stem from women and children being educated or beginning to work. Thus leaving the family home. Consequently, this results in some migrant men feeling they are not sufficient providers.[9] Equally there are men who are loathe to countenance shifts in societal positions as their sense of masculinity is eroded by male-female equality in the work place, as well as being deemed to be racial others in the host society.[10]

The women writers themselves are immigrants who have managed to take advantage of socio-economic mobility or were refugee children. While they represent a range of geographical origins and values, they have all settled in either France or Canada, and write in French. Contrary to most women of their time, in their countries of origin, they have been educated and have overcome the obstacles imposed upon them due to their gender. While they do portray women in their texts, their treatment of men and the relationship between masculinities and the experiences of

[7] For more on this notion see the work accomplished by Donaldson, Hibbins et al. (2009), Carabí and Armengol (2014). See also Vasquez de Aguila (2014), Idriss (2017).

[8] See also Silverman (1992).

[9] In cases where it is the women who have emigrated to work, leaving the men to take care of the household and childcare duties, as is the case in Vietnam, this has led to considerable pressures to live up to masculine ideals while undertaking traditionally feminine roles. See Ahn Hoang and Yeoh 2011).

[10] See Kimmel et al. (2005), Kimmel (2013) and Hearn et al. (2013).

(im)migration enables me to thread through the common vectors of their narratives. As with Devi, in *Les Hommes*, these immigrant women writers adopt a different approach to masculinities as suffering under the yoke of patriarchy, to men as bearing the burden of their communities and being weighed down by traditions. The initial experiences of nostalgia for the country of origin, the lack of linguistic ability for those who have little grasp of French, the experience of rejection due to physical alterity, the clash of cultures or different permutations of the above are present in the texts I examine. The texts grapple with nostalgia, family commitments, desire, control, power and how these are manifested along gender lines.

In 1995, Raewyn Connell published a foundational text, *Masculinities*, which articulated the notion of hegemonic masculinity. The text altered the ways in which masculinity was understood as simply being a set of characteristics attributed to men. Masculinities became relational to femininity, hierarchical with 'weaker' men being deemed inferior; they became something that could be women's purview too. There were many criticisms levelled against Connell's concept, which she later addressed,[11] but she remains one of the pioneers of masculinity studies who recognizes that men too can be victims and thus vulnerable.[12] I engage with Connell's concept several times in this book. For me, it is imperative to address the following questions: Is vulnerability necessarily a weakness or is it a way of emphasizing the humanity linking human beings? Do immigrant women writing about men introduce a completely different perspective to masculinities as they change through immigration, and indeed, through the new environment and values? Do masculinities acquire a different aspect which women writers can harness through their imagination, their narratives?

In a recent article published in *Men and Masculinities*, Stephen Horlacher explores the links between narrative and masculinities. For Horlacher, the concept of 'masculinity' seems to:

> differ from culture to culture, from location to location, and from historical era to historical era [...] synchronically as well as diachronically, leading to a kind of contemporaneity of the noncontemporaneous (sic); it differs intersectionally according to age, religion, education, ethnicity, and so on [...]. (2019: 76)[13]

[11] See Connell and Messerschmidt (2005).
[12] See also Reeser and Seifert (2008), Reeser (2010).
[13] See also Buchbinder (2013).

Masculinities are understood as 'having a largely discursive, textual, or narrative relational structure and as consisting of complex, differentiated, and dynamic subject positions' (2019: 76). The critic underscores the need to pay 'special attention to stories and genres as the paramount components of historical and current constructions of masculinities', since, after all, it is more productive to understand masculinities as a 'performative and narrative concept' (2019: 76–77). Horlacher aligns himself with Winfried Fluck's notion of 'self narrative', which stresses the fact that 'social narratives [...] may provide cultural frames of and furnish genre and plot structures for self-narration, but we still have to turn these into the scripts of our own life' (2013: 52). I draw on his concept in the first chapter, with reference to Thúy's text, *Vi*, since Horlacher states that 'literature can be regarded as a particularly effective medium for the creation of alternative masculinities beyond what is deemed acceptable within a specific culture' (2019: 82).

Significantly, Anne M. François writes that 'post-colonial literature [...] has revalorized the neglected female experience and agency as well as the notion of migration' (2011: xv). Discussing Caribbean women writers, François underlines the fact that women's writing must feature prominently in discussions of migration. Similarly justifying her inclusion of Francophone women writers from all parts of Africa in *Francophone African Women Writers: Destroying the Emptiness of Silence*, Irene Assiba d'Almeida argues that:

> Francophone women writers from different parts of the continent have different intellectual, social, and religious backgrounds, they hold various ideological stances: they are endowed with different writing skills. Yet they also have much in common: they share a history of colonialism, they generally live in highly patriarchal societies, and their life experience is informed by the fact that they are women. (1994: x)

The critic's point regarding the plausibility and possibility of comparing a range of backgrounds based on their commonality of experience as women living under patriarchy, albeit with singular understandings, informs my choice of comparing a range of writers in this analysis. Crucially, for her, 'for women's position to change, society has to change, and therefore they have become social critics to create insight into, and a vision of, what the future could hold' (1994: 123). While Assiba d'Almeida's purport was specifically geared towards altering the perception of women's writing and its position in Africa, I discuss new visions of masculinities in immigrant women's writing as a compelling and novel notion which merits further examination.

In *Le Masculin dans les œuvres d'écrivaines françaises*, Françoise Rétif argues that women who write about men are doing so '[en] bravant tous les aspects de l'assignation générique, qui voudrait si possible leur refuser de croire à l'écriture' (2016: 7). Rétif elucidates this further:

> Représenter les personnages masculins, cela consiste pour elles dans un premier temps à transgresser des frontières pour s'interroger sur un genre en quelque sorte inconnu, cet autre […] soi disant pourvu de tout ce qui leur manque et ayant accès à tout ce qui leur est interdit ou dont elles sont exclues. (2016: 8)

For Rétif, coming to writing for women ineludibly involves a 'mise en question' of masculinities and the masculine world in its different manifestations. Literature creates the conditions for such an interrogation to occur. In many cases, women writers have been confronted with prejudice and patriarchal oppression, which they foreground in their texts. Yet coming to writing (about) men is not a process of revolt or subversion. Rather, in the midst of writing, immigrant women writers accentuate the transformative experience of migration, and the evolving faces of masculinities. Their texts expose a distinct conceptualization of men and women as equal in suffering, and vulnerability as generated by migration and contact with their host country. The pain endured due to displacement and especially, the lack of hospitality and belonging experienced by (im)migrant men in their host societies, are depicted sensitively as a means of highlighting the suffering of men who are taught to remain stoic as part of the values inculcated to them in their home societies, as portrayed in the texts. The act of writing (about) men thus becomes a way of interrogating gendered experiences of (im)migration for women writers.

The process by which I arrived at the shortlist of works to be included was a complex one as I wanted to focus exclusively on women writers who have immigrated into France or Canada, who write from within these spaces and whose main protagonists have migrated into the same countries as they did. It was important that they should be writing from these two contexts so that I could compare how each space shapes the ways in which (im)migrant masculinities are envisaged. Thus, writers towards whom I had originally oriented my research were subsequently excluded, such as Maryse Condé, who is based in the USA and Guadeloupe, and whose works are firmly set in her native island; and Nina Bouraoui, who was born in France, to a French mother and Algerian father, and who spent the first part of her life in Algeria and moved to France as a teenager. Similarly Nathacha Appanah whose text *Blue Bay Palace* (2005) I initially thought of including, did not make it to the final list as the narrative is set in Mauritius. Two of the women writers whose works initially interested me, Faiza Guène (*Un homme ça ne pleure pas* (2014)) and Saphia Azzedine (*Mon père est femme de ménage* (2009)), were later eliminated as the first was born and raised in France, and the second immigrated as a very young child and, therefore, grew up in France.

My final choice of Chen's *Lettres chinoises* (1993) and *Lenteur* (2014), Thúy's *Ru* (2009) and *Vi* (2016), Devi's *Les Hommes* (2011), Mokeddem's *Mes hommes* (2005), Djebar's *Nulle part* (2007), Diome's *Ventre* (2003), and Miano's *Afropean* (2008a), *Tels* (2008b), and *Crépuscule 2* (2017b), alongside her essays, offers a diverse corpus spanning a range of geographical terrains and socio-political backgrounds. With the exception of Chen, who is Chinese by birth, they hail from former French colonies. However, Chen was born in Shanghai in the area formerly known as the French concession (1849–1943). At a time when university admissions examinations were reinstated, Chen obtained a place to read Modern Languages instead of Chinese language and literature as she had wished. All the other women writers were introduced to French from a young age either since they were born during the French colonial rule (Djebar, Mokeddem) or after decolonization in a country which maintained its place in the Francophonie (Miano, Diome). Others hailed from a country that has a special relationship with the French language (Devi), or, indeed, had to learn French upon arrival in their host country, despite France having formerly colonized their country (Thúy).

The works I have shortlisted are written by women who have never returned to their home country except for short visits. Miano arrived in France from Cameroon as a student, as did Mokeddem and Djebar, from Algeria. Diome left Senegal and arrived as a Frenchman's wife and subsequently enrolled at university to remain in France when they separated. Mauritian Devi settled in France near the Swiss border as her husband, and later she herself, worked in Geneva. Chen emigrated to Canada after studying French and French literature, working as a translator, and subsequently settled there, whereas Vietnamese Thúy represents a different form of migration through the refugee and asylum immigration policy in

Canada. Thúy's family left after the second Indochina war, which was marked by the fall of Saigon in spring 1975.

Understanding the ways in which these immigrant women writers write (about) men is important, since they all originate from patriarchal societies where women were considered to be inferior, as I examine through their works. The men they portray range from brothers and fathers to lovers, as well as other men who might have influenced their lives. Aside from Miano's text, where Amok's non-heteronormative sexuality is discussed, romantic relationships, if they are present, are predominantly heterosexual, although it was not a deliberate choice on my part not to include a range of sexual orientations. While I have looked elsewhere at female identity and subjectivity in some of the texts, with Devi, Mokeddem and Thúy, in particular,[14] the way in which these women writers actually examine the transformations operating within men as they seek to integrate a new society has spurred me to undertake this project. Together the texts I have chosen span over twenty-five years, with Chen being the earliest voice to describe such shifts in men and Miano being the most recent one.

The comparative element covering such a vast geographical terrain permits an interrogation of the extent to which migration into France and Canada by these women writers and, indeed, their protagonists, might impact the ways masculinities are conceived even as women's status and education, as well as their place in the household, transform in the host society.

Hospitality

Probing migration shifts the focus to the country one might migrate to, and the ways in which migrants are welcomed, or not. The second chapter situates migrants vis-à-vis the society which they have joined. I focus both on how society views the newly arrived and on the manner in which the latter are affected by the host society. Hospitality itself is not a novel notion in that it is rooted in the idea of the welcome extended to strangers across centuries. One of the most prominent proponents of hospitality was Immanuel Kant whose concept of 'universal hospitality' is famously delineated in the 1795 essay *To Perpetual Peace: A Philosophical Sketch* (rep. 2003). Enshrined in Kant's 'universal hospitality' is the idea that all human beings are equal, free, independent and are indubitably egalitarian

---

[14] See Kistnareddy (2010, 2011a, 2011b, forthcoming).

members of the human community.[15] In a more recent context, Emmanuel Levinas in *Totalité et infini* (1961) advocates an ethics of hospitality predicated upon a recognition that the relationship between the self and the other is crucial to the formation of subjectivity. For Levinas, 'la limitation ne se conçoit que dans une totalité où les parties se définissent réciproquement. La définition loin de faire violence à l'identité des termes réunis en totalité—assure cette totalité' (1961: 197). Hospitality hinges upon language. If 'la différence absolue, inconcevable en termes de logique formelle, ne s'instaure que par le langage' (1961: 169), then hospitality itself can also only be actualized through language. The power of speech, of the address to the other inaugurates the relationship of the self to the other, as much as it unifies the self to itself. For Jacques Derrida, in *Adieu à Emmanuel Levinas,* Levinas's hospitality is ethics and precedes the political, the ontological and all conceptuality (1997c: 61). Hailing Levinas's work as the first philosophy of hospitality (1997c: 20), Derrida interrogates the universalist Enlightenment model. Hospitality becomes a very complex and structured notion requiring a discussion of the philosophy underpinning it, the ethical questions framing it and how it is lived and experienced in the empirical world.

Derrida's hospitality is structured upon the dialectic of the host and the stranger, and the stakes of its absolute or conditional nature. However, the word 'hôte' is very particular in French insofar as it refers to both the host and the guest, placing the two in an interdependent and blurred relationship. This interchangeability intensifies the intimate relationship between the host and guest in French. Hospitality can be on an individual level, with the welcome arising between friends or individuals, or at national level, with countries extending hospitality to refugees or (im)migrants. Hospitality is a two-fold concept inasmuch as it can be open, along the lines of Kant's universal hospitality and Levinas's ethics of hospitality, but it may also be policed and limited by laws and the judiciary, thus

---

[15] Kant wrote this essay in the aftermath of the French Revolution and in the Enlightenment period and, as such, his 'universal hospitality' is underpinned by the very tenets of 'Liberté, égalité, fraternité' which became the founding values of the French Republic. Yet such doctrines do not always translate into the empirical world when, for instance, concomitantly the colonial enterprise was justified by the barbaric and inhuman qualities of the colonized or when the laws of hospitality dictate who is permitted entry into a nation or not. In fact, to a certain extent, it might be said that the Kantian ideal is an abstraction that cannot relate to empirical fact and the subjugation of slaves is an aporetic paradox. See Zavediuk (2014).

controlling who can enter, who is excluded from the welcome and who has outstayed their welcome.

Derrida initiates his reflection on the concept of hospitality in *De l'hospitalité* by posing the question of the 'étranger' (1997a: 11), which in French refers to the 'strange', the 'stranger' and what is outside of reason or conformity. For Derrida, thus, the concept of hospitality is not distinct from the questioning of the ontology of the stranger, of 'être-en-question', of being in question and being questioned. From this perspective, Derrida argues that a stranger must by definition be 'strange'. Nonetheless, hospitality, as originally defined in the Enlightenment period, hinges upon equality, identity, similarity with the self. By bringing into focus the strangeness of the stranger to whom hospitality is given, Derrida enables us to question whether hospitality is extended when there are differences of race, sex and class at play. A stranger, for Derrida, is de facto someone who was born outside of the host nation: 'l'étranger est l'étranger par naissance et de naissance' (1997a: 81). Conversely, being 'strange' can entail behaviour and norm defying thought processes. Thus, Derrida writes:

> l'Etranger craint qu'on ne le traite de fou (*manikos*). Il redoute de passer pour un fils-étranger fou [...] un fou qui renverse tout de pied en cap, de haut en bas, qui met tous les pieds sur la tête, sens dessus dessous, qui marche sur la tête. (1997a: 17)

Here, psychological dislocation is not the reason behind the strangers being perceived as 'fou'. Instead, their thoughts and actions contravene the social mores and values of the host society. The laws of hospitality dictate that strangers must follow the rules and regulations imposed upon them. Yet how can someone who is not fully cognizant of all social norms in the host nation and of the accepted values ever not be 'fou'? Furthermore, an individual who was born in the country but does not conform to the norms is not a stranger by Derrida's definition, but he can be 'étrange'. These interrogations are central to my questioning of the hospitality, or the lack thereof, proffered to (im)migrants in the second chapter. They also form the basis for patterns of exclusion from the French community in the second chapter.

Similarly, reading Derrida allows me to understand the different layers hospitality comprises. For him, hospitality is both the Law of hospitality and the laws of hospitality. In *De l'hospitalité*, Derrida identifies 'l'hospitalité inconditionnelle' and 'l'hospitalité circonscrite par le droit et le devoir'

(1997a: 11). The latter, governed by the laws of hospitality,[16] is conditional, contingent upon knowing the name of the stranger. The host, and especially in the context of national hospitality, the host nation, extends hospitality according to the laws of hospitality which are well defined. The stranger in this paradigm is welcomed according to set criteria but can also be excluded as per the same. Conditional hospitality is constructed as a pact binding both the stranger and the host nation: 'ce pacte, ce contrat d'hospitalité qui lie *à* l'étranger et qui lie *réciproquement* l'étranger, il s'agit de savoir s'il vaut au-delà de l'individu et s'il s'étend ainsi à la famille, à la génération, à la généalogie' (1997a: 25). The question this raises is whether the immigrants who were welcomed in France in the aftermath of the post-war economic crisis, and later the agricultural and industrial crises, remain strangers. Likewise, it is important to examine whether the children who were born to immigrant parents, following the *rapprochement familial* of the 1970s, should still be considered strangers. According to Judith Still, 'the host community may be welcoming or may respond violently' to those she calls the 'interlopers', 'neither response excluding the other; the host (or guest) need neither be considered as homogeneous nor as free from contradiction' (2010: 6). Laws granting strangers access within the remit of the nation also exclude other strangers who are deemed to be unworthy, thus creating a structure of hostility within hospitality, or 'hostipitalité' (Derrida 1999). Thus, the limits of hospitality are explored by Derrida who identifies the sovereignty of the host. As the master of the house, the host has the right of choice in deciding whether to permit entry and the terms by which this hospitality is defined. The knowability of trespasses or derogations is predicated upon the notion of surveillance and restrictions in the case of *hospitalité de droit*.

---

[16] In *Les lois de l'hospitalité* (1965) Klossowski adds another dimension to the notion of hospitality, wherein the hostess is seen as an object of desire by the guests. '[…] les lois de l'hospitalité chez nous ne peuvent toujours s'observer à souhait' (1965: 27) due to the fact that the guest's gaze has already penetrated the hostess's 'charmes voilés' (1965: 27). Yet the narratorial voice deplores such laws as incomprehensible even as 'on ne prête un objet précieux et rare qu'avec les plus grandes réticences. Mais comment prêter son épouse à d'autres hommes?' (1965: 27). If the hostess is faithful to her husband, she will fail to accommodate her guest and if she is not, she contravenes the laws of hospitality. Still, in *Derrida and Hospitality* (2010) explores the gendered aspect of hospitality through the notion of the mother (2010: 125), as well as the idea that the mistress of the house also plays an important role in hospitality, even though the master's role is foregrounded the most. For Still, hospitality effectively takes place between men, and women are objectified or side-lined as secondary actors, despite the fundamental role they play in welcoming guests (2010: 125).

During the Enlightenment period, with the advent of secularism and the promulgation of science, the Law of hospitality was understood as an equal reciprocal value system wherein both the host and the guest acknowledged their sameness and openness to the other. Following Levinas's theory that 'le sujet est un hôte', thereby enunciating the idea that subjectivity begins with the ability and willingness to extend hospitality to an other, for Derrida, the Law of hospitality is open and absolute as it involves 'l'accueil sans question' (1997a: 31). However, the aporia at the core of this concept remains the extent to which hospitality can remain universal or equal insofar as colonialism, for example, was instituted on the concept of inequality based on the superiority of the white European man, thereby positing women and non-Europeans as inferior in their strangeness.[17] In addition, for Derrida, there are limits to how much unconditional or absolute hospitality can be practised as the guest can become a 'parasite' (1997a: 57). This image is evocative insofar as the host nation is portrayed as a self-policing and self-sufficient entity with *ipséité*. When frontiers are traversed, laws and limits are the only means of regulating the guest in the host nation, justifying Derrida's assertion that the guest must remain a guest under the laws of conditional hospitality which prevail (1997a: 67).

In her preface to *Postcolonial Hospitality: The Immigrant as Guest,* Mireille Rosello asserts that:

> My theoretical point of departure is that hospitality is a form of gift, and that, like most forms of gift-giving, the practices that transform two individuals or two communities into, respectively, the host and the guest, are meticulously prescribed by sets of laws that differ from culture to culture, and vary depending on historical contexts. (2001: viii)

Rosello clearly understands that there are variations according to cultures though the schema of host-guest remains similar insofar as there is a power structure at play even if is constantly being re-envisaged. As with Rosello, central to the notion of absolute hospitality for Derrida is also the notion

---

[17] According to Chakrabarty, concepts such as state, society, public and private, individuals, modernity and so on find their roots in Europe and the Enlightenment period (2000: 4). Even Postcolonial theory engages with universals dating from the period. Yet, such supremacy of European thought was always constructed upon the inferiority of other cultures and forms of thought (ibid.: 118).

of the gift he develops in *Donner le temps* (1991). Derrida asserts that 'on ne peut pas traiter du don sans traiter de ce rapport à l'économie' (1991: 18). Reciprocity and exchange are at the heart of the economization of the gift by nature. The gift should not be returned, it should never circulate back to the one who gives, and thus, Derrida concludes that 'c'est en ce sens peut-être que le don est impossible' (1991: 19). The act of giving for him is the act of subjectivization insofar as the 'donateur' comes into being through the act, as if the gift in turn validates the one who presents it (1991: 23). Nonetheless, the act of 'rendre' or restitution annuls the very fact of giving, whether such an occurrence happens immediately or in a distant future (1991: 24). For a 'don' to take place, it is vital that the 'donataire ne rende pas, n'amortisse pas, ne rembourse pas, ne s'acquitte pas, n'entre pas dans le contrat' (1991: 26). The very act must not be acknowledged by the 'donateur' (1991: 29), it must be completely forgotten (1991: 31). Yet forgetting the gift would eradicate the identity of the 'donateur' as the subject. This aporetic paradox is found in absolute hospitality wherein the nation state or the individual bestowing hospitality does not forget the act. Rather, in individual circumstances, as Derrida would argue, hospitality between friends consolidates their relationship and involves remembering the time spent together in each other's homes. At national level, while refugees or asylum seekers are offered hospitality, the laws of hospitality still govern their insertion into the host nation. The pact or contract is present, thus rendering absolute hospitality an (ethical) impossibility.

In *Cosmopolites de tous les pays, encore un effort!* (1997b), Derrida defines the intimate relationship between ethics and hospitality as follows:

> L'hospitalité, c'est la culture même et ce n'est pas une éthique parmi d'autres. En tant qu'elle touche à l'éthos, à savoir à la demeure, au chez soi, au lieu du séjour familier autant qu'à la manière de se rapporter à soi et aux autres, aux autres comme aux siens ou comme à des étrangers, l'éthique est hospitalité, elle est de part en part co- extensive à l'expérience de l'hospitalité, de quelque façon qu'on l'ouvre ou la limite. (1997b: 42–3)

For Still, this is the 'law of absolute welcoming, in which the other is received beyond the capacity of the self' (2010: 8). Similar to Levinas's concept of the other's vulnerability as contingent upon the self's own intrinsic vulnerability, hospitality presupposes an openness to the other as ethically unequal insofar as the other *is more important than the self.* Thus, the ethics of hospitality has an implied inequality. For me, this raises the question of whether strangers are actually perceived in the Levinasian perspective of being superior to the self.

For Rosello, when the Pasqua laws were enacted in the 1990s, 'They reflected an increasingly repressive and restrictive philosophy, turning the clandestin (illegal immigrant) into an enemy of the state, the most easily identifiable national scapegoat (2001: 1). Although in the early days after the French Revolution, France had positioned itself as 'universal host' (2001: 4), very soon decrees would be written to expel those who were at war with France (Wahnich 1997: 108). The figures of host and guest became a problematic framing of the laws of hospitality as the government began to forget its earlier need for workers and began to see the others they invited in as unwelcome strangers. The 'single male migrant worker' of the 1950s and 1960s had become the Beur generation of the 1980s (2001: 5), leading to a profound malaise in the French society. Rosello reminds us that for the French, the stranger is everyone except white French nationals: 'the "stranger" being a foreigner, a recently arrived immigrant, the naturalized child of immigrants, or even a French child born to non-European parents who continues to be treated as an other' (2001: 5). Despite its origins as a philosophical principle, hospitality is still regimented by the laws of hospitality, leading to sociologists such as Monique Chemillier-Gendreau to write books with very evocative titles such as: *L'injustifiable: Les politiques françaises de l'immigration* (1998). For Rosello, hospitality is in crisis not the least because it is constantly being redefined. Often, what states, such as France, must remember is the fact that immigrants were not 'invited' to be guests but to work, thus leading to an interrogation of the notion of hospitality itself: 'if a nation invites immigrants because they are valuable assets, because it needs them for an economic or demographic purpose, that country is not being hospitable' (Rosello 2001: 12). Rosello reminds us that the risk or threat that the host country detects in the immigrant is also shared by the latter for the immigrant can also be in danger from the host, as I discuss in Chap. 2 with both Miano's and Diome's texts.

It is also from this perspective that I draw on Julia Kristeva's *Etrangers à nous-mêmes* (1988) to explore the treatment of strangers in France from another point of view. Kristeva asserts that 'l'étranger nous habite: il est la face cachée de notre identité. […] De le reconnaître en nous, nous nous épargnons de le détester en lui-même' (1988: 9). For Kristeva, the stranger and the self are part of the same identity, and it is due to the stranger that the self can recognize itself. This schema implies an ethical openness to the other as other, given that otherness is a characteristic that is intrinsic to the self. Nevertheless, the alterity of the stranger in Kristeva's theory remains ungraspable, which prompts the theorist to state that 'toujours ailleurs, l'étranger est de nulle part' (1988: 21). The dialectic of belonging and non-belonging is crucial here as the host nation can close its doors to protect itself from the stranger; however, the stranger belongs everywhere since s/he is from nowhere. This notion presents fascinating angles for exploration in both Chap. 2, with hospitality, and Chap. 3, with community. For me, this would imply that the stranger belongs in the host nation as much as s/he belongs to the outside world, thus positing the liminality of the stranger as a form of cosmopolitanism in Kristeva's work. Kristeva's other texts inform my analysis in Chap. 2 as 'Women's Time' (1981) permits a rethinking of the importance of utilizing one's power conscientiously in Mokeddem's narrative, while her concept of intertextuality furthers my discussion in Devi's text.

Migration also presents another significant aspect: that of language and its relationship to hospitality. To understand the role language plays in hospitality, I return to Derrida since the migrant might not speak the host society's language, or might not have a perfect grasp of it, as I examine throughout the first chapter. According to Derrida, in *De l'hospitalité*, the stranger contests dominant paradigms because s/he is outside the dominant logos. This position is deemed to be empowering through the example of Plato, who calls into question the laws of those who have summoned him to court using a language that excludes him from knowledge: 'l'étranger est d'abord étranger à la langue du droit dans laquelle est formulé le devoir d'hospitalité, le droit d'asile, ses limites, ses normes, sa police etc.' (1997a: 21). For Derrida, the stranger necessarily does not speak the host nation's language. Derrida exposes this as a form of violence against the stranger who is compelled to:

> Demander l'hospitalité dans une langue qui par définition n'est pas la sienne, celle que lui impose le maître de la maison, l'hôte, le roi, le seigneur, le pouvoir la nation, l'Etat, le père etc. Celui-ci lui impose la traduction dans sa propre langue, et c'est la première violence. (1997a: 21)

The imposition of the host nation's language on the stranger is recognized as a form of diktat, leading to an interrogation of the ethics of language in hospitality. For Derrida, if the host nation demands that the stranger be fluent in the language of the host country, then 'l'étranger serait-il encore un étranger et pourrait-on parler à son sujet d'asile ou d'hospitalité?' (1997a: 21).

Derrida had been coming to terms with the fact that language has played a significant role in his own notion of home as well as his alienation. Understanding the linguistic positioning of the stranger/guest and how this might affect his feeling welcome or not in the host society become crucial as I consider texts where protagonists come from a range of geographical contexts and speak French in varying degrees. In *Le monolinguisme de l'autre* (1996) Derrida explores the idea that the French language could be the only home for someone, who, like him, has been placed in a liminal position. When nationality and citizenship was denied to Algerian Jews during the Second World War, the notion of home and belonging became fraught. Language becomes a beacon for the weary traveller who has no other home. Similarly, in *De l'hospitalité* (1997a), Derrida emphasizes the mother tongue as 'le chez-soi qui ne nous quitte jamais' (1997a: 83), adding that it is 'une seconde peau qu'on porte sur soi, un chez-soi mobile [...] mais aussi un chez-soi inamovible puisqu'il se déplace avec nous' (1997a: 83). Yet Derrida recognizes the impossibility of ever possessing language even as it is a home 'je n'ai qu'une langue et ce n'est pas la mienne' (1996: 1).[18] Derrida's inhabiting of the space of language as home allows me to conceptualize one of the different ways in which his notion of hospitality is tested in the empirical world. Nonetheless, it must be nuanced to account for the multiplicity of experiences of migration and hospitality.

There is some risk that Derrida's hospitality remains a conceptual structure where the master/host and the stranger/guest are but figures. Accordingly, the shift from the abstract philosophical schema of hospitality to the empirical field is not necessarily feasible and it is this impossibility that deserves further reflection. Derrida's personal experiences of dislocation and his relationship with language as home are not always mirrored by those who seek hospitality in a host nation. This is certainly the case of those who arrive in countries such as France from former colonies insofar as these (im)migrants have been taught the colonizer's language at school and already make use of the language to a certain extent. The imposition of the dominant language often lingers after decolonization. In many of

---

[18] See also Harchi (2016) who discusses this notion from the point of view of 'second generation immigrants' born and educated in France.

the former colonies, French remains one of the official languages. Whilst the switch to speaking French represents a significant change, it is not always the violence that Derrida describes insofar as many of the (im) migrants have been educated in a French-speaking system. However, it can be a form of alienation. As Vietnam was a French colony for a long time, it was not uncommon for schooling to take place in French, certainly with the parents' generation, as I discuss with Thúy's texts. Equally the refugees who arrive in Québec without knowing the host nation's language join incubator communities to facilitate their integration into society.[19] For those who are fleeing war, learning a new language is comparably a lesser evil. In fact, love for French as a language is a leitmotiv with the authors under study, as Diome and Chen articulate. Rather, the question that is raised is: Given that the protagonists manipulate French, should they be considered strangers at all? By the same token, if home cannot be found in language, is homelessness the perpetual state of the (im)migrants depicted?

The emotional and physical experience of being a stranger joining a host society are concomitant and equally problematic. Thus, it became important for me to find a theorist or philosopher who explores the strangeness of the migrant from the latter's perspective. Sara Ahmed's work appealed to me as she focuses on strangers' embodied experiences of migration in a host society. Herself a woman of colour and an immigrant academic in the UK, Ahmed's perspective is important. In the context of the first chapter, my reading of *Strange Encounters* (2000) and *Queer Phenomenology* (2006) provides additional theoretical support to Derrida's hospitality. Indeed, for Ahmed, in *Strange Encounters,* 'the experience of leaving home in migration is always about the *failure of memory to make sense of the place one comes to inhabit*, a failure that is experienced in the discomfort of inhabiting a migrant body, a body that feels out of place' (2000: 91). The experience of being strange can be seen in different guises through the mode of arrival which Ahmed underlines in *Queer Phenomenology.* For Ahmed, 'an arrival takes time and the time that it takes

---

[19] Woon identifies two types of Vietnamese and Sino-Vietnamese immigrants in Canada: those he terms 'able' immigrants have been exposed to the language and culture of the host nation in their home countries. Those who are 'unable' struggle to cope because they have had no contact with the language and values before (1986: 349). Social class plays a great role in the ability of the immigrants and refugees as those of a middle and upper class had access to French/American schools in Vietnam (1986: 355). However, those with limited knowledge of the language did have restricted access to better paid employment.

shapes 'what' it is that arrives. [...] What arrives not only depends on time but is shaped by the conditions of its arrival, by how it came to get here' (2006: 40). Thus, the circumstances both of departure and arrival influence the experience for migrants. It is crucial to understand that the hospitality accorded to strangers in the host nation where they arrive colours their affective experience. In Chap. 3, I examine Mokeddem's dissent through the lens of Ahmed's *Willful Subjects* (2014a) and *Living a Feminist Life* (2017), as the Algerian woman recuperates her agency in the face of the patriarchal Islamic community she inhabits. In the third section of the same chapter, with Devi's text and the treatment of vulnerability and emotions in the second chapter, Ahmed's *The Cultural Politics of Emotion* (2014b) permits an interrogation of the extent to which the writer reshapes masculinities in her text, through depicting the anger the men around the author feel. I also draw on Ahmed's short discussion of Spivak's subaltern in Chap. 3 to situate the notion of 'speaking with' as I consider how Spivak's theory remains relevant in today's world.

In Chap. 2, I argue that the 'strangeness' of postcolonial (im)migrants in France lies specifically in their hypervisibility. Contrary to philosophical and ethical notions of hospitality, (im)migrants' alterity does not seem to be fully accepted in France as depicted in the texts. In fact, the condition of welcoming is based upon categorization and integrating a system which is already familiar to the host society. It relies on the continuation of a structure that assimilates the other but ghettoizes them. Such a gesture of mastery effectively disrupts the pact of the Law of hospitality, leading to various forms of violence perpetrated. The impossibility of real assimilation and integration is evidenced in the banlieues where immigrant populations have essentially been ghettoized and live outside of mainstream communities as I explore with Miano and Diome.[20] Conversely, Canada's immigration policy, in particular the Multiculturalism Act of 1971, accords the right to immigrants to preserve their cultures and traditions and should, in theory, permit their integration into society. Nonetheless, Québec itself privileges French-speaking immigrants, which might be

---

[20] Fassin (2012) argues that these boundaries between the white French population and migrants from Africa are not a recent invention, they have simply become more visible. Racial discrimination and ghettoization is equally echoed by documentaries and short films, directed by film makers like Diop (see *Vers la tendresse* (2017), which won the César for Best short film in 2017). This work showcases migrants' experiences of prejudice and racism in Parisian suburbs such as 'the 93' but also in French society at large. See also Niang's *Identités françaises* (2019), which especially underlines the experiences of women in the banlieues.

problematic, if one's French is subpar, as with Chen's epistolary novel. Equally, being allowed to keep one's culture might adversely affect the migrants as family structures might present a rigidity which alienates those who wish to integrate their host society fully, as I examine with Thúy's text. It is from this perspective that I choose to foreground the (in)hospitality which is the lot of these (im)migrants.

COMMUNITY

My exploration of the intricacies of what being welcomed implies has led me to another important question: that of belonging, and in particular, belonging to a community. I interrogate the relationship between giving hospitality and accepting an individual into a community in Chap. 3. On arrival, migrants are often positioned in the margins insofar as the existing community extends hospitality but does not perceive them as part of the community. For immigrants, who are determined to make this country their new home, the question of belonging becomes crucial as it is correlated with whether one is considered to be part of the community one is joining or excluded as an outsider. Whether the children born to immigrants are deemed to be a part of the community is also a significant point. This line of questioning has led to a complex examination of what community means and the role it plays in a society marked by mobility.

In the contemporary world, the term 'community' is evoked in a range of spheres, from the political to the sociological, via the philosophical and the postcolonial. The political dimension has proven onerous as communism—which Jean-Luc Nancy qualifies as 'le communisme dit réel' in *La Communauté désoeuvrée* (1983, rep. 1999: 13), as opposed to the ideal of communism, which would erase differences between the 'I' and the other—has garnered much criticism in the past decades. Community, in a traditional sense, is linked to morals, ethics and shared values.[21] The main complaint raised by communitarians is the loss of community in a world of individualism. Conversely, liberalist thinkers extol the virtues of the freedom of the individual and the moral neutrality of society. There is no imposition of views and thus each individual is free to behave as he or she wishes.[22] Similarly, philosophy offers a range of viewpoints with regard to community across centuries. The engagement with the notion of

[21] See MacIntyre (1971, 1988, 1995).
[22] See Rawls (1971, 1996).

community can be traced back to Jean-Jacques Rousseau from his nostalgic vision of a loss of community in *Discours sur l'origine et les fondements de l'inégalité parmi les hommes* (1755), to the tension he discerns between the need for people to bond together and the will to maintain their individuality in *Du Contrat social* (1762). For Rousseau, each individual is always a part of a community before being perceived in their individuality. Yet there is a fear of totalitarianism that pervades his notion of community.[23] The loss of community is glimpsed through a desire for an irrecoverable originary community, which is perpetually idealized. This notion is of paramount importance in a world of mobility: as people leave and integrate communities, society, its values and its self-perception alter. The concept of community compels a reassessment of the place it occupies in a world where individuality has garnered a great deal of importance, and where the collective has been relegated to a secondary position, without completely losing its currency. In fact, in many cases, when diasporas form after migration, there is often a concerted effort to build a diasporic community based on shared values and origin.[24]

Nancy's notion of community offers the necessary insight into the ways in which comprehending community and its limits might aid in envisioning how immigrant women writers reshape masculinities. Nancy argues that the return to an origin is problematic as it is not an originary community which must be sought but a new means of conceptualizing community. Nancy's insistence on 'rethinking' existing concepts is appealing since it is precisely what I suggest these writers accomplish in the texts under study. The links between 'rethinking' community and reshaping masculinities are significant here as immigrant men encounter resistance to their integration into communities. Taking as point of departure Derrida's argument in *De la grammatologie* (1967) that there can be no return to an origin as the origin would no longer exist or it would have changed, Nancy applies a deconstructive approach to community by conceiving of it as untainted by nostalgia. From this viewpoint, I argue that Nancy's notion of community is critical as it provides a means of contemplating plurality and singularity simultaneously, which is a central notion in my discussion of Miano's texts in Chap. 3.

As a philosopher, Nancy is inspired by several thinkers and philosophers who have defined and redefined 'community' and through whose lenses

---

[23] See Simon-Ingram (1993).
[24] See Kalra et al. (2005).

he re-examines the concept in *La Communauté désoeuvrée* and *Être singulier pluriel* (1996, rep. 2004). Investigating Nancy's conceptualization of community, Ian James argues that:

> Nancy's thought unfolds as a ceaseless engagement with, or reworking of, other thinkers or bodies of thought. To this extent philosophy in Nancy emerges as an experience of philosophical community or of a sharing of the sense of philosophy itself, a sharing which can be seen to exceed the propriety or identity of the individual philosopher. (2006: 4)

For James, Nancy's community is a reworking and reinterpretation of other philosophers and thinkers with whom he actively converses, as is the case with Maurice Blanchot, who wrote a response to *La Communauté désoeuvrée*, in *La Communauté inavouable* (1983), but also with Martin Heidegger and Georges Bataille whose thoughts pervade Nancy's work on community.

However, before exploring Nancy's reinterpretation of other philosophers' notions of community, it is imperative to discuss what is missing in the notion of community at the time that he writes *La Communauté désoeuvrée*, which precedes the fall of the Berlin wall. Nancy opens his reflections by quoting Marx and defining community. Communism is central to the notion of community insofar as, for Nancy, it is founded on the basic principle of equality with no subordination and no social divisions. The ideal of communism did not, however, translate clearly and unequivocally into the real world. *La Communauté désoeuvrée* thus becomes Nancy's way of redefining the principles that he finds lacking in community. This deconstructive approach to community is compelling as I consider what it means for immigrants to be outside of community in France in Chap. 3. I explore how this experience of non-belonging a reconsideration of the notion of community.

There is a shift between what liberalists and communitarians understand by community and how Nancy defines it. Beginning with Georges Bataille's notion of community, Nancy reconsiders what community might mean in a world where most things are categorized and labelled. Bataille's community, as discussed in *Acéphale* (1936–1939), is anarchic rather than utopian insofar as it refuses to acknowledge established communities and is presented as a new universal community. Rejecting labels, Nancy draws on Bataille's anarchic community as a stepping stone. In *L'expérience intérieure* (1943), Bataille articulates the notion that human beings are finite and simultaneously uncontainable, they operate in excess. Inspired by Bataille's notion that death links all human beings, Nancy sees community as shared finitude. As James formulates, Nancy sees 'communal identity as a collective relation to death' (2006: 174).[25] Nonetheless, Nancy does not solely adhere to Bataille's notion of community as he does not believe in Bataille's ideas about immanence and sacrifice. The superiority of one being over another is contrary to Nancy's philosophy, and represents what Martin Crowley calls 'the all-too-human attempt to gather disparity into hierarchy' (2019: 23).

Equally, Martin Heidegger's philosophy is also a part of Nancy's definition of community insofar as Heidegger defines community as 'being with' in *Being and Time* (1927). The *Mitwelt* which the Being or Dasein inhabits is shared with other Daseins. This very Hegelian language of self and other, and all binaries in general, remain problematic for Nancy. Community itself is a fraught term as it is associated with identitarian values. Nevertheless, Nancy envisions community as rupture or dispersal, which permits an interrogation of terms that have been deployed problematically prior to this, and simultaneously undermines the idea of immanence. Nancy's unconventional notion of community jars with its common acceptance. Its interrogation of patterns of inclusion and exclusion informs my understanding of how the concept of community is understood in the texts I analyse.

As early as *La Communauté désoeuvrée*, Nancy underlines the fact that 'on ne fait pas un monde avec de simples atomes. […] il faut une inclinaison ou une inclination de l'un vers l'autre, de l'un par l'autre ou de l'un à l'autre' (2004: 17). By definition a being exists in relation to an other that is always present. There is no 'I' without a 'You' and there is always another being that lives so that 'I' can say 'I' exist. Crowley explains that this is also due to Nancy's understanding of the human language as speaking 'on behalf of the plurality of beings' (2019: 26). Nancy does not develop this plurality as an ethical relationship, contrary to Maurice Blanchot, who in his response to Nancy, in *La Communauté inavouable* (1983), constructs a theory of community which is strongly based on Levinasian ethics. For

---

[25] Ironically, as Morin points out, 'death individualizes' (2012: 77). For Morin, Nancy exposes the finitude of beings as community, but it is in death that beings are the most individual as it cannot be actually shared. For Luszczynska, sharing is community's way of presenting finitude to us. Community is the exposition of the very finitude that beings share (2012: 60).

Blanchot the relationship between the 'I' and the other is a gesture of openness but also of ethical *rapprochement* where the self is always reliant on the other so that the other is actually superior to the self. Conversely, in Nancy's community, there is no hierarchical relationship between the self and the other.

Later, in *Être singulier pluriel,* Nancy reworks philosophical terminology in order to explicitly redefine his notion of community as 'être-en-commun', thereby drawing on Heidegger and building constructively on the German philosopher's concept of 'being with'.[26] Perhaps the most prominent recasting of community in Nancy is in this work, where the notion of 'être-en-commun' or being-in-common, in which Nancy reworks Heidegger's being-with to create a new notion of community as the 'en', the gap between, an absence rather than as a mode of identification or an essential identity. Thus, touch and skin surfaces become important in Nancy's philosophy as the other begins where surfaces touch and feel each other through 'côtoiements'. However, this is contiguity and not continuity. Each being is separate even as it shares space with another being and they touch without violence: 'l'altérité de l'autre, c'est sa contiguïté d'origine avec l'origine propre. Tu es absolument étranger parce que le monde commence *à son tour à toi*' (2004: 24). This brings to bear the idea that difference is inherent to all beings.[27]

In Nancy's philosophy gender and race are absent insofar as 'la loi du toucher, c'est la séparation, et plus encore, c'est l'hétérogénéité des surfaces qui se touchent' (2004: 23).[28] Thus, any external surface is other and different. Differences of gender and race have no place in Nancy's being-in-common, as whatever is not 'I' is automatically other to me. We have shared finitude and we only exist because the other exists. In essence we are co-dependent as we co-exist and yet reassert alterity simultaneously. This conceptualization is productive insofar as it eliminates the impulse for

---

[26] One of the criticisms levelled against Nancy was that he relies too much on Heidegger in his philosophy and thus his argument is not original per se. However, James argues that 'Nancy is neither more or less Heideggerian than are Blanchot, Levinas, and Derrida; that is to say all of these philosophers traverse the Heideggerian thinking of being in one way or another, but all do so in order to critique or otherwise radically transform and exceed that thinking' (2006: 7).

[27] This is equally the case between humans and animals as Crowley (2019) asserts. For Crowley, Nancy permits thinking beyond 'anthropocentrism' (2019: 23) as he builds upon Heidegger's human *Dasein* to see relation with 'all manner of beings' (2019: 23).

[28] See McMahon's (2008) analysis of touch in Nancy's and Duras's works.

segregation and discrimination and Nancy rejects the notion of negative alterity as inherent to community. Being-in-common is a mode of existence that exceeds individuality by reinforcing the inherent commonality of all beings. Since all existence is co-existence, it is not unreasonable to conclude, as Nancy does, that being is always simultaneously singular and plural. Thus, Heidegger's 'being with' has become a way of conceptualizing the world and community as always existing in tandem with, and in the same space and time, as other beings. Rather than a time where absolute thinking involved the existence of a Being or one Existence that might supersede others, Nancy asks us to think of being as co-existence, a notion which precedes community itself insofar as we begin not from individuals but from the fact that beings do not exist unless there is another being that proves its existence, which he calls 'co-ipséité' (2004: 64).[29] Co-ipseity for Nancy would thus involve equality between all beings, ensuring that alterity is not a form of discrimination but a simple fact of life. For Nancy community becomes potential: it is the rupture and the gap, the excess that allows us to think beyond boundaries and beyond the possible.

Nancy's philosophy thus permits a reconsideration of difference as being so inherent that it essentially should not be a means of segregating or marginalizing others since we are all other to each other. It focuses on the commonality and the 'en' as that which is productive and empowering. To me, it is difficult to posit the empirical world as operating through Nancy's being-in-common simply as some values and ways of creating community remain ingrained and erstwhile. According to James, most criticism of Nancy focuses on his concept of community 'on the grounds that his thinking seemingly ignores or misjudges the empirical realm of political events and struggles' (2006: 153). Whilst Nancy's being-in-common does present an enticing and empowering way of seeing community as shared and simply existing, some aspects do not map easily onto lived experience.

Community as a philosophical concept becomes 'the problem of community' in postcolonial thought, according to Celia Britton (2010: 1).[30] Indeed, discussing the particular context of the French Caribbean, Britton

[29] Whilst Levinas would argue that the other is actually more important than the self in this relation because I cannot define myself without the other, Nancy chooses to highlight the equality of all beings.

[30] In *Reinventing Community* (2005), Hiddleston explores what identity and difference signify in the aftermath of colonization. Drawing from philosophy and literature, the critic looks at relationality, as well as the relationship between language and identity in community.

argues that community generates a 'deep-seated anxiety' in Antillean society due to the tension between collective and institutional practices in the French Caribbean. Britton contends that the use of race as 'basic structuring principle' (2010: 2) has led to this sense of community as problematic, as well as the assimilation strategies that saw the French occupy a hegemonic place in the hierarchy, subsuming and sublating ancestral practices and stripping colonies of their own sense of shared values, of their own sense of community. In her discussion of Nancy as linked to Edouard Glissant's notion of community, Britton argues that Nancy's focus on 'beings', 'stripped down to the finitude of their bare existence, results in a rather abstract conception of collectivities, as existing in a social and cultural vacuum' (2010: 38). She thereby underlines one of the limits of Nancy's theory insofar as it does not take into account the complexities of the postcolonial context. Although Britton queries the concept of community itself, she acknowledges, like Nancy before her, that community remains a part of social and political discourse. Rather than attempting to eradicate it, the critic too seeks to 'rework it in a way which resists its traditional connotations of homogeneity and closure' (2010: 4). 'Reworking' the concept of community becomes a recurrent notion whether it be with Britton or with Nancy. If the concept remains challenging, it still allows for critical thinking and different modes of understanding what community might mean in different contexts as I discuss with Miano, Mokeddem and Devi in Chap. 3.

For Achille Mbembe, 'that colonies might be ruled over in absolute lawlessness stems from the racial denial of any common bond between the conqueror and the native' (2003: 22). Colonialism was justified on the basis of racial difference and skin colour as a means of imposing white European superiority over the coloured other. Community, from this point of view, is determined by having race-in-common, which is markedly different from Nancy's being-in-common. By definition, then, the shared values of Europeans and their notions of superiority creates a community which was opposed to a group of racial others considered to be inferior. Whilst Nancy's being-in-common relies on the common finitude of all beings, a community of humans, colonialism permits a conceptualization of Black Africans, for example, as inhuman, outside of humanity, and therefore outside of (white) community, to justify their subjugation. In this schema, Nancy's ideal of community is absent as equality is foregrounded in his thinking. In colonial thinking, the European community's alleged superiority generates a difficult position for colonized peoples who are not only outside of their community, by virtue of not being white, but also outside of Nancy's community since, in the case of slaves, their very humanity is denied. The presence of descendants of former slaves in white France calls into question notions of belonging and community, thereby creating patterns of inclusion and exclusion.

In *Peau noire, masques blancs* (1952), Fanon was the first postcolonial theorist to examine the challenging situation of the assimilated Black man in the all-white French community. His objectification and dehumanization on being referred to as Black rather than a man is seen as both emasculating and demoralizing. Being singled out as outside of community enabled him to begin a questioning of colour and gendered narratives in French society. Fanon was thus the first to connect being excluded from the French mainstream 'community' to questions of masculinities and race, which remain salient today, as I discuss in the first section of Chap. 3. Fanon's experience highlights the limits of Nancy's concept insofar as he demonstrates the extent to which race plays a significant role in French society as it attempts to protect itself from alterity, as discussed with reference to Miano's and Diome's texts in Chap. 2.

For James, whilst Nancy does not answer all the questions posed with regard to community, his philosophy 'does nevertheless open up new perspectives in which we might think about, and engage with, the world as a form of historical community and a site of struggle and decision' (2006: 154). Thus, in the context of migration and post-migratory identity crises, it becomes crucial to gauge whether Nancy's thinking of community can provide some ways of engaging with problems of identity. It is from this perspective that I examine the notion of myth, and particularly, the notion of 'interruption of myth' which allows for a rethinking of community and belonging. For Nancy, myth only has a place when the members of a community cannot find a means of creating a foundation, thus focusing on the idea of a mythical identity and seeking to bring about cohesion around this myth. I explore this aspect of Nancy's theory in the first part of Chap. 2 with particular reference to Miano's depiction of Afropeans in France and the difficulties they experience in recreating a history through African myths. Nancy's deconstruction of the myth enables a critical interrogation of the latter as an absence of identity and ultimately it is not conducive to a satisfactory notion of identity through community. Equally, the concept of writing community, which Nancy theorizes in *La Communauté désoeuvrée* presents a potential for thinking of writing and identity through community. Indeed, Nancy's own responses to Blanchot have aided in refining what community means to him. His prior reinterpretations of Heidegger, Bataille and Hegel are propitious for the concept of community as being-in-common to emerge. It is precisely this form of community of writing which I draw on to explore Devi's *Les Hommes* in the final section of Chap. 3, with a view to interrogating the ways in which a writer can create a family through the community of writing.

Thus, Nancy's concept of community plays a prominent role in my exploration of Miano's, Diome's, Mokeddem's and Devi's texts, even as I grapple with some of its limitations. Notwithstanding Nancy's denial of the intersectional (race, gender, class) differences which might affect the notion of community as being-in-common,[31] his notions still provide significant critical purchase and permit a rethinking of masculinities.

Women's Writing

For the immigrant women writers I focus on in this study, reading, writing and speaking become crucial aspects of their oeuvre as they write about men. Many of the writers hail from traditional communities which did not allow women to read or write. Writing can be subversive for women who live under the diktats of patriarchy,[32] be it for Djebar and Mokeddem, in the aftermath of the Algerian war, or for Diome, who was not even expected to know how to read as a girl, and much less in French, in decolonized Senegal. It is equally seditious for Devi whose husband and son blame her failures on her writing. In my quest to comprehend what writing represents for women who are deemed to be inferior by their home societies, I encountered several women whose works have redefined the act of writing itself. The most salient are Hélène Cixous and Djebar as they reflect on what it means to write when reading itself is not accessible to most women in their societies. Cixous's position as a 'Jewoman' at the confluence of cultures and languages (German and French) in Algeria,[33] and Djebar's identity as an Algerian woman who was allowed to read and write due to her father's education and love, and who subsequently emigrated to France, enable an interrogation of the extent to which

---

[31] See Crenshaw (2019).

[32] See Danticat (2010) and Baisnée-Keay (2018).

[33] In French, the term 'Juifemme' can be a play on the words 'Je suis femme', underlining the notion of femininity and multiple identities at play here, especially since Cixous's father was an Arab Jew and her mother a European Jew, adding further to complex notions of race, religion and gender.

geographical and identitarian considerations permit an examination of women's writing and the role it plays in the transformation of masculinities.

In *Coming to Writing* (1991),[34] Cixous discusses her first venture into writing, since as a woman she would normally be excluded from such an act. Cixous begins her own journey into writing both fiction and non-fiction as a subversive demand to leave 'no space for death […] to confront perpetually the mystery of the there-not-there. The visible and the invisible' (1991: 3). Writing becomes a way of keeping the other alive for, as Cixous states, 'I write and you are not dead. The other is safe if I write' (1991: 4). This is significant on two levels: the power of writing is viewed in its ability to recreate a world which suits the writer. Its alternative reality permits new conceptualization of the world. It is also the act of birthing, and creating oneself repeatedly, 'being [her] own daughter of each day' (1991: 6). Central to this is the notion that Cixous wishes to explore the possibilities afforded her through writing. I contend that the women writers whose works I study are precisely attempting to recreate a world according to their own ideals through their texts. Likewise, writing to keep the other alive is relevant as Djebar writes *Nulle part* following her father's death, to bring him back into her creative world, as I discuss in the first section of Chap. 4.

Moreover, Cixous sees writing as an imperative, and still, there are 'so many boundaries, so many walls, and inside the walls, more walls' (1991: 3). Imprisoned into her many 'cages', Cixous emphasizes the fact that she has had to write 'to see; to have what I never would have had' (1991: 4). Writing becomes a way to 'make room for the wandering question that haunts [her] soul and hacks and saws at [her] body' (1991: 7). For Cixous, writing is the means through which she can make sense of her own desires and material existence. It is the place, which in 'l'écriture féminine' as she defines it in *La jeune née* (1975) and *Le rire de la Méduse* (1975), can take place through its lack of boundaries and images of maternal milk and menstrual blood. Having discussed finding one's place through writing with Devi in Chap. 3, the first part of Chap. 4 foregrounds two women, Diome and Djebar, whose communities exclude women from writing and erect walls so that they cannot eschew the edicts of patriarchy. Cixous's image of the walls which attempt to keep women within well-defined boundaries and which writing breaks is crucial as I examine how fathers (or father

---

[34] I have not been able to obtain a copy of this text in the original French.

figures) provide the opportunity to these women to overcome obstacles on their way to education and social betterment.

While writing is an imperious demand, it is not without humility that Cixous engages with it. 'With what right?' she asks herself, for 'after all, [she] read them without any right, without permission, without their knowledge' (1991: 12). Cixous reinforces the idea that reading is a forbidden act carried out surreptitiously. How then can one write when one was not allowed to read in the first place? A product of her time, Cixous asserts that 'everything in [her] joined forces to forbid [her] to write: History, [her] story, [her] origin, [her] sex. Everything that constituted [her] social, cultural self' (1991: 12). Patriarchy, society, who she is excludes her from a realm to which she aspires. As with many women before her and after her, who live(d) in a traditional society, she believes that 'writing is reserved for the chosen. It surely took place in a realm inaccessible to the small, to the humble, to women' (1991: 13). The enumeration of those disallowed from writing is significant here as women come after the small and the humble. Cixous's exclusion from the space of writing as claimed by men is attributed to her having 'no legitimate place, no land, no fatherland, no history of [her] own' (1991: 15). The unmoored woman writer is thus not permitted to engage in the act of writing since she does not have a pedigree nor a sense of belonging. Her disarticulation is perceived as a stain marring the rules of legitimacy with regard to writing.

Furthermore, not belonging to Algeria since she is marginalized, French by nationality, an 'imposture' as she calls it (1991: 16), Cixous presents a double dislocation which further excludes her. It is from this bodily discomfort of being read as female, of not belonging anywhere that Cixous begins to conceive of the relationship between writing and the body. It is through writing on her body, writing her body and, thus recuperating it, that Cixous is able to find a home, a place to belong: 'in Books I became someone, I was "at home" there' (1991: 29). Elizabeth Anderson underlines the fact that Cixous 'configures writing itself as sanctuary' as it becomes the dwelling place of the stranger (2013: 365). Of particular interest to me is the fact that the immigrant women writers I study all see writing as home when they feel they do not belong in the society in which they live. This is especially true of Diome, Djebar, Thúy and Chen in Chap. 3, but also a recurrent notion in Devi's text as discussed with Nancy's writing community in Chap. 2.

Cixous identifies the state of loss as the beginning of writing, for it is when one has nothing, and nothing left to lose that one can find writing and be possessed by it. It is this notion of being possessed by writing, the madness it entails, that is central to Cixous's concept of writing. It is through the process of letting go, of releasing all pressures and demands on us that we can love freely: 'writing, loving: inseparable. Writing is a gesture of love' (1991: 42). It is through this love that a woman attains the possibility to live beyond 'codes' (1991: 49), and no longer walks 'between walls' (1991: 50). The freedom which is thus gained enables the woman to fully become a woman since she 'kills no one in herself' and instead nourishes herself and others (1991: 50). Thus coming to writing is coming to love and coming to freedom, which can only take place if the woman is unimpeded by the self-questioning which patriarchal society leads to. Postcolonial immigrant women writers, in particular in the texts that I examine in this book, understand coming to writing in two different ways. They foreground the woman's body, breaking boundaries and voicing, as outlined by Cixous, and writing about the other: men. Nurturing is not solely for the women but also for the men who might equally suffer in a patriarchal society, as I articulate in Chap. 3 with Mokeddem and Devi. I examine writing about and speaking with men in Chap. 4 and the range of ways in which coming to writing is intricately linked with writing about men in the texts studied. In so doing, I highlight the implications for writing gender in postcolonial Francophone women's writing.

However, coming to writing also entails another question which Cixous herself asked: in which language to write? For Cixous this question is prompted by the relationship between two languages which she masters: French and German. While she acknowledges that she cannot possess a language, as Derrida explores, Cixous argues that language can possess the writer and in so doing completely change one's relationship to language. Cixous's reflections on writing and, in particular, the relationship of the writer to the language which she chooses to employ brings me to another important figure in women's writing: Djebar. It was insightful to read what Djebar sees as the main problem of language in women's writing, especially given that all the women writers in my corpus speak several languages. The relationship they have with French is therefore crucial.

It is from this perspective that I read Djebar's own theory about language and voices in *Ces Voix*:

L'écrivain est parfois interrogé comme en justice: "Pourquoi écrivez-vous?
" A cette première question banale, une seconde souvent succède: "Pourquoi

écrivez-vous en français?" Si vous êtes interpellée, c'est bien sûr, pour rappeler que vous venez d'ailleurs. (1998: 7)

Djebar underlines the intricate and delicate relationship between the writer and the languages at her disposal. While the first question is deemed to be banal, it carries in its wake the very interrogation that Cixous has on the legitimacy of a woman writing. 'why do you write?' might seem innocuous but coupled with 'why write in French?', it can be read as questioning the legitimacy of the postcolonial woman writer. As a Muslim woman, Djebar is already breaking with tradition through her education and by voicing her opinion. By writing in French, she is perceived as a product of colonization, an impostor employing the French language to write her texts.. The right to write in French, about a subject which is not French nor related to France is interrogated, and yet it is an intrinsic part of postcolonial Francophone writing.

As with Cixous, who emphasizes the choice of writing in French and speaking German through her family, Djebar explicates the intimate relationship that Algerian women have with languages. Djebar's perspective is invaluable as she discusses the complexity of writing in the colonizer's language when it is the language one has grown up with. Closely linked with the choice of the language to write in, is the notion that one belongs to a culture through the language one uses. Djebar identifies four languages which the Algerian woman contends with: 'cette berbère [...] rebelle et fauve' (1998: 13), Arabic, which is 'la langue de la ferveur scandée', French, 'la langue des maîtres d'hier' (1998: 14) and the language of the body. Djebar calls this the 'tangage des langages' (1998: 13) at the core of postcolonial Algeria. The specificity of the Algerian situation is underscored here as there is a weaving of languages at play in the vernacular, the religious, the political and the corporeal senses. Being 'entre deux mondes/Entre deux cultures' (1998: 15), Djebar reinforces the in-betweenness experienced within the postcolonial nation itself, which is a recurrent notion in my analysis.

While Cixous addresses the impossibility of writing for women, due to their gender, Djebar exposes the multifocal impossibilities which haunt postcolonial women's writing from countries where women are oppressed by patriarchal society, religion and traditions, 'du fait de [leur] éducation musulmane' (1999: 18). For Djebar, writing becomes a way of acquiring a gaze 'totalement neutre, ni d'homme, ni de femme, ou plutôt de femme surgie d'un coup au soleil' (1999: 19). She addresses the notion of invisibility and its significance for a woman who was deprived of visibility in her society. Writing here is liberation, but it is also lived in a neutral way, devoid of exclusively male or female attributes, but rather encompassing both simultaneously.

What is at stake here is the desire to write and to write in a language which allows her to voice her ideas. To a journalist's questions on her being a 'voix francophone', Djebar responds that it is precisely what she does not want to be 'une voix'. It is when she does not speak that she can write 'alors, justement, mon écriture sort, surgit, coule soudain ou par moments explose' (1999: 25). For the writer, the act of writing is a function of not speaking, of enforced silence. Voicing here gives place to writing, which can only occur if the silence is unbroken. However, the language is not clear. Rather, quoting Cixous herself, she argues that her writing takes place in a 'hors-des-langues' but also as a 'mise en écrit de la voix' (1999: 26). This notion is significant as I discuss the use of writing to give voice to characters which otherwise remain voiceless in Chap. 4.

As a product of the political linguistic landscape of her country, Djebar identifies French as the language 'simplement mise à disposition' which leads to a 'lutte intérieure' due to Arabic being her maternal language (1999: 28). Discussing Djebar's work, Hiddleston asserts that 'the colonial context disrupts a sense of origin and leaves the colonized infant disoriented and rootless' (2011: 24). Rather than being a Francophone 'voice', Djebar practises 'franco-graphie' (1999: 29). Nonetheless, she is inhabited by the non-French voices which form part of her cultural heritage and it is this aspect of herself that she brings to her writing 'jusqu'à un texte français qui devient enfin mien' (1999: 29). Thus, contrary to Derrida who denies the ability to possess language in *Le monolinguisme de l'autre,* and Cixous who contends that a language might possess an individual even if the individual does not possess it, Djebar asserts that she can make French hers by weaving in other voices thereby creating her own singular language. More importantly, it involves duality and liminality 'entre-deux-langues' (1999: 30), in a 'francophonie où graphie et oralité se répondent comme deux versants face à face' (1999: 38), where the maternal language returns as a vibrant echo, a 'résonance' (1999: 39). Writing the language of the other becomes a work of re-appropriation, of acquiring the ability to say that she is 'femme, et de "parole française"', and that 'il n'en reste pas moins que [son] écriture, dans son texte original, ne peut être que française' (1999: 41).[35] Excluded from an education in Arabic due to the colonial political decisions to use French as a main medium for learning, Djebar can only use French to write. Nonetheless, the other voices remain present within the French, creating a 'parole pouvant être double, et peut-être même triple' and 'particip[ant] de plusieurs cultures' even though she can only write in French (1999: 42).

The postcolonial perspective which Djebar brings to women's writing is significant to my analysis as it also allows me to comprehend what it means for Djebar to be an educated women who speaks of a context where other women are not educated and who, in her fiction, foregrounds women who have been excluded from literature before her. Djebar's discussion of voices and giving the opportunity to different voices to come through is crucial as it informs my thinking about what it means to write (about) others. Since it is the postcolonial context, it becomes important to discuss a postcolonial theorist whose main focus has been to ensure that agency is given to those who are usually marginalized Gayatri Chakravorthy Spivak.

In particular, for the purpose of this analysis, I argue that Spivak's notion of the 'subaltern' and the need to speak on equal terms brings a significant perspective as the women writers in the texts I explore give voice to men and women and they are both subalterns. I find it particularly salient that in her famous essay 'Can the Subaltern Speak?' (1988), Spivak takes the work of Foucault and Deleuze and claims that both are oblivious to their own problematic positioning as intellectuals attempting to represent the underclass. For Spivak, in Deleuze's case, there are two concomitant ideas: 'representation as "speaking for", as in politics, and representation as "re-presentation", as in art or philosophy' (1988: 71). The issue is that theorists cannot 'speak for' those who are struggling (1988: 71). Drawing on Marx, she goes on to say that the subaltern does not have the power nor the subjectivity which will allow him/her to speak (1988: 74). Indeed, 'the S/subject [...] belongs to the exploiter's side of the international division of labour' and therefore cannot be simultaneously the subaltern (1988: 75). The intellectual who theorizes can to a certain extent be complicit in the 'persistent constitution of Other as the Self's shadow' (1988: 75). Spivak stresses the fact that the Western intellectual who wishes to represent or speak for the subaltern reinforces the binary dichotomy of self-other. Her contention is that this notion was

---

[35] Zimra calls the text 'a fully gendered engagement with history' (2004: 150).

exploited with the colonial other who needed to be saved. Central to her concerns is the fact that there is no single identifiable other, and that the colonized subject 'is irretrievably heterogeneous' (1988: 79).

Commenting on Ranajit Guha's and her own work in *Subaltern Studies*, Spivak asserts that there 'is no unrepresentable subaltern subject that can know and speak for itself' and therefore 'the intellectual's solution is not to abstain from representation' (1988: 80). This is especially salient in the case where 'what the work *cannot* say becomes important', notably with what she calls the '"figure" of woman', since 'the relationship between women and silence can be plotted by women themselves; race and class difference are subsumed under that charge' (1988: 82). Spivak's pithy remarks about the intersectional silence involved is probative as it also highlights her own concerns with specific aspects of the subaltern's ability to speak. Since the male is dominant in the structure she examines, woman as subaltern is central to her work for 'the subaltern has no history and cannot speak, the subaltern as female is even more deeply in shadow' (1988: 83). Furthermore, 'if you are poor, black and female you get it in three ways' (1988: 90).

Spivak stresses the necessity that is 'learn[ing] to speak to (rather than listen to or speak for) the historically muted subject of the subaltern woman', in order to 'unlearn' 'female privilege' (1988: 91). The question then shifts to 'Can the Subaltern (as woman) speak? (1988: 92). Spivak identifies her own readings as an 'inexpert examination, by a postcolonial woman, of the fabrication of repression, a constructed counternarrative of woman's consciousness' (1988: 95). Since *sati*, or widow self-immolation, in India was justified by men as the women's own volition, Spivak argues that the question of who speaks for these women is crucial here. Ultimately she concludes that 'the subaltern female cannot be heard or read' and that the 'female intellectual as intellectual has a circumscribed task which she must not disown with a flourish' (1988: 104). For me, Spivak raises a number of questions which are important in the context of immigrant women writers from non-Western countries who write about men: what happens when the subaltern woman transcends her own circumstances, acquires knowledge and speaks for herself and with those who are not able to speak? Does she remain a subaltern, does she 'evolve' into an intellectual who can speak? Does the new position imply another relationship with subaltern men? Can she speak for both the men and the women in her in-between positioning?

Thus, Cixous, Djebar and Spivak provide the critical framework to speak of writing vulnerability in the final chapter. The notion of coming to writing, and in particular, to writing about men, which language(s) to write in and how to write, as well as who to write about are significant here as a means of setting the stage to speak of immigrant women from a range of countries and cultures writing about men and masculinities and living in France and Canada.

In the course of this analysis, two additional voices accompany me in my exploration of how women writers reshape masculinities: those of bell hooks and Guilaine Kinouani. hooks's discussions of masculinities and home have been an important lens through which I have examined several aspects of the works under study. In Chap. 1, I draw on *Black Looks* (2015) and *We Real Cool* (2003) to underline the lived experience of being a Black man under patriarchy and how this impacts on the individual in an inhospitable society. Her reflections on changing masculinities in *The Will to Change* (2004) have been significant in my examination of Thúy's *Vi* and Mokeddem's *Mes Hommes*, while her meditations on the notion of the home allow me to draw together my conclusion to Chap. 2. hooks's notion of the 'gaze' permits a critical interpretation of French society's treatment of Black men in Chap. 3, while in Chap. 4, her conversations with Stuart Hall in *Uncut funk* (2018) provides the critical framework for my discussion of equal conversations between Black men and women. Equally important to this study is the recently published *Living While Black: The Essential Guide to Overcoming Racial Trauma* (2021), authored by French-born psychologist Kinouani, who has Congolese origins. Her incisive examination of lived experiences of being Black in France, UK and the USA informs my study of Black masculinities in France in Chap. 2. Her work on racial trauma and its effects on migrants, immigrants and their children as they struggle to belong frames some of my own analyses in Chap. 3, while the distinct experience of postcolonial racial trauma enriches my discussion of *Crépuscule 2* in Chap. 4.

Thus, my analysis of masculinities in this book is carried out through the lens of critical theories of hospitality, community, women's writing, affect and race theory. Chapter 2 focuses on the concept of hospitality as theorized by Derrida. It maps the different levels of inhospitality experienced by protagonists in Miano's *Tels and Crépuscule 2*, Chen's *Lettres chinoises*, Thúy's *Vi* and Diome's *Ventre*. I examine how the new beginning experienced by the protagonists during their journey from their home countries to their host country, changes and reshapes masculinities in the texts. Male protagonists' unease in a country, which rejects their alterity, in the case of Diome and Miano and renders them vulnerable, is central to this chapter. Kristeva's *Etrangers à nous-mêmes,* Ahmed's *Strange Encounters* and Kinouani's *Living While Black* serve as an alternative way of conceptualizing this embodied strangeness, as Black masculinities call into question the notion of a homogeneous French society. In other cases, it is the individual who interrogates his place in this new alienating environment, as is the case of Chen's protagonist in Canada. While Canada allows for multiculturalism and maintaining traditions, Chen problematizes the male protagonist's inability to harness the two cultures available to him. Here, Ahmed's notion of 'disorientation' comes into play as the unwilling guest is unable to adapt to the new environment and experiences psychological dislocation. Conversely, Thúy depicts Canada as a hospitable country to refugees, but where extant traditions lead to a nineteen-year old taking responsibility for his family in the absence of his father. While values are upheld, there are distinct shifts as the protagonist's notion of masculinity and his relationship with his sister change. Thus the texts all foreground migration as a deeply transformative experience which allows women writers to test, contest and reshape masculinities in their texts.

Chapter 3 focuses on the problematics of (non) belonging to a community in Miano's *Tels Afropean,* and her essays, Devi's *Les Hommes* and Mokkedem's *Mes Hommes.* Drawing on Nancy's notion of community this chapter examines the in-between positionality of Miano's male protagonists as immigrants' children in France, through a reading of Critical Race theory, Kinouani's *Living While Black* and Miano's own theories of community in her essays. The notion of myth, which Nancy envisages as undergirding the notion of community is examined through the 'Fils de Kemet' group in *Tels,* while the concept of being outside of community, and especially in-between France and Africa is explored with 'Afropean Soul'. In the second section, I discuss Mokeddem's text as a singular voice fighting against Islamic patriarchal masculinity, while herself adopting so-called macho behaviour through the lens of Ahmed's (2014a, 2017) notion of wilfulness. The protagonist's relationship with her father and her subsequent relationships with a range of men are analysed. It is through the vulnerability the narrator underlines in the men in her life that her love and her ability to forgive transcends the narration. Similarly, Devi's text creates a new community of men with whom she can dialogue and exchange ideas, a community of writers, a writing community, as outlined by Nancy, which allows her to recover her own individuality as part of a wider community who will not interrogate her very being as her husband and son have. Ultimately, the different forms which community takes in this chapter allow the writers to reconfigure masculinities as loving and vulnerable and equally affected by patriarchy as women.

Chapter 4 explores the idea of vulnerability through women writing about, on behalf of, and with, men through the lens of Cixous's *Coming to Writing* and Spivak's notion of 'speaking with' which she explicates in 'Can the Subaltern Speak?'. The concept inspires me to examine different variations of 'speaking with' in the chapter, as well as the original association with the subaltern. I focus on Diome's and Djebar's relationships with their father (figure) who is the source of knowledge and does not adhere to traditional patriarchal notions denying education and success to women. In their stories of father-daughter filiation, Djebar and Diome portray their father (figure) as a deeply loving man who is oppressed by traditions and society. The education which Djebar and Diome hold as a legacy is seen as a lasting one, beyond time and space. In the second section, the form which Chen (epistolary) and Diome (telephone conversations) utilize to write their texts unveils their intention to create a type of equal conversation between lovers and siblings, thereby giving another dimension to the notion of 'speaking with'. In the final section, I discuss the silences which are present in the text, which far from being detrimental to the relationships between women and men, allow for a re-conceptualization of silence and intimating as revelatory processes in women's writing about men.

Ultimately, the chapters examine the ways in which immigrant women writers rethink writing and use it as a means of creating close bonds with the men they foreground.

REFERENCES

PRIMARY TEXTS

Chen, Ying. 1993. *Lettres chinoises*. Montréal: Babelio.
———. 2014. *La Lenteur des montagnes*. Montréal: Boréal.
Devi, Ananda. 2011. *Les Hommes qui me parlent*. Paris: Gallimard.
Diome, Fatou. 2003. *Le Ventre de l'Atlantique*. Paris: Anne Carrière.
Djebar, Assia. 1998. *Ces Voix qui m'assiègent*. Paris: Albin Michel.

———. 2007. *Nulle part dans la maison de mon père*. Paris: Babelio.
Miano, Léonora. 2008a. *Afropean Soul et autres nouvelles*. Paris: Flammarion.
———. 2008b. *Tels des astres éteints*. Paris: Plon.
———. 2017. *Crépuscule du tourment 2: Héritage*. Paris: Grasset.
Mokeddem, Malika. 2005. *Mes hommes*. Paris: Livre de Poche.
Thúy, Kim. 2009. *Ru*. Montréal: Liana Levi.
———. 2016. *Vi*. Montréal: Liana Levi.

SECONDARY REFERENCES

Ahmed, Sarah. 2000. *Strange Encounters: Embodied Others in Post-coloniality*. London: Routledge.
———. 2006. *Queer Phenomenology*. Durham: Duke University Press.
———. 2014a. *Willful Subjects*. Durham: Duke University Press.
———. 2014b. *The Cultural Politics of Emotion*. Durham: Duke University Press.
———. 2017. *Living a Feminist Life*. Durham: Duke University Press.
Ahn Hoang, Lang, and Brenda S. Yeoh. 2011. Bread-Winning Wives and 'Left-Behind Husbands': Men and Masculinities in the Vietnamese Transnational Family. *Gender & Society* 25 (6): 717–739.
Amnesty International. 2018. Refugees, Asylum-Seekers and Migrants. Accessed 21 January 2020. https://www.amnesty.org/en/what-we-do/refugees-asylum-seekers-and-migrants/.
Anderson, Elizabeth. 2013. Writing as Sanctuary: Place, Movement and the Sacred in the Work of Hélène Cixous. *Literature and Theology* 27 (3): 364–379.
Appanah, Nathacha. 2005. *Blue Bay Palace*. Paris: Gallimard.
Assiba d'Almeida, Irene. 1994. *Francophone African Women Writers: Destroying the Emptiness of Silence*. Gainesville: University Press of Florida.
Azzedine, Saphia. 2009. *Mon père est femme de ménage*. Paris: Léo Scheer.
Baisnée-Keay, Valérie, Corinne Bigot, et al. 2018. *Women's Life Writing and the Practice of Reading*. Cham: Palgrave Macmillan.
Bataille, Georges. 1936–1939, rep 1995. *Acéphale*. Paris: Jean-Michel Place.
———. 1943. *L'Expérience intérieure*. Paris: Gallimard.
Blanchot, Maurice. 1983. *La Communauté inavouable*. Paris: Editions de Minuit.
Bond, Emma. 2018. *Writing Migration through the Body*. Cham: Palgrave Macmillan.
Britton, Celia. 2010. *The Sense of Community in French Caribbean Fiction*. Liverpool: Liverpool University Press.
Buchbinder, David. 2013. *Studying Men and Masculinities*. London and New York: Routledge.
Carabí, Angels, and Josep Armengol. 2014. *Alternative Masculinities for a Changing World*. London: Palgrave Macmillan.

Chakrabarty, Dipesh. 2000. *Provincializing Europe: Postcolonial Thought and Historical Difference*. Princeton: Princeton University Press.

Chemillier-Gendreau, Monique. 1998. *L'injustifiable: Les politiques de l'immigration*. Paris: Bayard.

Cixous, Helène. 1975. *Le Rire de la Méduse et autres ironies*. Paris: Galilée.

———. 1991. *Coming to Writing and Other Essays*. Harvard: Harvard University Press.

Coleman, David. 2015. Migrants and Migration in Europe. In *International Encyclopedia of Social and Behavioral Sciences*, ed. James D. Wright, 376–388. Elsevier.

Connell, Raewyn. 1995. *Masculinities*. Cambridge: Polity Press.

Connell, Raewyn, and James Messerschmidt. 2005. Hegemonic Masculinity: Rethinking the Concept. *Gender & Society* 19 (6): 829–859.

Crenshaw, Kimberlé. 2019. *On Intersectionality: Essential Writings*. New York: The New Press.

Crowley, Martin. 2019. The Many Worlds of Jean-Luc Nancy. *Paragraph* 42 (1): 22–36.

Dados, Nour, and R. Connell. 2012. The Global South. *Contexts* 11: 12–13. https://doi.org/10.1177/1536504212436479.

Danticat, Edwidge. 2010. *Create Dangerously: The Immigrant Artist at Work*. Princeton: Princeton University Press.

Derrida, Jacques 1967. *De la grammatologie*. Paris: Editions de Minuit.

———. 1991. *Donner le temps*. Paris: Galilée.

———. 1996. *Le monolinguisme de l'autre*. Paris: Galilée.

———. 1997a. *De l'hospitalité*. Paris: Calmann-Levy.

———. 1997b. *Cosmopolites de tous les pays, encore un effort!* Paris: Galilée.

———. 1997c. *Adieu à Emmanuel Levinas*. Paris: Galilée.

———. 1999. Hostipitalité. In *Pera Peras Poros: Atelier interdisciplinaire avec et autour de Jacques Derrida*, ed. Ferda Keskin and Önay Sözer, 20–115. Istanbul: Cogito.

Diop, Alice. 2017. *Vers la tendresse*. Paris: Les films du Worso.

Donaldson, Michael, Raymond Hibbins, et al. 2009. *Migrant Men: Critical Studies of Masculinities and the Migration Experience*. New York: Routledge.

El-Tayeb, Fatima. 2011a. The Forces of Creolization: Colorblindness and Visible Minorities in the New Europe. In *The Creolization of Theory*, ed. Françoise Lionnet and Shu-Mei Shih, 225–252. Durham: Duke University Press.

———. 2011b. *European Others: Queering Ethnicity in Postnational Europe*. University of Minnesota Press.

Fanon, Frantz. 1952. *Peau noire, masques blancs*. Paris: Seuils.

Fassin, Didier. 2012. *Les nouvelles frontières de la société française*. Paris: La Découverte.

François, Anne M. 2011. *Rewriting the Return to Africa: Voices of Francophone Caribbean Women Writers*. Lanham: Lexington Books.

Fluck, Winfried. 2013. Reading for Recognition. *New Literary History* 44 (1): 45–67.

Guène, Faïza. 2014. *Un homme ça ne pleure pas*. Paris: Fayard.

Guha, Ranajit, and Gayatri Spivak. 1988. *Selected Subaltern Studies*. New York: Oxford University Press.

Harchi, Kaoutar. 2016. *Je n'ai qu'une langue, ce n'est pas la mienne*. Paris: Pauvert.

Hearn, Jeff, Marina Blagojevic, and Katherine Harrison. 2013. *Rethinking Transnational Men: Beyond, Between and Within Nations*. New York: Routledge.

Heidegger, Martin. 1927, rep. 2008. *Being and Time*. New York: Harper Perennial.

Hiddleston, Jane. 2005. *Reinventing Community: Identity and Difference in Late Twentieth-Century Philosophy and Literature in French*. Oxford: Routledge.

———. 2011. The Mother as Other: Intimacy and Separation in the Maternal Memories of Assia Djebar's *Nulle part dans la maison de mon père*. *Journal of Romance Studies* 11 (2): 22–33.

hooks, bell. 2003. *We Real Cool: Black Men and Masculinity*. New York: Routledge.

———. 2004. *The Will to Change: Men, Masculinity and Love*. New York: Washington Square Press.

———. 2015. *Black Looks: Race and Representation*. New York: Routledge.

hooks, bell, and Stuart Hall. 2018. *Uncut Funk: A Contemplative Dialogue*. London and New York: Routledge.

Horlacher, Stefan. 2019. 'In Reality Every Reader Is, While He Is Reading, the Reader of His Own Self' Reconsidering the Importance of Narrative and Savoir Littéraire for Masculinity Studies. *Men and Masculinities* 22 (1): 75–84.

Hughes, Deirdre, Fusun Akkok, et al. 2019. Migration: Theory, Research and Practice in Guidance and Counselling. *British Journal of Guidance & Counselling* 47 (1): 1–5.

Idriss, Sherene. 2017. *Young Migrant Identities: Creativity and Masculinity*. London and New York: Routledge.

James, Ian. 2006. *The Fragmentary Demand: An Introduction to the Philosophy of Jean-Luc Nancy*. Stanford: Stanford University Press.

Kalra, Virinder, Kaur Raminder, et al. 2005. *Diaspora & Hybridity*. London: Sage.

Kant, Immanuel. 2003. *To Perpetual Peace: A Philosophical Sketch*. London: Hackett Publishing.

Kimmel, Michael. 2010. *Misframing Men: The Politics of Contemporary Masculinities*. New Brunswick, NJ: Rutgers University Press.

———. 2013. *Angry White Men: American Masculinity at the End of an Era*. New York: Nation Books.

Kimmel, Michael S., Jeff Hearn, and R. Connell. 2005. *Handbook of Studies on Men and Masculinities*. Thousand Oaks, CA: Sage.

Kistnareddy, Ashwiny O. 2010. L'ex-il/île ou l'île intérieure: l'île Maurice dans l'oeuvre romanesque d'Ananda Devi. *Palabres: Revue d'études francophones* XI (2): 93–110.

————. 2011a. Représenter l'altérité: le corps grotesque dans l'oeuvre Romanesque d'Ananda Devi. In *Ecrivaines mauriciennes au féminin: Penser l'altérité*, ed. Srilata Ravi and Véronique Bragard, 179–193. Paris: L'Harmattan.

————. 2011b. Interrogating Identity: Psychological Dislocations in the Novels of Ananda Devi. *Dalhousie French Studies Journal* 94: 27–38.

————. 2015a. *Locating Hybridity: Creole, Identities and Body Politics in the Novels of Ananda Devi*. Oxford: Peter Lang.

————. Forthcoming. 'Against the Flow': Exile and Willful Subjects in Malika Mokeddem's *My Men* and Kim Thúy's *Vi*. *Journal of Contemporary Women's Writing*.

Klossowski, Pierre. 1965. *Les lois des l'hospitalité*. Paris: Gallimard.

Kristeva, Julia. 1988. *Etrangers à nous-mêmes*. Paris: Folio.

————. 2007. *Cet incroyable besoin de croire*. Paris: Bayard.

Kristeva, Julia, Alice Jardine, and Harry Blake. 1981. Women's Time. *Signs* 7 (1): 13–35.

Levinas, Emmanuel. 1961. *Totalité et infini: Essai sur l'extériorité*. La Haye: Martinus Nijhoff.

Lusczynska, Ana M. 2012. *The Ethics of Community: Nancy, Derrida, Morrison, and Menendez*. London: Bloomsbury.

MacIntyre, Alasdair. 1971. *Against the Self-Images of the Age: Essays on Ideology and Philosophy*. London: Duckworth.

————. 1988. *Whose Justice? Which Rationality?* Notre Dame: University of Notre Dame Press.

————. 1995. *Dependent Rational Animals: Why Human Beings Need the Virtues*. Chicago: Open Court.

McMahon, Laura. 2008. Lovers in Touch: Inoperative Community in Nancy, Duras and 'India Song'. *Paragraph* 31 (2): 189–205.

Mbembe, Achille, and Libby Mentjies. 2003. Necropolitics. *Public Culture* 15 (1): 11–40.

Migration Observatory. 2020. Accessed 21 January 2020. https://www.amnesty.org/en/what-we-do/refugees-asylum-seekers-and-migrants/

Morin, Marie Eve. 2012. *Jean-Luc Nancy*. Cambridge: Polity Press.

Nancy, Jean-Luc. 1983, rep 1999. *La Communauté désoeuvrée*. Paris: Christian Bourgois.

————. 1996, rep. 2004. *Être singulier pluriel*. Paris: Galilée.

Niang, Mame Fatou. 2019. *Identités françaises: Banlieues, féminités et universalisme*. Leiden and Boston: Brill Rodopi.

O'Reilly, Karen. 2015. Migration Theories: A Critical Overview. In *Routledge Handbook of Immigration and Refugee Studies*, ed. A. Triandafyllidou, 25–33. Oxford: Routledge.

Rawls, John. 1971, rep. 1999. *A Theory of Justice*. Cambridge: Harvard University Press.

————. 1996. *Political Liberalism*. New York: Columbia University Press.
Reeser, Todd. 2010. *Masculinities in Theory: An Introduction*. Oxford: Wiley-Blackwell.
Reeser, Todd, and Lewis Seifert. 2008. *Entre Hommes: French and Francophone Masculinities in Culture and Theory*. Newark: University of Delaware Press.
Rétif, Françoise. 2016. *Le Masculin dans les oeuvres d'écrivaines françaises*. Paris: Classiques Garnier.
Rosello, Mireille. 2001. *Postcolonial Hospitality: The Immigrant as Guest*. Stanford: Stanford University Press.
Rousseau, Jean-Jacques. 1755, rep. 2011. Discours sur l'origine et les fondements de l'inégalité parmi les hommes, Les échos du Maquis. Accessed 18 June 2018. https://philosophie.cegeptr.qc.ca/wp-content/documents/Discours-sur-lin%C3%A9galit%C3%A9-1754.pdf.
————. 1762, rep. 2001. *Du contrat social*. Paris: Garnier Flammarion.
Silverman, Kaja. 1992. *Male Subjectivity at the Margins*. New York: Routledge.
Simon-Ingram, Julia. 1993. Rousseau and the Problem of Community: Nationalism, Civic Virtue, Totalitarianism. *History of European Ideas* 16 (1–3): 23–29.
Song, Sarah. 2018. Political Theories of Migration. *Annual Review of Political Science* 21: 385–402.
Spivak, Gayatri. 1988. Can the Subaltern Speak? In *Colonial Discourse and Postcolonial Theory: A Reader*, ed. Patrick Williams and Laura Chrisman, 66–111. New York: Harvester Wheatsheaf.
Still, Judith. 2010. *Derrida and Hospitality: Theory and Practice*. Edinburgh: Edinburgh University Press.
Vasquez de Aguila, Ernesto. 2014. *Being a Man in a Transnational World: The Masculinity and Sexuality of Migration*. London: Routledge.
Wahnich, Sophie. 1997. *L'impossible Citoyen: L'étranger dans le discours de la Révolution Française*. Paris: Albin Michel.
Woon, Yuen-Fong. 1986. Some Adjustment Aspects of Vietnamese and Sino-Vietnamese Families in Victoria, Canada. *Journal of Comparative Family Studies* 17 (3): 349–370.
Zavediuk, Nicholas. 2014. Kantian Hospitality. *Peace Review* 26 (2): 170–177.
Zimra, Clarisse. 2004. Hearing Voices, or Who Are You Calling Postcolonial? The Evolution of Djebar's Poetics. *Research in African Literatures* 35 (4): 149–159.

CHAPTER 2

Migrant Men: (In)Hospitality in France and Canada

Migration involves a dual process: leaving one's home, one's home country and arriving in a country which often operates with a different value system. The host country has a duty to welcome (im)migrants but their entry and exit are systematically regulated. Investigating the complexities of hospitality and immigration, Avril Bell asserts that:

> The discourse of hospitality is seemingly benign, generous, and inclusive. As a way of understanding relations of immigration it encourages good treatment of new arrivals and a positive self-perception on the part of the "host" community. Closer consideration, however, highlights the complexity of the language of hospitality and its limitations in making sense of relations of immigration. (2010: 236)

Bell's analysis underscores the complexity of Jacques Derrida's notion of hospitality due to the deconstruction of the nature of the host-guest paradigm it entails. In defining conditional hospitality as a 'relationship of unequal power, in which the host nation is sovereign', the generosity and openness of the discourse of hospitality is belied by the power relations involved (2010: 240). The imposition of conditions on the welcome and the decision underpinning inclusion in, and exclusion from, the host nation do not demonstrate hospitality.[1] Derrida's own interrogations of what hospitality implicates, and the aporia at its heart—specifically the differences between the Law of hospitality, which is absolute, and the laws of hospitality, which are conditional—permit a critical reassessment of what migration into a host country in the contemporary world encompasses.

As discussed in the introduction to this study, both Derrida's hospitality and Mireille Rosello's postcolonial hospitality raise an illuminating set of questions regarding affect, and, particularly, the ways hospitality must be reconsidered in line with a range of historical, cultural and geographical contexts. I examine immigrant women writers' works through the individual circumstances and concerns the writers themselves choose to accord pathos and prominence to. Throughout the texts, lived experiences of hospitality enable an interrogation of what being a stranger in a society represents when one is visibly different from the homogeneous society which one is (un)welcomed to.[2]

The affective experience of losing one's home or not feeling at home is thus a crucial aspect of hospitality. In this chapter, I contend that the experiences of emotional and physical rupture as a stranger joining a host society are concomitant and equally problematic.[3] I apply Sara Ahmed's explorations of the stranger in *Strange Encounters* to my analysis as some of the protagonists are either illegally in France or refugees in Canada or simply strangers in a society which exhibits fear and anxiety at their presence. I discuss Miano's *Tels*, with reference to its sequel, *Crépuscule 2*, Diome's *Ventre*, Chen's *Lettres chinoises* and Thúy's *Vi*, to gauge the extent to which France and Canada, as depicted through the texts, represent two different host societies with divergent immigration policies, which are inhospitable for a range of reasons, including the language that they speak. In the particular case of France, I also draw on Guilaine Kinouani's *Living*

---

[1] Even asylum seekers are tasked with proving their precarity in order to claim asylum. In addition, this is further complicated if the asylum seeker has sought access to another country and been rejected there, under the 'Dublin' policy. For the complex nature of asylum status in France, see Office française de la protection des réfugiés et apatrides (2020).

[2] I develop this notion further by drawing on Fanon, and Butler's reading of Fanon's predicament (Kistnareddy 2020).

[3] In *Strangers at Our Door* (2016) Bauman argues that there is a form of migration panic currently. However, as with socio-economic migrants, refugees and asylum seekers have always been part of humanity's history. For Bauman, it is the unknowability of the stranger which poses problem: 'strangers tend to cause anxiety precisely because of being "strange"' (2016: 8). According to Bauman, most people operate in a 'comfort zone' and those who are different are 'barred entry' (2016: 107).

While Black to discuss the experiences of racism as part of the inhospitable environment in France as depicted in the Miano's and Diome's texts. The impact on male protagonists is significant since migration leads to a range of transformations in terms of their masculine identity, which is reshaped as they feel dislocated and disarticulated in the host society. I examine how the forms of inhospitality experienced by each of the foregrounded male protagonist are conducive to an interrogation of what it means to be a man in a new society with incompatible values. To better situate these transformations, I separate the texts into two spaces: the Sub-Saharan African migrant experiences in France and the Chinese and Vietnamese protagonists' arrival and adaptation to Canada.

INHOSPITABLE FRANCE

France has a long history of immigration. Yet it has also been the site of numerous acts and forms of discrimination against (im)migrants.[4] For Gérard Noiriel, "'l'antisémitisme" et le "racisme" sont des idéologies et des programmes politiques qui sont nés à la fin du XIXe siècle, avec le développement de l'immigration et de la colonisation' (2007: 9). For the historian:

> Le "problème" de l'immigration a fait irruption dans le débat public français entre 1880 et 1900. C'est seulement à ce moment-là que l'opposition entre le national et l'étranger, qui nous semble pourtant si naturelle aujourd'hui, est entrée dans le sens commun. (2007: 17)

The opposition between the stranger and the 'peuple français' is instantiated in the fact that 'l'immigré, c'est avant tout l'étranger qui vient s'installer "chez nous"' (2007: 22). As with Derrida, Noiriel sets up an opposition between the home, 'chez nous', one's familiar space, and the stranger, or 'l'immigré'. However, where Derrida sees the relationship between host and guest as mutually benefitting and founded upon respect and loyalty, Noiriel underlines French society's enduring mistrust of the stranger: 'ils sont perçus comme une menace potentielle' (2007: 23), a notion shared by Rosello in her introduction to her book. This perception led to the beginnings of identity control in 1888. The Third Republic marked the configuration of 'l'appartenance à l'état' as sole criterion for

---

[4] See also Macé (2017).

nationality while immigrants were officially managed as from the First World War (2007: 288). Racial discrimination was officially made illegal in the 1958 Constitution, and in 2018, MPs concurred that since in France, race does not formally exist, then the word must be taken out of the Constitution.[5] However, as Noiriel himself argues, there is a discrepancy between public discourse and what is said 'tout bas' (2007: 9), insofar as racism and racial discrimination do prevail. I explore this further in the next chapter, with the notion of community, but what interests me here is the lack of hospitality accorded to Black (im)migrants in France and the ways such unwelcoming behaviour affects those who are on the receiving end.

This notion of racial difference is underscored by Kinouani who begins her book *Living While Black* with her own experiences of growing up as a Black child in France. As a psychologist, she comes into contact with a range of men and women who are permanently scarred by the racism they encounter on a daily basis, thus showing signs of 'psychological distress' (2021: 29). For her, 'the refusal, overt or covert, to confront the lived reality of racism in the lives of Black people is a tell-tale sign of institutional racism' and this disavowal can lead to racial trauma (2021: 33). Examining 'either migrants or children of migrants in a country that was overtly hostile towards them' reveals a range of coping mechanisms (2021: 41) and a problematic sense of home and belonging as they are confronted with a society that does not want to welcome them.

In 2016 and 2017 Diome and Miano published *Marianne porte plainte!* and *Marianne et le garçon noir*, respectively. Whilst Miano focuses on the sacrificial figure of the young Black man as a victim, adopting a gender-specific approach, following the two horrific instances of police brutality against young men of colour (Théo Luhaka and Adama Traoré) in France in 2016, Diome focuses on the notion of xenophobia in the French context at large. Taking Marianne, the female figure of the French republic, as a point of departure, both authors denounce the inhospitality of the French nation towards those who are strangers by their hypervisibility, thus problematizing the fundamental tenets underpinning the French republic: Liberté, Egalité, Fraternité. In their fictional work, both writers are concerned with the treatment of (im)migrants in France as the latter suffer from racism and discrimination issues.

---

[5] See Ndiaye (2018) for a problematization of this notion.

Miano's *Tels* is a polyphonic novel written from the perspectives of Amok, Amandla and Shrapnel, with an unidentified narrator opening and closing the narrative. Amok and Shrapnel hail from an unnamed country on the African continent, but where Amok is of a wealthy background and is legally in France through studies and, subsequently, employment, Shrapnel is an illegal immigrant. Amandla, who is from a DOM-TOM, thus a descendant of former slaves transplanted as labour, is a French national by birth. The absence of clear markers as to their specific birth countries speaks to a deliberate generalization of their experiences on Miano's part, insofar as the text evokes Black individuals as undergoing similar situations and identity issues in France, regardless of their birth countries and origins. All three are positioned as outsiders to the society depicted and inhabit a space called *intra muros*, thus highlighting the patterns of inclusion and exclusion at play in the novel.

Diome's text is narrated from Salie's point of view. Diome has admitted that the character of Salie is heavily inspired from herself, and the events in the book are drawn from her own experiences.[6] Salie is from Niodior, a small island off Senegal. Much as Diome herself, she resides in Strasbourg, working as a maid to fund her studies. Previously married to a white Frenchman, whose family rejects her due to her skin colour, she lives alone and maintains contact with her brother Madické, who dreams of coming to France to become a football player, as do most of the boys in the village. Through anecdotes and stories which are weaved into her own reminiscences, Salie portrays France as a deeply racist society towards Black individuals. Her final message to her brother, and to all the boys who want to emigrate, is to focus on their studies and change their own society so that there is no need to dream of Europe.

In this section, I examine the ways in which Miano's and Diome's texts centre on the suffering of postcolonial strangers who are unwelcome in French society, while uncovering different ways of dealing with the identity issues which emerge as the protagonists learn to acclimatize to the host society.

[6] Diome herself admits that the story is 80% based on her own experiences in a television interview 'Fatou Diome: Le mythe de la France Eldorado' (Youtube, INA 2014).

Cartographies of (In)Hospitality in Tels des astres éteints

Le Nord ne leur ouvrait pas les bras. Il se fichait de leur rêve. Il ne pouvait accueillir tous les rêveurs du monde.
—Miano, *Tels*

Amok's critical statements on the discrepancy between the expectations of those who leave African countries with dreams of an Eldorado in France and the reality of their (un)welcome, unveils the deep-seated disappointment endured by immigrants from the African continent upon their arrival in France (called le Nord) in Miano's novel. The gesture of greeting imbricated in the act of 'ouvrir les bras' is set against the cavalier 'fichait', which itself is positioned as a counterpoint to the 'rêve' invoked. Yet the subsequent sentence underlines the impracticality of welcoming everyone's dreams and meeting all expectations, thereby mitigating the dismissiveness of the previous utterance. From this perspective, I argue that Miano's text underscores the aporia at the heart of absolute hospitality by foregrounding its impossibility. However, bonhomie seems absent in this case. The deployment of the imperfect tense with 'ouvrait' denotes a never-ending cycle of hope and disillusionment as waves of immigration reach French shores where hopes are promptly dashed. Miano's novel portrays a society instituted upon the laws of hospitality, as elucidated by Derrida. These are dictated by policies and involve both legal and illegal immigrant. This reality problematizes the very term 'hospitality' as both are equally unwelcome in Miano's novel.

For Derrida, conditional hospitality entails that for the migrant to become a guest he must provide his name (1997: 7). Access to the country is given following set criteria, to enter the nation space along with his family.[7] Naming enables the host nation to recognize and identify, thereby aiding in the categorization of (im)migrant strangers into specific pockets of French society. While nomenclature provides order, it can also foster a form of segregation rendering the host nation inhospitable. Discussing naming and skin colour in Miano's *Tels*, Myriam Brussosa points out that 'jamais ni Amok, Shrapnel ni Amandla ne sont désignés par leur patronyme' and finds this fact astonishing (2013: 144). For Brussosa the absence of a last name represents a genealogical rupture. While Shrapnel

---

[7] Still observes that hospitality happens between men and that women are excluded from this system (2010: 125).

was born to an unwed mother and does not bear his father's name, Amok refuses his 'patronyme' since his grandfather was a war collaborator. Conversely, Amandla, much as Shrapnel, is fatherless, but unlike him, she is not accorded a history since she is a descendant of former slaves who were sold in the French islands. Her mother attempts to recreate her filiation by adopting African names. All three live the absence of a last name as a 'vide nominatif' (2013: 143). However, I contend that this fissure is further exploited when individual identities are effaced due to the way French society, as depicted in the novel, alienates those whose name does not sound 'French'. This is evidenced through the call centre where Amok finds employment.

The transformation of Amok into 'Daniel Laurent' is doubly disparaging. Firstly, he is deprived of his own identity insofar as 'on se faisait passer pour qui on n'était pas' (Miano 2008: 113). Secondly, the message transmitted to the guest is that identity can not only be policed, but it can also be imposed. This attitude is discussed through the concept of 'assimilation' by Kinouani in her chapter entitled 'Working While Black'. For the psychologist, it is 'the expectation that Black people leave their Blackness at the door […] that they whiten themselves to be accepted' (2021: 122). In the text, the whitening is imposed by the employer and the dislocation that this may cause is not considered. At first glance, this 'identité creuse' is regarded as empowering for Amok as his patronym is a source of shame for him (2008: 113). However, the choice of the word 'creuse' highlights the emptiness felt by the guest whose strangeness is arbitrarily moulded to fit into society's idea of normalcy.[8] I see such problematic uses of renaming for order as symptomatic of the failure of the host nation to come to terms with a heterogeneous (im)migrant workforce which undermines its sense of identity, in line with Rosello's observations in *Postcolonial* Hospitality.

Conditional hospitality serves as means of policing but also of assimilating the other into identifiable and controllable spaces. This implied need for a new start for (im)migrants is reinforced by Amandla's observations as a pro-return to Africa activist in the text:

Le Nord ne pouvait donner rien d'autre […] que le vague à l'âme, la suspension dans le vide. Il ne serait jamais à eux, puisqu'il leur demandait de laisser leurs bagages à l'entrée. […] Il les voulait vides, sans âme, malléables, assim-

---

[8] This notion is explored further in the short story 'Afropean Soul' as I discuss with the concept of community in the next chapter.

ilables, modelables à merci. Réticent à les laisser l'habiter, il exigeait de les investir totalement. (2008: 93)

Thus, contrary to the Law of hospitality that would acknowledge the stranger's entity as worthy of respect, the implied laws of hospitality delineated here invoke a stripping down of values, of identity, to fulfil France's need to control its incoming (im)migrants. If the culture and values are strange, they are jettisoned at the border as unwanted baggage. In turn, this is conducive to a 'vague à l'âme, la suspension dans le vide', that is, a complete sense of disengagement and disconnection. Yet compliance does not lead to integration either and the government is accused of having 'ourdi cet insuccès' (2008: 58), since it marginalizes (im)migrants even if they do follow the rules. Writing about the particular context of Maghrebis in France, Tahar Ben Jelloun argues that 'la France a opté dès le départ pour une "hospitalité contrôlée", ce qui est un non-sens puisque l'"invitation" s'est faite dans la violence' (1997: 19).[9] The writer refers to the displacement of Maghrebis to France, in the aftermath of the Second World War, to provide manual labour. For him, France does not have a problem with immigration itself, but with its colonial past (1997: 21).[10]

According to Rosello, migrants 'often have to rely at first on the generosity of members of their community who arrived before them' (2001: 68). Rosello envisions this as a form of community which is already there and on whose support the newly arrived individual can count. In Miano's text (in)hospitality is complexified as older sub-Saharan African guests mistreat and abuse new guests. From the book's inception, Amok calls the police as he witnesses verbal and physical abuse by immigrants over another immigrant who works for them. The victim is told that 'elle n'était rien. [...] Elle avait voulu vivre chez les Blancs. Eh bien, il y avait un prix à payer' (2008: 24). Emphasis is placed on the fact that 'ceux qui lui parlaient avaient le même accent. Peut-être un peu atténué par des années de vie loin du Continent' (2008: 24). Thus, while the predominant discourse centres on the inhospitality of French society towards postcolonial strangers, the linchpin of Rosello's argument in her book, Miano highlights the

[9] Silverstein observes that the presence of these Muslim immigrants in 'postindustrial France' is deemed to be 'unnecessary' and now only constitute 'a problem to be managed' (2018: 23).

[10] This notion is problematic as France has had multiple cases of xenophobia and rejection of others across its history. See Noiriel (2007) and Weil (2005). See also Gilroy (2005).

fact that inhospitality is present in various forms and can equally emanate from those who are immigrants themselves. The corollary to legal immigration is the presence of those who enter the country through illegal means. Miano's text deplores the power play exercised by those who take advantage of their own legal status by exploiting illegal immigrants, here termed 'les faibles' (2008: 128). The 'immigrés clandestins' (2008: 50), and those who are legally in France, are nonetheless compelled to live in the same ghetto due to the rarity of accommodation at affordable prices. For postcolonial (im)migrants, be they legal or illegal, France only provides 'la froideur et la misère' (2008: 124).

The positioning of Shrapnel, Amok's best friend as an illegal immigrant in the text provides an additional perspective to Derrida's concept of controlled hospitality, classification and prejudice. In lieu of weakness, Shrapnel displays majesty and a sense of self-identity which instils fear in its eccentricity. He is depicted as a stereotypical gangster from the ghetto, whom Miano uses to shed light on the prejudice of the society through the process of litany and anaphora: 'on s'écartait sur son passage. On changeait de trottoir. On serrait son sac à main contre soi. On retenait son souffle' (2008: 52). The short sentences reflect the fear inspired by the Black stranger's masculinity and physical dominance.[11] The 'on' underscores the generalized fear he rouses in men and women alike. For Kinouani, Black individuals are 'supposed to be both inhuman and superhuman' (2021: 57). Kinouani's observation underscores the prejudices that are rife surrounding Black bodies and the way they inhabit the world, forcing them to be resilient and invulnerable. Shrapnel's alterity, his larger-than-life attitude is not assimilable in this society and the latter remains unwelcoming, bringing to bear the aporia and impossibility that Derrida identifies at the heart of hospitality in the relation between absolute and controlled hospitality.

This lack of welcome is particularly potent when the language used to dehumanize the other is the colonizer's language, which was imposed on the former colonies. Here, in particular, what interests me is the fact that decolonization has rendered French less pervasive in the home country and this generates problems for some (im)migrants. In *Not Like a Native Speaker: On Languaging as a Postcolonial Experience* (2014), Rey Chow opens her analysis with a discussion of Frantz Fanon and what she calls 'racialization as an encounter with language' (2014: 2). Chow stresses that

[11] On Black masculinity in this text, see Kistnareddy (2019) and Murray (2019).

it is in 'naming' the other, following Walter Benjamin's writings on human language, that 'we derive knowledge of the world' (2014: 3). For Chow, 'the instant the black man is visually objectified is the same instant he feels being hailed into existence, as it were, through the names "dirty nigger" and "negro"' (2014: 4). In the former colonies, Chow asserts that language issues centre around a form of 'coerced bilingualism at the expense of indigenous languages' (2014: 12). Nonetheless, Chow indicates that the 'colonized's encounter with the colonizer's language offers a privileged vantage point from which to view the postcolonial situation, for precisely the reason that this language has been imposed from without' (2014: 14).

Chow discusses Derrida's *Le monolinguisme de l'autre* as an important take on the colonial situation wherein Derrida focuses on French even though Algeria boasts many languages. In reiterating 'je n'ai qu'une langue et ce n'est pas la mienne', Derrida does not lay claim to a more 'originary language', which is a source of surprise for Chow (2014: 20). Instead, Derrida 'foregrounds the important question of the relationship among language, property ownership, and a sense of belonging' (2014: 20). In the context of postcolonial (im)migration what happens when the (im)migrant is ill at ease in a language? In Miano's novel, language and identity are closely linked to social class and the colonial origins of the strangers who arrive in the host nation. Indeed, the first level of linguistic competence is emphasized through the illegal immigrants who 'baragouinaient tout juste la langue pour laquelle des multitudes avaient été abattues sommés d'oublier la leur' (2008: 125). The ties between colonial conquest and the loss of language in the home society are underscored, without however creating tension between the protagonists and the language. The 'ils' are set up in opposition to Shrapnel who learnt to master French to be able to work towards a future in France. Thus, education becomes a significant aspect of immigration insofar as those who have been able to attend French classes are in a superior position to those who were taught in indigenous languages. For those who belong on the bottom rungs of society in their home country, French is creolized to the point that 'eux seuls pouvaient s'y reconnaître et la comprendre' (2008: 64).

Conversely, French is the only language spoken by the prestigious elite in the home country. Amok belongs to this social class and is referred to as a 'Mukala', or white man, since 'il parlait mal la langue du pays' (2008: 198). In his chapter on the Black man and language in *Peau noire, masques blancs*, Fanon asserts that the Black man can only be similar to the white man if he speaks French: 'le Noir Antillais sera d'autant plus blanc, [...] qu'il aura fait sien la langue française' (1952: 14). While people in his home country might call Amok 'Mukala' in the text due to his mastery of French, the reality is that he is not white and his Blackness is deemed to be problematic in France, hence his transformation into 'Daniel Laurent' at the call centre, as demonstrated earlier. In his home country, his inability to speak a pre-colonial language leads to an identification with 'les noirs de l'Ouest' as they too were deprived of their 'langue naturelle' (2008: 71). The quest for identity and belonging is crucial here as language problematizes identity for Amok, who has a 'statut identitaire hybride. Lui qui ne parlait pas la langue de ses ancêtres [...]. La langue de ses pères ne lui avait pas été transmise par des parents ayant intériorisé l'idée de leur infériorité' (Miano 2008: 71).[12] Nonetheless, Amok's 'trouble de l'identité' (Derrida 1996: 40) is not the equivalent of the disjuncture experienced by African Americans. The interruption of language transmission is effected across diasporic spaces as second and subsequent generations of Black individuals are born and raised in America. In Amok's case, children born to privileged classes in former colonial countries are not taught pre-colonial African languages since the latter regard themselves as superior to the rest of the population. Amok's disarticulation is thus enacted by social class and is not a result of generations of assimilation. If there is a Derridean 'première violence' here (1997: 21), it is ironically perpetrated by the elite of the home country and not the host country, thereby complexifying the relationship between language and identity in former colonies.

Derrida's notion of language as a home which one can never truly possess is relevant here as Amok suppresses his 'accent subsaharien' and significantly, 'au reste du monde il réservait un parler standard, dépouillé des expressions imagées de son pays' (2008: 315). The accent is crucial as Derrida himself acknowledges his Algerian accent as a painful reminder that he does not speak pure French (1996: 79). In emotional moments, such as anger, the accent appears, demarcating him as *étranger*. Similarly, Amok's accent is imperceptible until he speaks with his lover, Amandla, 'parce qu'ils étaient proches' (2008: 315). Thus, while the immigrant can morph his language to fit into the mould of the host society, affect does play a role in his own (in)hospitality as it symbolizes a form of alienation

---

[12] For more on hybridity in Miano's Afropean novels see Unter Ecker (2016).

requiring self-policing. Amok's linguistic duality testifies to his willingness to adapt to fit in.

Ineluctably, a prominent aspect of mobility is the implied ability to return home. Miano interrogates the possibility of the return in her texts as she highlights the mutability of both the home society and the host society and the effect of such changes on (im)migrants. According to Ahmed et al.:

> The affectivity of home is bound up with the temporality of home, with the past, the present and the future. It takes time to feel at home. For those who have left their homes, a nostalgic relation to both the past and home might become part of the lived reality of the present. (2003: 9)

They underscore the importance of the notion of home in the lived reality of the migrant stranger who arrives in a host society. Earlier in *Strange Encounters* Ahmed had evinced the idea that 'the question then of being-at-home or leaving home is always a question of memory, of the discontinuity between the past and the present' (2000: 91). Indeed, strangers' perception of the host society and their positioning in the latter are contingent upon their relationship with their home and the past. However, this is not a collective experience, but a subjective one affecting each individual in numerous ways. For Ahmed et al., 'mobility can be foisted upon bodies through homelessness, exile and forced migration just as the purported "home" may be sites of alienation and violence (for women, children, queers)' (2003: 7). While the critics qualify forced migration as imposed on 'women, children, queers', Miano portrays Amok as a young Black man who is expected to study in France due to his social class, but who also chooses his own displacement due to paternal domestic violence. Thus, migration is seen as empowering, as 'un espace vierge où deployer l'énergie que la terre natale écrasait' (2008: 41). Whilst Amandla and Shrapnel focus on the collective experience of inhospitality and rejection experienced by Black individuals in France, Amok's subjective experience of home and migration lead to a vision of France as hospitable, due to the fact that 'l'histoire familiale' in his situation is more significant than 'l'Histoire' (2008: 304), that is collective history.

As I articulated with reference to Still and Rosello in the introduction to this book, as with any guest, the stay is not permanent. For the protagonists foregrounded in Miano's novel, France is a 'lieu de transit' (2008: 81). The notion of home is problematic in this case as Amandla is a French citizen since she comes from an overseas French territory but does not 'feel French' due to her Sub-Saharan African origins. For Amandla, France does not belong to 'Africans',[13] who are perpetual guests who must perforce return as 'installer son lit sous le toit d'un autre, c'était se condamner à n'avoir jamais de demeure à soi' (2008b: 230). Such a notion is aligned with Kinouani's assertion that 'as a result of the transatlantic slave trade, many of us have been born away from our ultimate ancestral lands. This disconnection already renders home making complex' (2021: 62). Yet the return is also fraught. Miano further complicates the notion of controlled hospitality by transposing it to the embassy's questioning of Amandla's trip to Amok's home country to accompany the latter on Shrapnel's demise. If France as master/host is depicted as inhospitable to Black individuals, so too is Africa, as descendants of slaves who do not have a 'patronyme subsaharien' and have French citizenship are denied visas (2008: 358). Thus, Amandla must rely on her relationship with Amok to gain access to his country. The concepts of home and belonging become challenging for descendants of displaced Black individuals who are refused hospitality in both the original home and in the adoptive home. Derrida's aporia and impossibility at the heart of hospitality takes on a distinct facet here as the boundaries between home and host countries are blurred, rendering France and Africa into non-hosts and especially the guests as non-guests or, indeed, guests of both nations. In this narrative, there is no home left for those who have emigrated. To counter this notion, Miano promulgates a return which is not predicated on the home nor the host country through Amok's meditations: 'le pays c'était l'enfance. C'était la source. Pas la destination. [...] l'*intra muros* apportait l'apaisement. Aucune réponse cependant. Ici, non plus, ce n'était pas chez lui. Il n'y avait jamais déposé ses valises' (2008b: 324). However, in *Crépuscule 2*, Miano provides Amok with a putative home through a recuperation of repressed otherness within himself.

Crépuscule 2 is the re-articulation of identity through recognition of the strangeness as natural. According to Véronique Petetin, in the two volumes of *Crépuscule du tourment*, 'les êtres sont féminins, même s'ils sont des hommes. Beaucoup de ses personnages sont à cette frontière des races et des sexes, refusant d'être sommés de choisir: être homme ou femme,

---

[13] Amandla groups all people of African origin under the same term in keeping with the fact that she argues that the society cannot tell the difference between those who were born in France or DOM-TOMs and those who were born on the African continent.

être Noir ou Blanc, être Européen ou Africain' (2017: 86). Miano sub-
verts gender binaries in the novel as thoughts of repressed sexuality bring
to the fore the love of 'le genre trouble', 'l'entre-deux' in Amok (2017b:
131). His preference reveals an unbounded attraction for transgender
individuals who have breasts and a penis. The reference to Judith Butler's
Gender Trouble (1991) is crucial here as Miano plays with gender roles and
heterosexual practices which are constrictive for the protagonist. The
notion of creating new spaces for a different conceptualization of gender
has been further explored by Butler in *Undoing Gender* (2004), where she
identifies fantasy as the realm of the possible insofar as it allows for the (re)
imagining of ourselves and others otherwise. Butler argues that situating
gender in the imaginary would enable the possible, and the possible is that
which allows for progress and evolution. The theorist adopts the view that
the body is a becoming, as it is in constant process:

> (Masculine/Feminine) both categories are still in process, underway, unful-
> filled [...] we must use this language to assert an entitlement to conditions
> of life in ways that affirm the constitutive role of sexuality and gender in
> political life, and we must also subject our very categories to critical scrutiny.
> (2004: 37)

Promulgating a similar vision of gender to that of Butler, Miano asserts in
an online interview with Alain Mabanckou: 'pour moi, dès qu'on dépasse
la question biologique, le féminin et le masculin sont des constructions
sociales et culturelles' (in Mabanckou 2006). Since gender is constructed,
it can also be deconstructed and reconstructed. For her, when women
write about men, they reshape masculinities through a distinct lens that
blurs gender boundaries: 'Lorsqu'on décrit des caractéristiques de la littérature dite féminine, on se rend compte que bien des hommes ont une
sensibilité féminine' (in Mabanckou 2006). I contend that reshaping masculinities is reworking the affect into experiences of masculinities, where
men in immigrant women's writing are the products of their circumstances
and they live and feel in new and transformative ways because of the movement into a different physical and mental space. Whilst Miano's interview
with Mabanckou highlighted her opinion in 2006, in 2017, she calls for
new alternative masculinities in *Crépuscule 2*.

In his analysis of the relationship between music and masculinity in
Crépuscule 2, Thomas Murray comments on Amok's choice of playing
Curtis Mayfield's 'Beautiful Brother of Mine' as lacking since it celebrates

a new confident African American masculinity honouring love for beautiful Black women. For Murray 'Amok, dont la sexualité s'écarte de l'hétéronormativité attendue, sait que son identité ne correspond pas à cet idéal sexuel' (2019: 158), and in due course, he chooses another song by the same singer, 'Sweet Exorcist', in which suicide is evoked as the only way out for someone who fails to negotiate his (sexual) identity. I argue that in *Crépuscule 2*, rather than surrender to melancholia, Amok's inward turn leads to a reconsideration of his own masculinity and sexual needs:

> l'homme souhaitait lui aussi retrouver son corps, l'habiter sans se reprocher d'en avoir un, prendre du plaisir sans y voir, ensuite, un avilissement. Ne plus souffrir de tant aimer pratiquer les actes auxquels il avait été contraint enfant. Accepter que cela lui avait laissé des désirs peu communs. [...] Pour l'heure, conscient d'avoir durablement refoulé ses pulsions sexuelles, de les avoir presque éteintes, il comptait les retrouver par l'imagination d'abord. Le souvenir de Mabel lui serait précieux. (2017b: 269)

Through the process of a journey into repressed memories, Amok comes to terms with his own masculinity, which is not constituted through heterosexuality, but with the help of sexual practices which are not traditional and yet are still valid and valuable. The journey to finding himself through his sexuality creates a new home through intimacy for Amok.

It is from this perspective that I turn to Svetlana Boym who writes about intimacy and the home. Boym articulates 'the notion of intimacy [a]s connected to home' (2000: 227). Writing specifically about the relationship between the diaspora and the home, Boym claims that 'diasporic intimacy can be approached only through indirection and intimation, through stories and secrets' (2000: 227). In Miano's *Crépuscule 2*, intimacy is lived both as the renegotiation of the intimate space of identity as recuperated through sexual practices, which were repressed through the diktat of colonialism as an oppressive space, and also as the acceptance of masculinity as not predicated upon heteronormative sexual practices. Thus, Amok uncovers the affective power of intimacy through a rediscovery of his sexual attraction for Mabel, who blurs the boundaries between masculine and feminine, and in so doing, enables him to comprehend his own sexual identity.

The return to the intimate space of the childhood home is conducive to the recuperation of the sexual self that need not question his own masculinity anymore, nor his place in the world. Indeed, acceptance of alterity commences with the acknowledgement that otherness is part of oneself as Kristeva has argued in *Etrangers à nous-mêmes*. The premise is that one should not fear the other or the strange as it is a part of every individual. Nonetheless, where migration and Black masculinity are a point of contention, Diome offers us an alternative to the migratory space in her novel.

Rejection of French (In)Hospitality in Le Ventre de l'Atlantique

> [...] une image de la France jamais vue sur les cartes postales.
> —Diome, *Ventre*

Moussa's predicament in the French prison prior to his deportation back to Senegal as an illegal immigrant exposes the hidden face of France, not as an Eldorado but as a country whose immigration policy dehumanizes those it considers to be strangers. Moussa's alienation echoes the cartographies of inhospitality delineated in the discussion of Miano's text, while simultaneously stretching the notions of racism and rejected alterity further. This section thus considers the migratory experience of the Senegalese (im)migrants in Diome's novel and underscores the range of ways in which stereotypes exacerbate the already inhospitable nature of France's immigration policies. I examine Diome's offering of education and sensitization on the African continent, thereby permitting a new way of reshaping masculinities from within the home society itself.

According to Rosello, 'infinite hospitality (greeting the stranger whoever he is, wherever she comes from) must deploy infinite naiveté, or perhaps a certain indifference to the possibility of seeing one's hospitality abused' (2001: 78). Thus, to uphold the Law of hospitality, French society would need to completely accept the other without suspicion and see only their positive aspects. Indubitably, as I have underlined in Miano's text and as I discuss in this section, France chooses not to adopt such a magnanimous position. In fact, as Kristeva argues, 'Nulle part on n'est *mieux* étranger qu'en France' and yet, 'nulle part on n'est *plus* étranger qu'en France. [...] les Français opposent à l'étranger un tissu social compact et d'un orgueil national imbattable' (1988: 58–59). These statements might be seemingly dichotomous, nevertheless, what is salient is the fact that difference is at the forefront of both attitudes.[14] Kristeva underlines one of the thorniest issues with immigration and hospitality in France: French society's fascination and rejection co-exist as there is a veritable fear of change. Homogeneity is seen as crucial to maintaining identity, and the presence of the other in this 'tissu social compact' calls into question French society's own identity (1988: 59).

According to Kathryn Lachman, 'Diome's debut novel, *Le Ventre de l'Atlantique*, articulates an impassioned critique of French immigration policy and racism, while advocating the reform of patriarchal institutions and educational and economic policy in Senegal' (2014: 34). Along with such important messages, it is also a depiction of forms of performative masculinities which are disavowed through racial discrimination against Black men. Diome's portrayal of spurned masculinities stems from the inhospitable nature of France's immigration policies along with its inherent sense of malaise towards Black individuals as Fanon suggests. Thus, characters such as Moussa become emblematic of policemen's drive to segregate and hunt down illegal immigrants who are mostly male.[15] Reduced to working illegally after his failure to keep his long coveted place on a football team, Moussa's incarceration is excruciating, to the extent that his food becomes 'mouriture' as he sees 'une image de la France jamais vue sur les cartes postales' (Diome 2003: 109). In Moussa's case, alterity is perceived as a reason to control and expel Black bodies. The discrepancy between the image of France, as advertized to him, and the France he experiences as he fails to achieve socio-economic prosperity, is stark. Moussa's dislocation is a direct corollary of both racism and the laws of hospitality which police borders and lead to a justification of his mistreatment. The image that the French police officers who incarcerate

[14] Speaking as the mayor of Paris in 1991, Jacques Chirac underlines 'il est certain que d'avoir des Espagnols, des Polonais et des Portugais travailler chez nous, ça pose moins de problème que d'avoir des musulmans et des Noirs' (in Fassin 2012: 5). However, speaking as the President in 2005, in the aftermath of the suburban riots, Chirac condemns 'le poison pour la société que sont les discriminations. Nous ne construirons rien de durable si nous ne reconnaissons pas et n'assumons pas la diversité de la société française. Elle est inscrite dans notre histoire. C'est une richesse et c'est une force' (2012: 5). Chirac's shifting position is testament to the changing terrain of politics regarding race in France. However, Fassin argues that these boundaries between the white French population and migrants from Africa are not a recent invention, they have simply become more visible. In this way, notions of colour and race, due to hypervisibility in a white French society, thus become highly significant.

[15] See Cazenave and Célérier (2011).

Moussa reflect to him is tainted and recoded with their own racist interpretation and Moussa cannot decolonize his mind.[16] As an individual
experiencing egregious police brutality and inhumane conditions in
prison, it can be difficult to not interpret such treatment as pure racism.[17]

Privileging the lived experiences of people who are part of Niodior
where Salie comes from, Diome weaves together a complex tapestry show-
casing the discrimination against Black (im)migrants in France. As Mbaye
Diouf remarks:

> Le métadiscours et les monologues intérieurs sont les modalités narratives
> privilégiées pour donner corps à ce discours. Que ce soit par le biais de per-
> sonnages comme Ndétare ou Moussa, ou par la narratrice elle-même, le
> sujet de la justice et de l'intégration des Noirs en France fait l'objet d'un
> véritable débat. (2010: 61)

The writer employs metanarrative to highlight the problematic marginality of Black men in France, through the author-protagonist Salie, the
homodiegetic narrator who provides the main backdrop even as she
recounts stories of Senegalese men's experiences.[18] Alternating pathos and
humour, Diome paints a bleak picture of the latter's lives post-migration.
Thus, the success story of Niodior, l'homme de Barbès, who eventually
opens a shop on the island, is juxtaposed with the realities of his suffering:

> avait été *un nègre à Paris* […].[19] Jamais ses récits torrentiels ne laissaient
> émerger l'existence minable qu'il avait menée en France. […] il avait d'abord
> hanté les bouches de métro, chapardé pour calmer sa faim, fait la manche,
> survécu à l'hiver grâce à l'Armée du Salut avant de trouver un squat avec des
> compagnons d'infortune. (2003: 88–89)

---

[16] The race of the field policemen involved is never overtly enunciated, whether in de
Maillard et al.'s factual study (2017) of the stop checks carried out by the police in France,
or in Miano's and Diome's novels. That these policemen might belong to the dominant
white French segment of the population is taken for granted and leads to a generalization of
the collective comportment of policemen in France.

[17] In the USA multiple protests tore the fabric of the nation in the aftermath of George
Floyd's death at the hands of a white Minneapolis police officer in May 2020. Instances of
police brutality and the embeddedness of racism are flagrant in both France and the USA, as
seen with Luhaka and Traoré. See also Traoré and De Lagasnerie (2019).

[18] See Genette (1980).

[19] Diome refers to Dadié's (1959) novel of the same name here. It unveiled the vicissitudes
of life for Black migrants in Paris.

Enumeration is deployed to underscore the series of trials and tribulations he endures before finding a temporary home. The ghettoization I examined in Miano's novel is exposed further here as poverty leads all those living in precarity to converge, regardless of their immigration status. As with Miano's novel, here too, French society is portrayed as ruthless to anyone who cannot contribute to its economy, irrespective of their origins. The society is equally inhospitable to its own white members if they are not deemed to be valuable contributors to the economy. Nonetheless, Diome's treatment of such dejection is humorous. In employing a homodiegetic narrator adopting the stance of a heterodiegetic narrator, Diome distances Salie from the characters endowing them with the status of figures serving a specific purpose. Thus, l'homme de Barbès is set up as a caricature and a hypocrite who hides behind wealth gained after decades of dire precarity in Niodior. Similarly, Moussa is constructed as a deeply tragic figure who dies a martyr due to his home society rejecting him as he returns empty-handed from France.

Elucidating the reasons behind her discourse against migration, Diome's narrator foregrounds a hierarchy in the levels of alterity in the French society: 'en Europe, mes frères, vous êtres d'abord noirs, accessoirement citoyens, définitivement étrangers' (2003: 176). The first level of categorization is skin-deep, the second level is nationality-based and the third is the fact that they are strangers. Thus, Derrida's non-distinguishable stranger is here lost behind other (more important) considerations for the master-host nation who decides who is permitted to stay, who belongs and who should be discarded. However, Diome underscores the fact that beyond considerations of humanity, colour and race have pride of place in the French society she portrays. Diome's generalization of the experiences of Sub-Saharan (im)migrants in France emanates from the notion that French society does not distinguish between migrants and immigrants or those who were born in France, which Pap Ndiaye's study *La Condition noire* (2008) questions. Ndiaye underlines that the lighter-skinned individuals are better treated, which might account partially for the obsession with lightening creams and skin bleaching.[20] In addition, Diome herself is evidence that success is possible in France as she has become a renowned writer. However, this is due to her own intellectual pursuits and the strong emphasis placed on education. Lastly, Diome does not think of returning

---

[20] Miano also reflects on this propensity for women to bleach their skin. See Kistnareddy (2020).

home, and neither does Salie. Her own lived experience of life in both countries leads her to choose the path of non-return as France, despite the society's ambivalent attitude towards race,[21] empowers Salie to make her own choices since her home society rejects her as an illegitimate child, as discussed in Chap. 4.

Just as Miano complexifies the notion of host and guest in the inhospitality foregrounded in *Tels*, Diome also employs irony as a means of questioning the home nation's inhospitality towards those who have migrated.[22] Diome deconstructs the concept of hypermasculinity in *Ventre* through the demystification of polygamy, one of the social ills the writer seeks to tackle in her novel. Thus, El Hadji, a former migrant in France, is called 'monocouille' in Niodior (2003: 146), as he practises monogamy. The derision towards El Hadji testifies to the significance of exhibiting one's masculinity through sexual prowess in Niodior. The failure of El Hadji's second marriage, due to jealousy, after decades of monogamy, supports Diome's subsequent message on the need to rid the society of such outdated practices if the youth wish for change to occur. Whilst Diome's view of destitution and underdevelopment in Senegal could be interpreted as the observation of an intellectual imbued in contemporary French society, she is indomitably a fervent proponent of non-migration due to the level of racism experienced by Black individuals in France.

Following Ahmed's notion of 'feeling out of place', in the case of Black male individuals, such a sentiment is not only attributed to their living on the margins of society, but also to the unease felt vis-à-vis their body. The experience of being other due to one's skin colour leads to the characters' emotional and psychological malaise. 'Feeling out of place' and out of home are important facets of migration which Diome explores in her work but she conflates such experiences as a collective identity crisis, unlike Miano, Chen and Thúy as I examine in the next two sections of this chapter. Whilst the other writers accentuate the deeply personal shifts operating in migrant men as they cross borders, Diome addresses an audience of young men whom she attempts to dissuade from emigrating. Thus, France's inhospitality becomes a deterrent through the use of nostalgia, as well as the feeling of dislocation experienced by those who return. Ahmed argues that no place remains unchanged, and no (im)migrant remains the

---

[21] Conversely Wassink and Hagan (2020) note that nearly half of all international migrants return to their country of origin within five years of emigration.

[22] See also Ahluwalia (2007).

same person who has left. Thus, the (im)migrant is a stranger both in the host society and in the home society:

> Les Africains, toutes vagues confondues, vivent en majorité dans des taudis. Nostalgiques, ils rêvent d'un retour improbable dans leur pays d'origine; pays qui, tout compte fait, les inquiète plus qu'il ne les attire, car, ne l'ayant pas vu changer, ils y sentent étrangers lors de leurs rares vacances. (2003: 176)

The threat of non-belonging is used as a means of dissuading the young men from Niodior from undertaking the voyage. In many ways, Diome's text is echoed by Kinouani's statements regarding the homelessness of Black migrants in France. Indeed, she observes, 'it is tough to feel secure in one's home when your skin forever marks you as an outsider. As not belonging. As not really from 'here', especially when the threat of dispossession or deportation always looms' (2021: 62). For those to whom community is a significant part of their life, the feeling of non-belonging would be deemed to be a convincing disincentive.

Whilst in Miano's novel Amok's return is a necessary passage to the reappropriation of his own personal history, here the collective rejection of Moussa as a failure leads to his inner fragmentation and to his suicide. Diome invokes Moussa's incapacity to come to terms with his home country, which while familiar, has become an unfamiliar space that drives to perdition, as delineated by Ahmed. Unlike Amok who still has the possibility of returning to France, Moussa now has no host country and is rejected by his home society. The text explicitly discusses this as a deeply mentally disparaging experience. As Diome's Salie poetically remarks: 'Partir c'est mourir d'absence. On revient certes, mais on revient autre' (2003: 227). In Moussa's case, he is not recognized as a man since he cannot provide for the family. Diome foregrounds characters who are compelled to emigrate and find employment in France by their largely extended families.[23] Diome's narrator is lucid about the pressures that these young men contend with:

> La plupart de ces garçons ne reçoivent que des bouches à nourrir en guise d'héritage. Malgré leur jeune âge, beaucoup sont déjà à la tête de familles nombreuses et on attend d'eux ce que leurs pères n'ont pas réussi: sortir les

---

[23] See Zadi (2010) and Cazenave and Célérier (2011).

leurs de la pauvreté. Ils sont harcelés par des responsabilités qui les dépassent et les poussent vers les solutions les plus désespérées. (2003: 182)

For Salie, Senegalese society needs to change, and the idyllic vision of France must be altered as it is deeply erroneous.[24] In her analysis of emigration and immigration in Diome's novels, Audrey Small writes that 'Diome's work restores complexity to the discussion of migration, showing that "immigration" cannot be understood in isolation from "emigration", and exposing the lethal myth-making about migration that persists on all sides' (2019: 45). Diome's endeavour in this text is ostensibly one of denouncing French society's lack of hospitality to counter the discourse of France being an Eldorado which pervades societies across the African continent. The use of the term 'Africains' attests to her concern with the perception of France across the continent.

In this way, whilst the message targets Sub-Saharan young men who dream of becoming rich in France, the individual stories Salie relates are personal experiences which nuance her didactic *propos*, such as with Moussa. I again turn to Ahmed from this perspective since in *Queer Phenomenology* the theorist argues that 'our body is not in space like things, it inhabits or haunts space. [...] bodies move through space and are affected by the "where" of that movement' (2006: 53). I contend that the movement from the African continent to France places Black male bodies in an affective space conducive to an examination of what it means to inhabit a different body and a liminal space, a limbo. Rather than focusing on the racial component, Ahmed's assertion permits a shift to the emotional and subjective as each character grapples with their own individual identity and sense of self in the host society. In Diome's text, the negotiation of home as a space (ideal vs real) and time as something which is deeply problematic since the passage of time solidifies migrants' diasporic reality and distances them from their country of origin. Although diasporas idealize the notion of home, which fosters nostalgia and the feeling of dislocation, as discussed with most of the texts in this chapter, there is an increasing lucidity emanating from the text regarding the subjective experience of migration, which ultimately impacts on the conception of masculinities.

---

[24] Recently, Kustov (2020) published a salient article arguing that there are now several countries which reject the notion of emigration and are proponents of creating opportunities locally.

Diome presents a description of masculinities as deeply patriarchal in Salie's Senegal. Describing Salie's brother, Madické, the narrator explains:

> Les hommes n'aimaient pas les détails, dit-on, et lui, tout petit déjà, on lui avait fait comprendre qu'il devait se comporter en homme. On lui avait appris à dire "ouille!", à serrer les dents, à ne pas pleurer lorsqu'il avait mal ou peur. [...] on lui avait bâti un trône sur la tête de la gent féminine. Mâle donc, et fier de l'être, cet authentique guelwaar savait dès l'enfance, jouir d'une hégémonie princière [...] et avoir le dernier mot devant les femelles. (2003: 40–41)

From this viewpoint, hooks's vision of black masculinity in *We Real Cool* as constituted upon traditional notions of patriarchy is significant for Madické is taught by his society to *be a man* by ignoring his feelings and reigning over women. However, hooks argues that this is a vision of masculinity shaped by white patriarchy. Diome sees stoicism and repression as a characteristic of patriarchy in general, since Madické is portrayed as an 'authentique guelwaar', thereby underlining Senegalese society's role in oppressing masculinities.

Equally, liminality is important here as Salie's positioning on the margins of the society empowers her to interrogate this vision of masculinities which relies on feminine abetment as the 'femelles' perpetuate these values.[25] Contrary to the women of Niodior, Salie understands the pressure boys experience in her society. Akin to Derrida's stranger who is outside of Reason (Logos) by virtue of being born elsewhere and can thus be perceived as mad (1997: 17), Salie feels split between Europe and Africa. Yet, in her in-between position, she envisages the society she hails from, from an outsider perspective, enabling her to unveil its shortcomings. She remarks that virility is a 'trône fragile' (2003: 42), for boys and men are constantly required to demonstrate stoicism. The problematic nature of 'feeling' in men is evinced through the friendship between Moussa and Ndétare in the text. The villagers' perception of the closeness between Ndétare and Moussa as homosexual belies the fact that homosocial closeness does not arise in this particular setting. Since sharing feelings is prohibited, their intimacy is perceived as unnatural. Whilst in Miano's novel homosexuality is recuperative and seen as redemptive, here it is symptomatic

---

[25] This concept is explored by Connell in *Masculinities* (1995) through the notion of hegemonic masculinity, which is reinforced by women who also perpetuate the idea that women are inferior to men.

of the lack of understanding of Senegalese society which does not con-
done affection between men. Just as Moussa experienced exile in France,
Ndétare was sent to Niodior as a political exile. Mutual suffering becomes
the cement that joins the two characters in their blatant rejection of migration and its ramifications.

Drawing on the model of Moussa's failure, the narrative focuses on
situating the home country as the source of changes and the space where
the future is for the youth:

> D'accord, soyez prêts au départ, allez vers une meilleure existence, mais pas
> avec des valises, avec vos neurones! Faites émigrer de vos têtes certaines
> habitudes bien ancrées qui vous chevillent à un mode de vie révolu. La
> polygamie, la profusion d'enfants, tout cela constitue le terreau fertile du
> sous-développement. (2003: 179)

The power of education and thought is highlighted here as the text
encourages Senegalese youth to acknowledge where progress in their society lies instead of necessarily emigrating to France. Accordingly, Salie provides the means for her brother Madické to open a shop in Niodior and
relinquish the dream of going to France. As explored in Chap. 4, Madické's
transformation is evident as his energy is gradually channelled towards settling down and making a home in his own community. He is likely to be
the next success story of the village, without going through emigration,
thereby exemplifying other options available to the young men. The narrator advocates a complete change undertaken from the roots in Senegalese
society. However, the restoration of feelings for the young man is not
foregrounded as such. Madické's love for his sister is expressed simply as a
suggestion that she return 'home', as I examine in Chap. 4. The emotional
charge is attenuated by Diome's didactic enterprise. Salie's own aptitude
to finance her brother's new start in the home society was only actualized
by her own migratory experience. Her lucidity is a consequence of her
liminal position, however, for her, racism against Black men is significant
enough to deter the boys of her community back in Niodior from
emigrating.

Much as with Miano, Diome is a proponent of the restitution of feelings and love to boys and men who are deprived of a means of expressing
their emotions. For Miano, it is crucial to stop history from repeating itself
by constantly passing on the burning legacy of slavery and racism, for,
'accepter la succession de ses pères revient à prendre en charge le passif de

leur action, pas à le faire passer pour de l'actif. Ce serait cela, aujourd'hui cette grandeur dont on voudrait prévenir la fuite' (2017b: 21). Through the new embodiments of Black men in society, art and literature, Miano wonders whether 'des alternatives à la masculinité classique se mettent-elles en place de façon à ce que l'individu s'affranchisse des normes et s'invente d'autres espaces?' (2017b: 27). Indeed, she follows the same train of thought as hooks who contends that:

> If black men no longer embraced phallocentric masculinity, they would be empowered to explore their fear and hatred of other men, learning new ways to relate. [...] Most black men will acknowledge that black men are in crisis and are suffering. Yet they remain reluctant to engage those progressive movements that might serve as meaningful critical interventions, that might allow them to speak their pain. (2015: 112)

hooks examines the need for finding new ways of conceiving masculinity, including through using her brother as her model for 'reconstructing black masculinity': 'affectionate, full of good humor, loving, my brother was not at all interested in becoming a patriarchal boy' (2015: 87). Her ideal version of masculinity promulgates benevolence, love and kindness, and the men she remembers,

> [she] remember[s] them because they loved folks, especially women and children. They were caring and giving. They were black men who chose alternative lifestyles, who questioned the *status quo*, who shunned a ready made (*sic*) patriarchal identity and invented themselves. By knowing them, [she] ha[s] never been tempted to ignore the complexity of black male experience and identity. (2015: 88)

hooks proposes a reshaping of black masculinities which considers the affective circumstances in which they are constituted. Ways of seeing and categorizing Black men must be altered:

> Spaces of agency exist for black people, wherein we can both interrogate the gaze of the Other but also look back, and at one another, naming what we see. The "gaze" has been and is a site of resistance for colonized black people globally. (2015: 116)

hooks inexorably gives pride of place to the ways in which Black masculinities must be re-appropriated in America due to the enduring negative discourses prevailing in American society, but she recognizes that the experience is shared by others.[26] As Miano and Diome demonstrate, such a re-appropriation is crucial both on the African continent and in France for Black men to feel at home and accepted for the human beings they are.

Unlike Miano, however, Diome presents a different relationship to the French language due to the writer's own trajectory. Much as Chow underscores the vantage point afforded by the ability to manipulate the colonizer's language fully, Christopher Hogarth remarks that:

> Diome [...] credits her ability to write in French with her liberation, while criticizing the simplicity of any view of French as a language of oppression. In this way, she contributes to a Senegalese discourse on the role of French as Senegal's language of literary expression. (2019: 82)

As I suggest in Chap. 4, Salie does not herself exhibit a difficult relationship with French, since she chooses to learn it for both its aesthetic attributes and for the education it affords her. Yet, through her metanarratives, the reader is able to comprehend that not everyone is in the same position. Firstly, her own brother cannot speak French, since he attends Islamic school instead of the French education system. In learning French from Ndétare, Madické grows closer to his sister as 'il comprenait de mieux en mieux [ses] petites phrases françaises, intercalées par inadvertence dans [leurs] discussions' (2003: 91). Equally noteworthy are Diome's humorous portrayals of characters such as l'homme de Barbès who 'malgré son illettrisme, avait commencé à prononcer le *r* à la française' (2003: 31). While the accent is problematic for Derrida because it signals his otherness in French, here, the accent distinguishes l'homme de Barbès from the rest of the community since they cannot roll the letter 'r' as the French do. In gaining an accent, he becomes an other who is envied in this case.

Both Miano and Diome underline the challenges of being other and speaking French 'correctly' in their novels. (Im)Migrant Black men's dislocation is thus also contingent on 'sounding' different, and on their capacity to blend into French society. Nonetheless, both writers demonstrate that language becomes a locus for different possibilities to negotiate one's identity for the characters. Conversely, Canada presents a different

---

[26] Indeed, as George Floyd's death has demonstrated in the USA, racism and its impact have far-reaching consequences, which are echoed with Traoré in France as I underline in the next chapter.

context wherein East Asian masculinities are accepted in their difference, but their own limitations and the inability to change creates problematic identity issues and forms of unwelcoming, as I discuss with Chen's *Lettres chinoises* and Thúy's *Vi*.

CANADA THE WILLING HOST

Canada was colonized by both the French and the British. Its aboriginal population rebelled against the government in 1870–1871 and 1885, due to consistent lack of respect for the terms of aboriginal rights policies. Equally, the French were dissatisfied with the lack of protection of the French language and interests as per the British North America Act of 1867. Although Québec was given a 'Special status', it was not until 1976, after the Multiculturalism Act of 1971 was enshrined in the law, that 'Bilingualism and Biculturalism' was introduced.[27] The Multiculturalism Act stipulates in its most salient article that:

> 3. (1) it is hereby declared to be the policy of the government of Canada to (a) recognize and promote the understanding that multiculturalism reflects the cultural racial diversity of Canadian society and acknowledges the free-dom of all members of Canadian society to preserve, enhance and share the cultural heritage.

It delivers a clear message to anyone who inhabits the country and to any-one who elects to immigrate: they are welcome, and they can bring their culture and values from their home country to their host country. This Act was further developed in 1988 with the policy of 'Bilingualism and Multiculturalism', permitting people to freely practise their culture of origin.

Examining 'Multiculturalism' in the case of Canada, David B. Macdonald argues that Canada has 'long promoted itself as a world trend-setter in Multiculturalism' (2014: 66). However, he observes that this is a form of 'colonial multiculturalism' it denies the rights and culture of Aborigines as existing before colonialism (2014: 67).[28] Arguably, there are some struc-tural challenges which are already present within the concept, which is

---

[27] Naidu contends that this was 'too little, too late' for the French Canadians (1995: 2).

[28] For a detailed discussion of Multiculturalism in Canada and Europe see Mielusel and Pruteanu (2020).

exacerbated by the fact that in reality racism still persists in Canadian society,[29] despite its official declaration of openness to other cultures and religions.[30] In a gesture which differentiates it from France, which does not recognize racial difference in its 1958 Constitution, and in 2018 voted to take the word 'race' out of the Constitution, Canada acknowledges difference but perceives it as empowering and necessary in the contemporary world. Nonetheless, racist attitudes still persist. To a certain extent, it can be argued that Canadian immigration laws satisfy the principle of equality upon which the Law of hospitality is predicated. This does not change the fact that immigration is still policed, and the laws of hospitality prevail insofar as visas are granted and migrants are authorized entry under particular conditions.[31] In 1976 ethnic considerations were removed from the immigration policy. Since then, Canada has accepted hundreds of thousands of immigrants through either family reunification, socio-economic migration or on humanitarian grounds. The official figures from the Canadian government reveal that currently 300,000 people 'make Canada their home each year'.[32] Chinese immigrants have been part of the Canadian immigration landscape since the nineteenth century,[33] and most settled for socio-economic reasons. In the aftermath of the Vietnamese war, between 1975 and 1976 Canada admitted 5608 Vietnamese immigrants. By 1985, 110,000 Vietnamese refugees had settled in Canada, many in Québec, due to their affinity with the French language given that France had formally colonized the country. Québec can select its own immigrants by law but takes a quota of refugees who are pre-selected every year.[34]

While the protagonists in Diome's and Miano's novels are perpetually marginalized due to their racial difference and their lack of connection with France, Canada is regarded as an empowering space insofar as immigrants are encouraged to be at home in their otherness. Kristeva's notion of the recognition of the other as necessarily part of the self is significant here (1988: 9), as the host nation thrives in its display of differences as

[29] Bissoondath calls this 'selling illusions' (1994).

[30] See Mullings et al. (2016).

[31] Exceptions are made to an extent for refugees, who are unequivocally welcomed, but they also are controlled eventually and integrated into the Canadian community through the laws of immigration.

[32] See the Canada Government Website (2020).

[33] See Price (2013).

[34] See Immigration Gouvernement Québec (2020).

reflecting the multicultural fabric of any migrant society. Nonetheless, the host-guest relationship at stake here is not the same colonial-postcolonial one prevailing in France. Canada did not colonize China, nor Africa nor India. The presence of descendants of former colonized peoples does not foster the tension present in France, nor do immigrants perceive Canada as the nation of those who dehumanized them through slavery or subjugation. Instead, its own native population was subjugated and discriminated against. Yet immigrants' lives in Canada might not be the perfect experience of hospitality as it is also the role of the guest, in Derrida's structure of hospitality, to accept such hospitality, as I examine with reference to Chen's *Lettres chinoises* and Thúy's *Vi* in this section.

Chen's text is a three-way epistolary exchange written between Yuan, a Chinese student in Montréal, his fiancée, Sassa, who has remained in China to apply for her visa, and Da Li, Sassa's best friend who has also emigrated to Montréal. The letters attest to the transformation which occurs in a young man from China, where the values differ from Canadian society. He cannot come to terms with his host society even as the latter advocates freedom of choice and culture. In *Vi*, Thúy explores changing gendered identities in a Vietnamese refugee family in Québec in the aftermath of the Communist takeover of Saigon, where the affluent family lived. Since they left the husband/father behind, the consequences on Long, the eldest son and the family itself become crucial elements to the narrator, Vi's story.

Chen's Unwilling Guest in Lettres chinoises

In this section I am particularly interested in the perceived differences between China and Canada as depicted in Chen's *Lettres chinoises*. The text offers a distinct perspective on the arrival of a young man who begins his letters to his fiancée on notions of freedom and new beginnings as he leaves China to study in Canada, where he hopes Sassa will follow him soon. My reading hinges upon the divergent perceptions of China and the host society as the narrator writes to Sassa. First, it is important to remember that China is a communist society and it is founded on the precepts of Confucian values. According to F. Tsai, 'Confucius believed that political order must be established on social order, and social order must come from individual cultivation' (2005: 159). Tsai quotes Confucius's principles as encapsulated in the power of self-cultivation, which leads to 'their families [being] regulated. Their families being regulated, their States were rightly governed. Their States being rightly governed, the whole kingdom was made tranquil and happy' (Confucius 1991: 359). Confucian values dictate that from the individual's self-control stems order in society and such self-control is extremely important in the Chinese society Yuan, the protagonist references in his letters.

The epistolary exchange between the three protagonists becomes a gradual appraisal of the differences between the home country and the host country, Canada, and Québec in particular. Yuan extols the virtues of his host country, by aggrandizing the idea of migration itself as a form of rebirth (1993: 17). Ecstatic upon his arrival, he writes: 'je suggérerais à tout le monde de s'expatrier' (1993: 17), and deems migration to be 'nécessaire' (1993: 38). Importantly, as Julie Rodgers underlines, 'the emphasis is not necessarily on arriving at a place but, rather, the act of transposition itself' (2015: 54). Yuan cannot foretell what his life will be as he arrives and is merely carried away by the possibilities that mobility and the transformations which it entails, create for him, although this is not always a constructive experience. In this section, I examine the extent to which the host society's hospitality can be challenging due to the guest's own affective experiences. I explore Yuan's homelessness as he remains in a form of limbo between both countries.

Central to Yuan's vision of his new life are the stereotypes associated with North America as a land where all freedoms are attained. Much as inhabitants from former French colonies in Africa in relation to France in Miano's novels, in Chen's narrative, both Yuan and Da Li, Sassa's friend, have an idealized notion of what North America embodies. For instance, routine life itself is perceived as something extraordinary:

> J'aime l'Amérique. Ici, on vit dans les champs et on meurt dans une tombe. Une vie parfaitement normale, n'est-ce pas? Or, dans notre ville natale, j'ai l'impression que, faute d'espace, on vit sur la pointe des pieds, et quand on est mort, il faut que notre corps disparaisse dans les feux. (1993: 41)

Da Li's comments evoke the expanse of North America compared to the narrowness of life in overpopulated China, but also of the perceived opportunities and openness of her host country as opposed to the closed nature of her home society. Nevertheless, in the novel, stereotypes are slowly debunked as the freedom obtained in Montréal, where Yuan and Da Li live, is interrogated. While the laws of hospitality in the host country police behaviour and following them is mandatory for (im)migrants, here the laws are more relaxed than in China. This new paradigm compels Yuan to wonder about the extent to which he is truly free. Soon enough, he writes: 'J'ai voulu me libérer un peu en quittant Shanghai. [...] J'ai choisi tout cela: je me sens donc presque libre. Mais crois-tu que je le suis vraiment ici plus qu'ailleurs?' (1993: 21). His question leads the reader to interrogate freedom as a necessity in society. When laws are less restrictive in the host society, does hospitality change? Is this new society in reality freer than the one he has left behind? Here the guest's own limitations are conducive to a form of self-policing which tests the limits of the possible: 'je suis libre [...] je suis le seul responsable de moi-même. Et si l'idée me prenait de me tuer? [...] Pourtant, je commence à avoir peur de cette liberté qui m'attire comme un trou inconnu' (1993: 35). In Yuan's case, the freedom proffered is unwelcome since it symbolizes a lack of boundaries. In turn, this absence of curtailment is unfamiliar and is seen as inhospitable, thereby calling into question Yuan's sense of identity. *Contra* Rosello and Still for whom the guest might outstay his welcome and Derrida's theory that the guest might become a parasite if hospitality is unconditional, here the guest rejects who he might become as fewer restrictions are placed on him than in his home country. This fear of change prompts an over-attachment to the values he was raised with, fostering a sense of being in limbo between two modes of living and two countries.

Writing about what home means to the stranger, Ahmed argues that 'home becomes the impossibility and the necessity of the subject's future (one never gets there but is always getting there) rather than the past that binds the subject to a given place' (2000: 78). As the home is the locus of memories and attachment, for the stranger it becomes the goal that is to be attained in the future. Indubitably, nostalgia plays a crucial role in the (in)hospitality of the space Yuan inhabits. Rather than feeling he belongs in Québec, Yuan feels increasingly alienated from it and clings to his home country: 'je ressens un profond besoin de reconnaître mon appartenance à mon pays' (1993: 10). Significantly, the absence of government control beyond his immigration documents as a student in Québec, and the lack of directionality given by the prior edicts and laws in Shanghai, incapacitate him as he negotiates life without these parameters in the host nation. Similar to the in-betweenness highlighted by Ahmed,[35] Yuan cannot process the differences between his home and host countries and experiences

---

[35] The concept of identity in the 'in-between' or 'third space' is also explored by Bhabha (1994).

culture shock, leading to an increased attachment to the home country: 'c'est en quittant ce pays que j'apprends à mieux l'aimer' (1993: 10). Nonetheless, Chen swiftly debunks any notion that such nostalgia is conducive to a better sense of identity for him. Thus, through the character of Sassa, Chen critiques diasporic nostalgia insofar as it confers to the home country aspects and characteristics that are imaginary: 'on blâme son exil et on se console avec les souvenirs de sa mère patrie, purifiés et embellis par l'imagination grâce à la distance et au temps écoulé' (1993: 27). In so doing, Chen highlights the effects of space and time on migrant imagination and the negative effects of living in the past.

Moreover, Chen also foregrounds the problematics of living between cultures through the deteriorating relationship between Sassa and Yuan. Since Confucian masculine values dictate that men are stabilized through their relationships and their position in the family,[36] the loss of the home country, and Sassa, call for an interrogation of masculine identity in Chen's novel. *Lettres chinoises* sets itself apart from Miano's and Diome's texts by situating the perceived loss of masculinity and identity through the loss of love. As I have demonstrated so far, Yuan's own unwillingness to accept the host nation fully hinges upon his inability to negotiate two identities: as a Chinese man and as a guest in Canada. The inclusion of Sassa's and Da Li's letters to each other enables us to gauge that Yuan and Da Li have grown close as Yuan has been meeting Da Li regularly. Though Da Li does not reveal that it is Yuan whom she has fallen in love with, the letters lead us to believe that it is the case, as I discuss in Chap. 4. Of particular interest here is the fact that the two women narrators represent the two countries: Da Li (host society) and Sassa (home country). In his analysis of this text, Emile Talbot contends that Yuan 'transforme son amour pour sa fiancée, Sassa, en un véritable projet de mémoire' (2005: 150).[37] He argues that more than love it is what Sassa represents which drives Yuan: the home country. But as Sassa argues, 'un amour suspendu entre deux terres perd son énergie dans l'air' (Chen 1993: 124).[38] Neither relationship remains at the end of the exchanges as Da Li leaves and Sassa ends all communication with Yuan, leading to his ultimate loss.

Distance affects their relationship, but it is also the fact that Yuan attempts to keep Sassa as his idyllic fiancée whom he serenades about the

[36] See Scott Morton (1971) and Louie (2003).
[37] See also Yun (2007, 2013).
[38] See Dufault (2001).

glories of his motherland, while simultaneously beginning an intimate relationship with Da Li. Yuan's status as Sassa's fiancé dictates that he treat her well and that he give her a similar status as he would his wife. With Da Li, he wants to shed his conservative values and engage in sexual intercourse, telling her that she is too 'traditional' when she asks if he loves her, as I examine in Chap. 4 in my discussion of the epistolary form. Although Sassa writes: 'nous ne pouvons pas vivre dans un monde sans relâcher un peu, sinon complètement, les principes et habitudes d'un autre monde' (1993: 129), this does not imply that he should cheat on his fiancée with her best friend. Whether in Canada or China, such a behaviour is unacceptable. Cognizant of his transformation, Yuan is vocal of his fear of not being the same man who left China anymore: 'je sais que je suis en train de vivre une métamorphose qui peut-être ne me mènera nulle part [...] si je ne reste pas fermement moi-même, si je n'essaie pas de rester Chinois, je ne serai rien du tout' (1993: 133). The in-betweenness he feels, which Jack Yeager calls 'halfway house of culture' (2004: 140), is not productive. Yuan's liminal position fosters an understanding of the host nation as a space for rebirth, much as with Amok in Miano's novel. However, here the experience proves to be destructive as the protagonist tries to embrace two women as he would two cultures. Had he not associated the women with the two countries, Chen's Yuan would perhaps have been able to adapt to his host country. In line with the words of Confucius I quoted at the beginning of this section, in not controlling himself, in not keeping his relationship intact, Yuan has failed in the views of his home society and in his own eyes. The nostalgia he experiences, his inability to open to the host country and to the possibilities that are open to him there as an individual lead to his ultimate collapse.

Having demonstrated the ways in which Yuan himself made Canada an inhospitable space for himself, I now turn to the external factors that contribute to his downfall. In particular, I argue that linguistic inhospitality is an important facet of Chen's narrative. The writer herself is not a native French speaker, nor does she originate from a country where French is still used in official contexts as is the case with Miano and Diome. Given her affinity for languages, Chen was compelled to learn Modern Languages at university as per the Chinese government rules. Her subsequent decision to emigrate to Québec led to her embracing French further.[39] Her choice

---

[39] See Bouvier-Lafitte (1999) for an extended discussion of language and identity in Franco-Chinese writing.

to write in French marks her as an exophone writer.[40] Nonetheless, writing in another language can be a difficult task and is often related to a form of translation.[41] In *Beyond the Mother Tongue* (2012), Yasemin Yildiz draws on Derrida's theory of monolingualism to develop the concept of the 'postmonolingual' (2012: 5). Asserting that the 'mother tongue' represents affective and 'natural kinship' (2012: 10), Yildiz recognizes the potential of writing and speaking a language which is not one's mother tongue as creating a 'new linguascape' or uncommon language combination (2012: 109), as is the case of Mandarin and French with Chen here. In her own examination of Japanese-born Yoko Tawada's writing in German, Yildiz identifies the latter's use of 'bilingualism as a literary strategy of detachment from any language's claim on the subject, rather than as a basis for a claim to a double belonging' (2012: 112).[42] In *Lenteur*, Chen reveals that '[elle] parle mal français', which is 'presque impensable quand on est considéré comme un auteur d'expression française' (Chen 2004: 84). In the text, Chen does not employ Mandarin at all in the text, despite the title of the work being *Les lettres chinoises*. While bilingualism would have perhaps corroborated Yildiz's claim that the language utilized does not have a 'claim on the subject', in *Lettres chinoises* Chen demonstrates her particular affinity for French, which she calls 'un grand amour que viendrait appauvrir toute explication' (Chen 2004: 37). Thus, Chen herself does not share Yuan's difficulties as a newly arrived migrant who cannot understand French, thereby setting up a contrast between herself and Yuan, who feels disoriented in Québec.

Investigating the notion of disorientation in *Queer Phenomenology* Ahmed argues that it is necessary as 'the point is what we do with such moments of disorientation, as well as what such moments can do—whether they can offer us the hope of new directions, and whether new directions are reason enough for hope' (2006: 158). This moment of disorientation represents potent possibilities for a re-conceptualization of identity for Yuan since he arrives in Québec seeking for a form of rebirth as quoted earlier. Nevertheless, Chen chooses instead to demonstrate the consequences of over-attachment to the home country's contrastive values. Yuan does not take advantage of this moment of possibilities re-root himself on his own terms, with his own definition of his identity. Instead, he

---

[40] For a discussion of exophony in a European context, see Arnt et al. (2007).

[41] See Suga (2007). Chen also discusses this herself in *La Lenteur des montagnes* (2014: 84).

[42] See Porra (2011).

exemplifies the feeling of loss experienced by those who are psychologically disorientated in the host nation, and this is demonstrated through a form of linguistic disaffection.

Contrary to the experience of migration for Amok and Shrapnel in *Tels*, Yuan does encounter Derrida's 'première violence' in Montréal (1997: 21). For Derrida, language is home, but it is a home that cannot be appropriated. Yuan's lack of language skills leads him to feel out of place in the host community: 'quand tu te trouves parmi des gens dont tu ignores jusqu'à la langue' (1993: 10). The distance he experiences is due to his mastery of French being perfunctory so that he must take additional language classes in order to follow his course. While colonizers imposed their language in their colonies, in the cases of Cameroon and Senegal, and emigrating to Québec also involves a measure of linguistic imposition, here it is a violence that he has chosen. For Maude Labelle, in this text, 'la perte des repères langagiers est associée à une transformation radicale de l'identité' (2007: 48).[43] Yuan admits that 'très souvent [il] ne [comprend] pas les questions' (1993: 17). Ineludibly the lack of comprehension does mar his perception of the host nation. Since Canada has an established Chinese community spanning several generations as I discussed earlier, Chen shows that only the absence of language would distinguish the newly arrived Chinese man from the extant Chinese community; and it is precisely '[s]on accent' (1993: 12). Yuan's visible difference is exacerbated by both his inability to completely master French and his undisguisable accent, which intensify the feeling of disorientation he experiences.

Disorientation is recurrent in the text, including with various types of racial stereotyping in the novel. In his study of *Lettres chinoises*, Yeager argues that the text presents the search for an identity 'new, rooted or hybrid—and the seeming impossibility of finding such an identity when one is a visible outsider' (2004: 140). In the text, while multiculturalism is celebrated, it is also not recognized in its specificity: 'généralement, les gens d'ici ont tendance à mettre tous les asiatiques dans le même sac' (1993: 58). Though racism is at the extreme end of the spectrum, it is also problematic to not comprehend the fact that East Asians also have different origins, cultures and languages. The ignorance of the Québécois depicted in the novel is thus symptomatic of a hospitality which is simply legal and remains at surface level. Thus, the willing host might just as well lead the willing guest to a slippery slope of inhospitality insofar as the

---

[43] See also De Balsi (2018).

immigrant's identity is conflated with so many others'. For Yuan resistance against change can also be a rejection of a form of Québécois inhospitality: 'si je ne reste pas fermement moi-même, si je n'essaie pas de rester Chinois, je ne serai rien du tout' (1993: 133). Nevertheless, Yuan's choice to refuse these changes is not perceived as empowering in the novel. Rather, the fiancés' exchanges end on the evocative image of Yuan as a stringless kite which will eventually be lost.

Yuan remains unable to re-root and re-orient himself in the host society. His failure to blend in, his lack of language and his incapacity to harness the possibilities afforded to him by living in Québec lead to his internal lack of cohesion and complete sense of loss. While Québec is hospitable, it asks that the immigrant speak French, and integrate into the society seamlessly, which is impossible in Yuan's case. By contrast, the Vietnamese's refugee status, their capacity to understand and navigate the city using French, allows for a different perspective for Thúy's protagonists.

Host and Home in Vi

In her concluding chapter on hospitality's imperfections, Rosello asserts that: 'if the guest is always the guest, if the host is always the host, something has probably gone very wrong: hospitality has somehow been replaced by parasitism or charity' (2001: 167). Rosello argues, much as Still does, that guests must leave or their status changes from that of a guest. The critic believes that the continuum between guest and host is at risk of imbalance with guests being compelled to prove that they can reciprocate and outperform their hosts and vice versa, leading to what she calls 'ostentation' (2001: 168). But what of the refugee who is given asylum? Try as they might, they might never reciprocate the gift of a new home, grateful as they may be.

Derrida's notion of hospitality hinges upon a humane interpretation of hospitality with regard to asylum seekers and refugees. Based upon the ethical interpretation of hospitality promulgated by Levinas, the welcoming of refugees is an important facet that should always be upheld as it demonstrates our humanity. For those who partake of a stable and economically viable lifestyle, providing basic needs for those who are in a precarious position becomes a matter of ethics and humanity. Canada is one of the countries whose doors is open to refugees.[44] Yet the ability to use either English or French, in the case of Québec, is essential to integration. *Vi*, Thúy's third narrative after *Ru* (2010) and *Mãn* (2013) is set in both Vietnam and Québec as a family's history is revealed through the eyes of an eight-year-old girl, Vi, whose brothers are due to join the military at the age of eighteen. Grandchildren to a well-educated lawyer who doted upon his only son, their father, the children grow up protected by their mother until their escape in the aftermath of the Communist takeover of Saigon in 1975. Written in what critics have called 'vignettes' (Sing 2016: 181), and in anecdotal form,[45] *Vi* is the narrator's retelling of her experiences as a refugee places Canada as the first country to provide aid to the refugees stranded in refugee camps: 'la délégation canadienne a été la première à nous recevoir' (2016: 47). Vi's mother's role as French-Vietnamese interpreter for the delegation ensures that the family is given asylum in Québec. However, Canada is an unknown destination at the time and 'parce que nous avons fait partie de la première grande vague de réfugiés vietnamiens acceptés au Canada, nous n'avions pas entendu d'échos concernant ce pays' (2016: 47). Here Canada itself needs to prove that it can be a hospitable nation to refugees. But such hospitality on the part of the delegation is reliant on the fact that the family speaks French.

A working knowledge of French is one of the criteria that qualifies the family to be considered for entry into Québec. Since Vietnam was a French colony, many of those who were educated within the French system do not experience Derrida's 'violence première' (1997: 21), the deprivation of one's mother tongue and the need to learn a language which is completely different from one's mother tongue by its intonation, its lexical and its written forms.[46] Vietnam's decolonization post-1954 led to many of the schools reverting to Vietnamese as its main language, but the wealthier Saigon-based families still sent their children to French medium schools, as is the case with Vi's elder brother, Long. The latter's ability to speak

---

[44] As Robinson (1998) has observed, for two decades, between the 1970s and mid-1990s, the UNHCR registered a total of 839,228 ethnic Vietnamese and ethnic Chinese in numerous refugee camps throughout East and Southeast Asia. Many of these would make their way to Canada.

[45] See Buss (2018).

[46] As Vietnam was also simultaneously influenced by the American presence, English was also a medium of communication. In *Vi*, Ha, the family friend uses English with her American friends. It later enables her to communicate with the other countries who need a translator in the refugee camps. She ultimately also lives in the USA with her husband.

French is conducive to his integration in the Québecois society since 'ses années d'apprentissage du français dans les écoles de Saigon lui avaient permis de saisir rapidement le fonctionnement du réseau de transport' (2016: 51). Thúy constructs Long's journey to integration through small empowering victories. With a touch of humour, Thúy depicts his conquering of the transport system due to his knowledge of French. The host society's language is thus vital to feeling at home, as is contributing to the economy and earning a living. Accordingly, Long rapidly finds employment in a Japanese restaurant while refugees who have to acquire the language before they can find employment find it difficult to adapt to a new society and a new language,[47] much as Yuan in Chen's novel.

Language, in Thúy's novel is thus a necessary indicator of whether the immigrant will fit in or not. Long consequently instructs his siblings in French: '[i]l nous apprenait notre adresse, notre numéro de téléphone et les salutations en français en donnant l'exemple' (2016: 49). Rather than mandating the use of the Vietnamese language to preserve their cultural values, Long seeks to facilitate the family's integration in Québec by privileging a French-language education. However, Vietnamese is still prevalent within a private setting: Thúy's own French prose is strewn with Vietnamese words, testifying to her own bilingualism, even as she elects to write mainly in French.[48] Following Yildiz, as I underlined with Chen, the ability to shift between languages reinforces the notion of a language which 'does not lay claim on the subject' (2012: 112), and instead, allows for a different, fluid relationship between language and identity.

The absence of concern for racism, as a Vietnamese man is not deemed to be incongruous in a Japanese restaurant here, is a function of what Pierre Bourdieu terms 'habitus' (1980). Discussing 'habitus', François Collet argues that: 'habitus relies on the observation that in our most conscious thoughts we cannot but take some things for granted' (2009: 420). Thuy's 'habitus' might be the view that Canada is a warm and completely multicultural society where no discrimination exists and to which the refugee families have adapted easily. Such an overwhelmingly positive attitude towards the host country has led to critics such as Vinh Nguyen to see her

[47] Describing how Vietnamese and Chinese refugees integrate different social strata in Victoria, Canada, Woon (1986) highlights the fact that knowledge of English leads to better paid jobs and maintenance of social status. By contrast, those who do not manipulate the language are restricted to lower paid employment which requires little interaction with others, thereby also causing a sense of dis-ease in migrants.

[48] See Mata Barreiro (2012) and Edwards (2018).

novels as emblematic of 'refugee gratitude' (2013). However, this open-ness has led to the immigrants' sense of malaise insofar as it creates a form of unwilling inhospitality which creates tension in the guests themselves. The conflation of all Asians, with Long passing for Japanese at the restau-rant, is significant here insofar as Québec is depicted as tolerating other cultures but not seeking to understand them, as evaluated earlier with Chen's novel. Yet, for the refugee starting anew in the text, individual recognition is less important than the ability to regain economic stability: 'd'un côté les clients nourrissaient leurs rêves d'exotisme. De l'autre, mon frère Long se dirigeait vers la réalisation de ses rêves' (2016: 52). Thus, lack of understanding on the part of the society is not experienced as a difficulty insofar as Long focuses on his role as provider. Derrida's model of hospitality's limits are also debunked here as there is no need to ques-tion the way in which strangers are perceived in this case. For refugees, survival trumps any sense of unease or lack of comprehension of others, at which others, such as Chen's Yuan, might take offence.

Subjectivation is crucial to masculinities in the text as Long grapples with shifting values as he comes to terms with the new society which welcomes him in Québec. 'Nous sommes arrivés au paradis!' exclaims Long upon arrival (2016: 48). Long's ecstatic words after weeks of precarity living in refugee camps in Malaysia, followed by arduous travel to Canada itself, is demonstra-tive of the sense of relief experienced by refugees on reaching a host society which seems to welcome them, and which epitomizes wealth and abundance. Though Thúy does not typically use direct speech in her texts, Long's exclama-tion attests to the importance his words, and indeed, he himself, play in the narrative. I contend that while the process of immigration and the experience of being a refugee is a new beginning for Long, who must begin a completely new life for himself and the family which depends on him, the Multiculturalism Act's ostensible openness is conducive to a tension between conservative values and innovation. This malaise shifts the focus from the collective experience of the refugee system to an examination of a brother's love for his sister through the affect, thus bringing to the fore the notion of reshaping masculinities.

As underlined earlier, the Multiculturalism Act recognizes difference and the plurality of cultures. As such, it represents a positive change in Canadian history, which is peppered with racist remarks and constraints against Asians of different origins.[49] The limitations of Derrida's laws of hospitality discussed in

---

[49] The growing Chinese populations led to the imposition of a head tax in 1885 (Price 2013). In 1914, the *Komagata Maru*, a ship carrying Asians was not allowed to dock and its passengers deprived of food and medical assistance as the Canadian government would not

the introduction to the book are a moot point here since the opening of borders itself is welcome in this case. After the advent of the Multiculturalism Act, waves of immigration from Vietnam create an incipient Vietnamese community which is encouraged to preserve its values, which is itself akin to the enclaves that Rosello underlines in her book, as I discussed with *Tels* earlier. The refugees are given the opportunity to integrate into society and actively participate in the country's economy through access to education and housing. Québécois society and its refugees could perhaps come the closest to fitting Derrida's paradigm since the host society opens its doors and the guests are relieved to partake of whatever hospitality is afforded them. Yet the guests are not truly guests in this case: they will also become part of the host society as there is no home to return to, which undermines Still's point that the guest must perforce leave one day and creates tensions for refugees. Equally significant here is the fact that Rosello's perceived imbalance and 'ostentation' that I highlighted earlier will also not be applicable as the guests will not be guests anymore.

According to Ahmed, applying Henri Lefebvre's discussion of Heidegger's concept of production as 'causing to appear' (Lefebvre 1991: 22), 'an arrival takes time and the time that it takes shapes "what" it is that arrives. [...] What arrives not only depends on time but is shaped by the conditions of its arrival, by how it came to get here' (Ahmed 2006: 40). In the case of the Vietnamese refugees, the circumstances of Long's and his family's arrival in Québec and the time they spend as refugees in Malaysia allows for an interrogation of their identity, but also of how to negotiate their family unit in the new space they are about to inhabit. This is very significant, especially for Long, due to the fact that as the eldest son he is to replace his father and inherit the responsibilities of masculinity in the new social space as per Confucian traditions.[50] According to the Confucian principles which are followed in Vietnam, women owe three obedience: to their fathers, to their husband and later, to their sons.[51] As she has left her husband in Vietnam, Vi's mother now owes obedience to her son.

accept more Asians into the country. In the aftermath of the Japanese attack on Pearl Harbour, Japanese immigrants were interned in camps, and their properties seized and sold (Price 2013). According to Price, 'persistent lobbying on the part of Asian Canadians and their allies, including Asian countries and newly independent countries of the Caribbean, finally put an end to racist immigration preferences in 1967' (2013: 637).

[50] See Louie on Asian masculinities (2003).
[51] See Gao (2003).

Migration can lead to a shift in family dynamics, and in many cases, may lead to a renegotiation of gendered relations. Between 1981 and 1996, when most Vietnamese refugees arrived in Canada, the number of single mothers increased by 29.5%, with 67% of single mothers being employed as they provided for their families (Gucciardi et al. 2004). Although in Canada, single parent families headed by the mother were widespread during the period within which the narrative is set, Thúy's Vietnamese family passes the responsibility to Long as the oldest male at nineteen, despite the fact that Long's mother's ability to speak French and teaching in the refugee camps is primarily the reason why they were considered for immigration in Québec. According to Li-Hsiang Lisa Rosenlee discussing Confucian women, 'Conventionally women are in charge of the *nei* (inside) and men the *wai* (outside). [...] women's education and duties are limited to house duties and managements, regardless of their actual literary achievement and virtuous ability' (2015: 197).[52] Masculinity and primogeniture are the only acceptable qualifications as they choose to uphold the values inculcated in them in their home country: 'étant l'aîné, mon frère Long a porté le poids du rôle de chef de famille. Il remplaçait à la fois mon père et ma mère. [...]' (2016: 51). The choice of the word 'poids' brings to bear the onerous responsibility placed on such a young man. That he is asked to replace both the mother and the father testifies to the little importance given to the mother, whose presence remains a constant in the novel despite her effacement from the social scene.[53] Long himself is only mentioned twice as a passive character in the novel until their arrival in Québec. The new beginning represented by migration thus brings forth Long's voice as he is the first, and only, character to 'speak' his feelings in the novel through direct speech. But this coming of age is ambivalent in the novel.

Earlier in Thúy's novel the mother is depicted as being in charge of both the domestic and the public space in Vietnam, albeit from the shadows.[54] In the Malaysian refugee camps, she organized classes and actively taught children and adults alike to facilitate their integration in a host

---

[52] In *La domination masculine* (1998) Bourdieu highlights the fact that in conservative societies such as the Kabyle population he observes in Algeria, male members of the family are the only ones allowed political agency and given the opportunity to operate in the public sphere.

[53] This is also linked to a form of Bourdieusian 'habitus' insofar as these values are ingrained in them and are perpetuated from generation to generation.

[54] See also my article on 'willful subjectivity' in this novel (Kistnareddy forthcoming-a).

society, thus demonstrating not only resilience, but also an unparalleled drive. The incipient life in Québec could have led to a new paradigm wherein she would officially occupy the space of head of the family. Instead, she chooses to efface herself and return to the domestic space again. Thúy depicts a family which carries over its values, abetted by the Multiculturalism Act which allows every inhabitant to practise his/her own culture and value system, so that a teenager replaces an absent father and is tasked with ensuring the family's rapid integration. Whilst the migratory space provided a new beginning whereby they could have adopted the host country's values, the family refuses such freedom, which is reminiscent of Yuan's own predicament in Chen's *Lettres chinoises*. The laws and edicts of the home society, which are absent in Derrida's schema as it focuses on the host society and forgets the singular experience and the history of the guest who arrives, prevail despite the comparatively liberal attitude of the host country—in fact, because of it. Here, the hospitable immigration and national laws permit a withdrawal into the home country's social values, allowing a teenager to become the head of the family, with his mother adopting a secondary role. Long must not only create opportunities for his siblings but also simultaneously pursue his own education, work and contribute financially to the household.

Crucially, it is important to remember that Vietnam was a French colony until 1954 and South Vietnam, where Vi's family originates from, was an American ally until 1975.[55] The maintenance of divisions between men and women, male children and female children is evocative of the lack of parity which endures in the country while in France the first wave of feminism is taking hold and women are becoming more outspoken about their rights.[56] American women, too, are beginning to interrogate their status and women's empowerment is a driving force. That French colonization and allyship with the USA have not brought about changes for women and gender parity gestures to the former colonizer's and the USA's will to keep the status quo in the country. As Thúy herself exposes in *Em* (2020), her most recent text, American GIs were more interested in sexual relationships with Vietnamese women than adjudicating for their rights or status.[57] Often the fallout from war was a loss of family, position and the

---

[55] See Opper (2020).
[56] See de Beauvoir (1939 [1976]).
[57] In her autobiography *When Heaven and Earth Changed Places* (1989, rep 2017), Le Ly Hayslip describes the lives of the women who survived by entertaining the American soldiers, including her own sister.

need to find a means of surviving. For those who did not own land or were in the rural areas, precarity was rife, leading to many women turning towards prostitution in Saigon where the US soldiers were stationed. In the aftermath of the fall of Saigon, many men in the south were sent to re-education camps, leaving women to find means of surviving along with the children.[58] Clearly, the family that Thúy depicts in *Vi* does not experience such drastic circumstances, and the mother organizes their departure so that neither Vi nor her brothers encounter any difficulties, reminding us that social class also played a significant role in the fate of women and men in Vietnam.

Nonetheless, Long is depicted as having a dual perception of his role and identity as the first-born son, and Thúy subtly also demonstrates how Vietnamese masculinities are reshaped in Québec, when the individual is willing to open to the host society and the experiences which allow for betterment of both men and women. As Ahmed has argued, the circumstances surrounding the arrival are crucial in determining the perception of the world but also the object that arrives. Here, since it is a human being that arrives, migration allows for a disarticulation of Long as a young male Vietnamese from an affluent family and his re-articulation as an emotional human being who has lost his home and needs to acclimatize himself with the host society's mores and values to survive along with his family.[59] Refugees can be divided into two camps as per Woon's definition: they are either 'willing immigrants' or those who live at the margins of society and choose to turn down the opportunities given to them by their host society (1986: 349). Long belongs to the category of 'willing immigrants', so-called because they are ready to become part of the host society and contribute to it. Thus, the first decisions made by Long in Québec are for the education of his siblings with a view to their rapid integration: 'dès notre emménagement sur la 3ᵉ Avenue à Limoilou, il a voulu nous mettre sur les rails du présent en nous inscrivant à l'école le plus rapidement possible' (2016: 54).

Since the protagonists of *Vi* fled their homeland, it is understandable that living in Québec would be seen as a chance to begin anew, and in many ways to re-root themselves. Ahmed et al.'s notion of 'regrounding' (2003) focuses on the potential of a new space to permit different modes of thinking. In Thúy's protagonist's case, his 'regrounding' begins with a

---

[58] See Hai (2009).
[59] See my discussion of masculinities in *Vi* (Kistnareddy forthcoming-b).

disavowal of the home country in many ways. Whilst there is a constant congregation of Vietnamese friends at Long's house ('il était rare qu'il n'y ait pas d'invités autour de notre table puisque notre appartement était devenu le lieu de reunion des étudiants vietnamiens qui créaient ensemble un journal, une équipe de foot, de badminton ou de ping-pong en vue des olympiades' (2016: 54–55)), at no point do Long nor his brothers discuss politics back in Vietnam nor the life they have left behind. According to Jean-Louis Dorais, 'Nowadays, the social organization and collective memory of the Montréal and Québec City Viêt Kiêu is best expressed through shared cultural values stressing the primacy of the family, education, work, and economic integration, rather than being concerned with formal institutions and ideological discourses dealing with homeland politics' (2010: 101). Thus, the return to Vietnam is not necessary for the continuation of their family history and values. The refugee system in Québec, and in Canada at large, serves as an incubator which generates a new beginning, giving them the opportunity to showcase their specificity but without needing to think about a return that is fraught.

Nevertheless, I argue that Long does exhibit a willingness to change. Firstly, the writer emphasizes the entrepreneur aspect as Long sets up a business and chains of the Japanese restaurant he first worked in since he was given the opportunities offered by life in Québec. Derridean hospitality is highlighted here as it does empower the refugees to integrate society if they are willing immigrants. Here, they are not seen as guests but as new masters themselves insofar as there is no return and, thus, Québec becomes the new home. However, Thúy also underscores Long's extant Vietnamese values as he is the head of the family, and his wife, Hoa, is expected to live in his shadow: 'elle savait [...] être très discrète et extrêmement habile pour se tenir dans l'ombre de Long sans l'encombrer' (2016: 56–57). Xiongya Gao asserts that 'Confucianism acknowledges women only for the purpose of reproduction' (2003: 117), noting that Chinese Yin, 'literally meaning "overcast" or "shade", is often used to refer to the female [...], standing for all things dark, secret, hidden, cold, weak, and passive' (2003: 115). That Hoa should perchance be an obstacle or burden to him through her very presence speaks to ingrained patriarchal values. Love itself is seen not in outright expressions of affection but in the act of cooking: 'chaque bouchée [qui] renfermait des heures de travail, d'humilité et d'obéissance de la part de Hoa' (Thúy 2016: 57–58). Long and the friends he invites are unaware of the amount of energy Hoa invests in preparing meals   under   his   mother's   direction   (Thúy   2016:   57).   Hoa's self-effacement and patience is perceived as the enduring Vietnamese Confucian values and her absence of expectations towards Long is underlined. In this way, there is a tension in Long between such values and openness to the world, but it is not overtly criticized nor denounced.

Writing about *Vi* Robert Everett-Green observes that 'Non-Asians and Western ways show up in [Thúy's] novel most often as escape hatches from traditional practices, and as manifestations of alternative means of showing emotion' (2018). I argue that Long's singular experience of migration, and his 'regrounding' in Canada as a very young man compelled to take on his family's responsibility, lead to this disruption of Vietnamese values where the notion of gendered roles begins to be eroded. Exploring the need to change the notion of masculinity in *The Will to change: Men, Masculinity and Love*, hooks underlines the importance of love and affection in undermining patriarchal values. For hooks, the 'recovery of the self' is as important as the 'emotional right to love and to be loved' of men (2004: 16). Long is thus seen as a loving brother willing to challenge patriarchal values and his mother's views in order to educate his sister and enable her to make her own decisions. This is particularly demonstrated in two situations: her education and her love life. Indeed, contrary to her mother who was educated only to carry on her family's business, as aligned with the Confucian principles for women I underlined with Rosenlee earlier, Vi's brother has the ambition of 'le chemin stable et facile [...] en pharmacologie ou en médecine' for her (2016: 69). Her choice to study translation and law are marked acts of subjectivation as she begins to negotiate her own identity. Long, as the head of the family, authorizes her to do so. Shifting to Montréal and living in an unsupervised space are additional freedoms which are aggregated as she negotiates her own life.

Secondly, Vi's choice to have pre-marital sex with her boyfriend, Tân, and subsequently rejecting him for his reprehensible behaviour towards her, elicit anger in her mother who rejects her. Unlike the latter, all three brothers send her money and a letter saying 'Reviens nous voir pendant la semaine des vacances si tu peux' (2016: 90). The opposition between the mother's attitude and the brothers' acceptance of her decision, and their support, is significant as it demonstrates their diverging values, their rewriting of their own narrative of masculinity. Their sister and her happiness are accorded more importance than the values with which they were raised. In telling her that they want to see her, they demonstrate a different, more open-minded attitude towards their beloved youngest sibling, thereby generating a new form of understanding Vietnamese masculinity to emerge in Québec. This change in perception of what Long can do as the head of the family, and what the brothers elect to do, is only possible in the host society due to the circumstances of arrival, as delineated by Ahmed, having strengthened the emotional and affective bond between the siblings.

As I discussed with respect to Horlacher (2019) in the introduction to this book, while it is important for men to construct what Fluck calls a 'self narrative' (2013: 51), which is contingent upon culture and the social framework in which they operate, it is crucial to create one's own reference points, one's own narrative. As Fluck argues, cultural narratives 'may provide cultural frames of interpretation and furnish genre and plot structures for self-narration, but we still have to turn these into the scripts of our own life' (2013: 52). Long's decisions to change with the time and according to the society in which they now live in Québec is seen as empowering. Along the same lines, Long alters their family surname to simply 'Lê' since their father had 'perdu ce privilège le jour où il avait laissé sa femme et ses enfants se battre seuls' (2016: 123). Nonetheless, indubitably the son remains heartbroken at his father's choice to abandon his family as he would have liked his father to witness his ascension and his flourishing business.

Moreover, rather than follow in paternal footsteps in the mistreatment of women, Long respects his wife and takes the time to treat her to dinners and shows affection. While Long is still bound by the rules of his community's values, he also eschews its fetters by creating and sustaining a loving relationship with Hoa. Nonetheless, rather than a hybridized form of masculinity which takes on both Québécois and Vietnamese characteristics, I contend that it is the narrative of masculinities which Long adapts to his own circumstances. This narrative of masculinities is fluid and flexible and can be rewritten as and when the individual wishes it to be, as per Fluck and Horlacher. In this way, Long is constantly re-writing the narrative of the masculinity which suits him from circumstance to circumstance and in his different relationships with his family, including his father.

A Note on the Men Who Stayed Behind

This chapter would be incomplete without a brief discussion of those who did not make the journey to France or Canada. While my intention has been to examine the ways in which migration affects men and changes them, I want to underline the fact that the men who do not emigrate are also influenced by migration in different ways. Earlier, with Madické, Salie's brother, I indicated that the young man would likely become the success story in his home village without actually leaving. Clearly migration does have an impact on him for it is after all due to his sister emigrating and is earning money in Europe that he is able to set up a business in Niodior. Without her financial help, such a positive outcome would have been impossible.

There are many ways in which the texts I explore in this book gesture towards the effect of migration on the men who stay behind. For instance, Amok himself returns home to confront his father in Miano's *Crépuscule 2*. The confrontation itself would not have occurred had Amok not left his country, lived through the immigrant life in France and then returned to come to terms with the life and the father he left behind. The father, too, is moved by his son and this leads to an acknowledgement of past hurts and pains and the recognition that they must learn from their own mistakes. The return to Vietnam is also the way in which Vi reconnects with her father whom her mother had left behind to save her children. While the narrative does not delve into the final meeting, the fact that the father is a broken and ill man demonstrates the effect of his family leaving him behind and the changes that have occurred in him in the aftermath of their departure. Thúy does not give him the space to express his story, but leaves us with the impression that Vi will meet her father and take him back to Canada to reunite with his family.

Similarly, it is only after travelling across Algeria, and onwards to France and retracing her past through her book that Malika, Mokeddem's narrator, is able to reconcile with her father who has never travelled away from Béchar, as I discuss in Chap. 3. Assia Djebar whose 'return' to her father is belated and takes place after the latter's passing, still reveals the ways in which her movement away from the family home to study, and later to France, has enabled her to realize the impact that her father has had on her life and the secrets she has had to keep, as I examine in Chap. 4.

All these left behind men, in many ways are indebted to migration for the change in their relationship with their sisters or daughters or sons. While they personally did not undertake the journey that permits such a paradigm shift for them, those who migrate come home altered and change those who were left behind.

REHOMING MASCULINITIES

In this chapter, the notion of hospitality has been explored through the gaze of authors who foreground male protagonists whose identities change and evolve through the process of migration. Derrida's aporetic paradox that hospitality is an impossibility serves as a platform to examine the affective experiences of migration in the narratives. Hospitality, or rather, in many ways, the inhospitality experienced in the host nation by immigrants, leads to a re-conceptualization of masculine identity that is strongly predicated on the notion of home in the novels. According to hooks,

> home is no longer just one place. It is locations. Home is that place which enables and promotes varied and everchanging perspectives, a place where one discovers new ways of seeing reality, frontiers of difference. One confronts and accepts dispersal and fragmentation as part of the constructions of a new world order that reveals more fully where we are, who we can become. (1999: 171–172)

hooks's vision of home underlines the plurality of the spaces that can represent the home for the migrant. In Amok's case, home is the country he fled, as well as France, but it is also where his heart takes him in love, with Mabel. Miano reshapes erstwhile visions of masculinities using the affect and desire for an individual who blurs the boundaries between both genders. Mabel is the home that was repressed due to a lack of understanding of Amok's own sexuality, which he only recovers when he returns to the country where he was born. Similarly, Diome encourages her brethren to stay at home to develop the country, but it is her own experiences of leaving home and recreating a home in France which allows her to accomplish this task. Chen's Yuan is symptomatic of immigrants who cannot come to terms with the 'dispersal and fragmentation' that hooks views as empowering. This fragmentation leads to incoherence and a form of death, which is implied for Yuan. Thúy's refugees' homelessness and reconstruction of the home space in Québec generate opportunities for the protagonists to see new perspectives and frontiers as outlined by hooks. All of the writers have also reshaped migrant masculine identities in their texts by interrogating the notion of hospitality. The paradox at play here is that inhospitable France allows characters to 'find' themselves, homing in on their bare desire, their sexuality and their core identity and hospitable Canada becomes reifying, alienating and leads to loss in Yuan's case.

I have outlined the multifarious ways in which Black (im)migrants, Chinese and Vietnamese (im)migrants are compelled to interrogate their own identity as men in their host societies. Whilst these reconsiderations have triggered some powerful transformations on one hand (Amok in Miano's narratives, Long and, by extension, Vi, in Thúy's text, Madické in Diome's text), the inability to adapt and change has led to self-annihilation and loss on the other hand, as is the case with Chen's Yuan and Diome's Moussa. As writers living in France or Canada, Thúy, Chen, Miano and Diome provide the readers with new perceptions of masculinities which are empowering in their love and affection for those around them.

References

Primary Texts

Chen, Ying. 1993. *Les Lettres chinoises.* Montréal: Babel.
———. 2004. *Quatre mille marches: Un rêve chinois.* Paris: Seuil.
———. 2014. *La Lenteur des montagnes.* Montréal: Boréal.
Diome, Fatou. 2003. *Le Ventre de l'Atlantique.* Paris: Anne Carrière.
———. 2016. *Marianne porte plainte!* Paris: Flammarion.
Miano, Léonora. 2008. *Tels des astres éteints.* Paris: Plon.
———. 2017a. *Marianne et le garçon noir.* Paris: Pauvert.
———. 2017b. *Crépuscule du tourment 2: Héritage.* Paris: Grasset.
Thúy, Kim. 2010. *Ru.* Montréal: Liana Levi.
———. 2013. *Mãn.* Montréal: Liana Levi.
———. 2016. *Vi.* Montréal: Liana Levi.
———. 2020. *Em.* Montréal: Libre Expression.

Secondary Sources

Ahluwalia, Pal. 2007. Origins and Displacement: Working Through Derrida's African Connections. *Social Identities* 13 (3): 325–336.
Ahmed, Sarah. 2000. *Strange Encounters: Embodied Others in Post-coloniality.* London: Routledge.
———. 2006. *Queer Phenomenology.* Durham: Duke University Press.
Ahmed, Sarah, Claudia Castañeda, et al. 2003. *Uprootings/Regroundings: Questions of Home and Migration.* Oxford: Berg.

Arnt, Susan, Dirk Naguschewski et al. (Eds). 2007. *Exophonie Anderssprachigkeit (in) der Literatur.* Berlin: Kulturverlag Kadmos.

Bauman, Zygmunt. 2016. *Strangers at Our Door.* Cambridge: Polity Press.

Bell, Avril. 2010. Being "At Home" in the Nation: Hospitality and Sovereignty in Talk about Immigration. *Ethnicities* 10 (2): 236–256.

Ben Jelloun, Tahar. 1997. *Hospitalité française: Racisme et immigration maghrébine.* Paris: Seuil.

Bhabha, Homi. 1994. *Locating Culture.* London and New York: Routledge.

Bissoondath, Neil. 1994. *Selling Illusions: The Cult of Multiculturalism in Canada.* Toronto: Penguin.

Bourdieu, Pierre. 1980. *Le Sens pratique.* Paris: Editions de Minuit.

———. 1998. *La domination masculine.* Paris: Seuil.

Bouvier-Laffitte, Béatrice. 2013. Francophonie chinoise: Langues et identités en tension dans les œuvres de Dai Sijie, Gao Xingjian et Ying Chen. *International Journal of Francophone Studies* 16 (3): 263–280.

Boym, Svetlana. 2000. On Diasporic Intimacy: Ilya Kabakov's Installations and Immigrant Homes. In *Intimacy*, ed. Lauren Berlant, 227–230. Chicago and London: University of Chicago Press.

Brussosa, Myriam Mallart. 2013. 'Tels des astres éteints de Léonora Miano: Habiter un nom, habiter une peau', in Cédilles, 3: 143–155.

Buss, Helen M. 2018. Kim Thúy's Ru and the Art of the Anecdote. *a/b: Auto/Biography Studies* 33: 605–612.

Butler, Judith. 1991. *Gender Trouble.* London and New York: Routledge.

———. 2004. *Undoing Gender.* London and New York: Routledge.

Canada Government Website. 2020. Understanding Canada's Immigration System. Accessed 15 June 2019. https://www.canada.ca/content/dam/ircc/documents/pdf/english/campaigns/2433_takeaway_en_rev.pdf.

Cazenave, Odile, and Pascale Célérier. 2011. *Contemporary Francophone African Writers and the Burden of Commitment.* Charlottesville: University of Virginia Press.

Chen, Ying. 2004. *Quatre mille marches: Un rêve chinois.* Paris: Seuil.

———. 2014. *La Lenteur des montagnes.* Montréal: Boréal.

Chow, Rey. 2014. *Not like a Native Speaker: Languaging as a Postcolonial Experience.* New York: Columbia University Press.

Collet, François. 2009. Does Habitus Matter? A Comparative Review of Bourdieu's Habitus and Simon's Bounded Rationality with Some Implications for Economic Sociology. *Sociological Theory* 27 (4): 419–434.

Confucius (Kong Qiu). 1991. *Confucian Analects. In the Chinese Classics.* Translated by J. Legge. Vol. I. Taipei: SMC Publishing Inc.

Connell, Raewyn. 1995. *Masculinities.* Cambridge: Polity Press.

Dadié, Bernard. 1959. *Un nègre à Paris.* Paris: Présence africaine.

De Balsi, Sara. 2018. Postures francophones translingues. L'exemple de Ying Chen. *Interfrancophonies* 9: 27–38.

De Beauvoir, Simone. 1939, rep. 1976. *Le Deuxième sexe I*. Paris: Folio.
De Maillard, Jacques, Daniela Hunold, et al. 2017. Different Styles of Policing: Discretionary Power in Street Controls by the Public Police in France and Germany. *Policing and Society* 28 (2): 175–188.
Derrida, Jacques. 1996. *Le monolinguisme de l'autre*. Paris: Galilée.
———. 1997. *De l'hospitalité*. Paris: Calmann-Levy.
Diouf, Mbaye. 2010. Ecriture de l'immigration et traversée des discours dans *Le Ventre de l'Atlantique* de Fatou Diome. *Francofonia* 58: 55–66.
Dorais, Louis-Jacques. 2010. Politics, Kinship, and Ancestors: Some Diasporic Dimensions of the Vietnamese Experience in North America. *Journal of Vietnamese Studies* 5 (2): 91–132.
Dufault, Roseanna. 2001. Identity and Exile in Shanghai and Montreal: Les Lettres chinoises by Ying Chen. In *Frontières flottantes: lieu et espace dans les cultures francophones du Canada/Shifting Boundaries: Place and Space in the Francophone Cultures of Canada*, ed. Jaap Lintvelt and François Paré, 161–167. Amsterdam and New York: Rodopi.
Edwards, Natalie. 2018. Linguistic Rencontres in Kim Thúy's Mãn. *PORTAL: Journal of Multidisciplinary International Studies* 15 (2): 6–19.
Everett-Green, Robert. 2018. How Novelist Kim Thúy Focuses on the "Invisible Strength of Women". *The Globe and Mail*, May 2019. Accessed 10 September 2018. https://www.theglobeandmail.com/arts/books/article-vietnamese-canadian-novelist-kim-thuys-latest-book-vi-focuses-on-the/.
Fanon, Frantz. 1952. *Peau noire, masques blancs*. Paris: Seuil.
Fassin, Didier. 2012. *Les nouvelles frontières de la société française*. Paris: La Découverte.
Fluck, Winfried. 2013. Reading for Recognition. *New Literary History* 44 (1): 45–67.
Gao, Xyongia. 2003. Women Existing for Men: Confucianism and Social Injustice against Women in China. *Race, Gender & Class* 10 (3): 114–125.
Genette, Gérard. 1980. *Narrative Discourse: An Essay in Method*. Translated by Jane Lewin. Ithaca: Cornell University Press.
Gilroy, Paul. 2005. *Postcolonial Melancholia*. New York: Columbia University Press.
Gucciardi, Enza, Nalan Celasun, and Donna Stewart. 2004. Single-mother Families in Canada. *Canadian Journal of Public Health/Revue Canadienne de Santé Publique* 95 (1): 70–73.
Hai, Anh. 2009. The Guava Tree. In *The Viet Kieu in America: Personal Accounts of Postwar Immigrants from Vietnam*, ed. Nghia M. Vo, 86–93. Jefferson, NC and London: McFarland & Company.
Hayslip, Le Ly. 2017. *When Heaven and Earth Changed Places*. Anchor Books.
Hogarth, Christopher. 2019. Gendering Migrant Mobility in Fatou Diome's Novels. In *Exiles Travellers and Vagabonds*, ed. Kate Averis and Isabelle Hollis-Touré, 54–70. Cardiff: University of Wales Press.

hooks, bell. 1999. *Yearning: Race, Gender and Cultural Politics*. Boston: South End Press.

———. 2004. *The Will to Change: Men, Masculinity and Love*. New York: Washington Square Press.

———. 2015. *Black Looks: Race and Representation*. New York: Routledge.

Horlacher, Stefan. 2019. "In Reality Every Reader Is, While He Is Reading, the Reader of His Own Self": Reconsidering the Importance of Narrative and Savoir Littéraire for Masculinity Studies. *Men and Masculinities* 22 (1): 75–84.

Immigration Gouvernement Québec. 2020. Québec selection process. Accessed 2 February 2020. https://www.immigration-quebec.gouv.qc.ca/en/immigrate-settle/humanitarian-immigration/humanitarianimmigration/sharing-responsibilities.html#quebec.

Kinouani, Guilaine. 2021. *Living While Black: The Essential Guide to Overcoming Trauma*. London: Ebury Press.

Kistnareddy, Ashwiny O. 2019. 'Le Pays, c'était comme la femme d'un autre': Reconceptualising African Migrant Masculinity in Fatou Diome's *Le Ventre de l'Atlantique* and Léonora Miano's *Tels des astres éteints*', Itinéraires. https://doi.org/10.4000/itineraires.6086.

———. 2020. Disrupting Homogeneous Nation-space: The Black Male Body and the Migrant Woman Writer's Gaze (Léonora Miano and Fatou Diome). *L'Esprit Créateur* 60 (2): 41–54.

———. Forthcoming-a. "Against the Flow": Exile and "Willful Subjects" in Malika Mokeddem's *My Men* and Kim Thúy's *Vi*. *Journal of Contemporary Women's Writing*.

———. Forthcoming-b. Postmigratory Identities: Changing Masculinities in *Vi*. In *Recipes for Exile Reading Kim Thúy*, ed. Miléna Santoro and Jack Yeager. Montréal: Queen-McGill University Press.

Kristeva, Julia. 1988. *Etrangers à nous-mêmes*. Paris: Folio.

Kustov, Alexander. 2020. "Bloom Where You're Planted": Explaining Public Opposition to (E)Migration. *Journal of Ethnic and Migration Studies*. https://doi.org/10.1080/1369183X.2020.1754770.

Labelle, Maude. 2007. Les lieux de l'écriture migrante: Territoire, mémoire et langue dans *Les lettres chinoises* de Ying Chen. *Globe* 10 (1): 37–51.

Lachman, Kathryn. 2014. The Transatlantic Poetics of Fatou Diome. In *Francophone Afropean Literatures*, 32–47. Liverpool: Liverpool University Press.

Lefebvre, Henri. 1991. *The Production of Space*. Translated by Donald Nicholson-Smith. Oxford: Blackwell.

Louie, Kam. 2003. Chinese, Japanese and Global Masculine Identities. In *Asian Masculinities: The Meaning and Practice of Manhood in China and Japan*, ed. Kam Louie and Morris Low, 1–15. London: Routledge Curzon.

Louie, Kam, and Morris Low. 2003. *Asian Masculinities: The Meaning and Practice of Manhood in China and Japan*. London: Routledge Curzon.

Mabanckou, Alain. 2006. Portraits d'écrivains (1). Dix questions à Léonora Miano: "Laissons les étiquettes aux commerçants et aux esprits sans imagination!". Accessed 7 October 2017. http://www.congopage.com/Portraits-d-ecrivains-1-Dix.

Macdonald, David Bruce. 2014. Reforming Multiculturalism in a Bi-National Society: Aboriginal Peoples and the Search for Truth and Reconciliation in Canada. *Canadian Journal of Sociology* 39 (1): 65–86.

Macé, Marielle. 2017. *Sidérer, considérer: Migrants en France*. Lagrasse: Editions Verdier.

Mata Barreiro, Carmen. 2012. Hybridité linguistique et culturelle dans les écritures migrantes au Québec: L'identité de la traversée. *Nouvelles Études Francophones* 27 (1): 66–84.

Mielusel, Ramona, and Simona Emilia Pruteanu. 2020. *Citizenship and Belonging in France and North America*. Cham: Palgrave Macmillan.

Mullings, Delores, Anthony Morgan, and Heather Quelleng. 2016. Canada the Great White North Where Anti-Black Racism Thrives: Kicking Down the Doors and Exposing the Realities. *Phylon* 53 (1): 20–41.

Murray, Thomas. 2019. La masculinité à travers l'Atlantique: Enjeux identitaires et musicaux dans *Crépuscule du tourment 1 et 2* de Léonora Miano. *Études littéraires africaines* 47: 147–162.

Naidu, M. 1995. Canadian Multiculturalism: A Discussion. *Peace Research* 27 (2): 1–22.

Ndiaye, Pap. 2008. *La Condition noire: Essai sur une minorité française*. Paris: Calmann-Lévy.

———. 2018. Gommer le mot race de la Constitution française est un recul. Le Monde Afrique. Accessed 10 August 2010. https://www.lemonde.fr/afrique/video/2018/08/10/pap-ndiaye-gommer-le-mot-race-de-la-constitution-francaize-est-un-recul_5341299_3212.html.

Noiriel, Gérard. 2007. *Immigration, antisémitisme et racisme en France (XIXe–XXe siècle)*. Paris: Fayard.

Office français de protection des réfugiés et apatrides. 2020. Accessed 10 January 2020. https://www.ofpra.gouv.fr/fr/asile/la-procedure-de-demande-d-asile/demander-l-asile-en-france.

Opper, Marc. 2020. *People's Wars in China, Malaya and Vietnam*. Ann Arbor: University of Michigan Press.

Petetin, Véronique. 2017. L'"Afrophonie" de Léonora Miano. *Etudes* 9: 83–92.

Porra, Véronique. 2011. *Langue française, langue d'adoption: Une littérature "invitée" entre création, stratégie et contraintes (1946–2000)*. Hildesheim: Georg Olms Verlag.

Price, Jonathan. 2013. Canada, White Supremacy, and the Twinning of Empires. *International Journal* 68 (4): 628–638.

Robinson, W. Courtland. 1998. *The Terms of Refuge: The Indochinese Exodus and the International Response*. London: Zed Books.

Rodgers, Julie. 2015. "On s'occupe du multiple, on tourne le dos à l'unité": Ying Chen and Nomadic Figurations of the Subject. *Québec Studies* 59 (1): 51–70.

Rosello, Mireille. 2001. *Postcolonial Hospitality: The Immigrant as Guest*. Stanford: Stanford University Press.

Rosenlee, Li-Hsiang L. 2015. Confucian Friendship (You 友) as Spousal Relationship: A Feminist Imagination. *International Communication of Chinese Culture* 2 (3): 181–203.

Scott Morton, W. 1971. The Confucian Concept of Man: The Original Formulation. *Philosophy East and West* 21 (1): 69–77.

Silverstein, Paul A. 2018. *Postcolonial France: Race, Islam, and the Future of the Republic*. London: Pluto Press.

Sing, Pamela. 2016. Kim Thúy: A Gentle Power. In *Ten Canadian Writers in Context*, ed. Marie Carrière, Curtis Gillespie, and Jason Purcell, 179–193. Alberta: University of Alberta Press.

Small, Audrey. 2019. Société d'accueil et de *teranga*: Emigration and Immigration in Three Texts by Fatou Diome. *Francosphères* 8 (1): 41–55.

Still, Judith. 2010. *Derrida and Hospitality: Theory and Practice*. Edinburgh: Edinburgh University Press.

Suga, Keijiro. 2007. Translation, Exophony, Omniphony. In *Yoko Tawada: Voices from Everywhere*, ed. Douglas Slaymaker, 21–34. Lanham: Lexington Books.

Talbot, Emile. 2005. Conscience et mémoire: Ying Chen et la problématique identitaire. *Nouvelles Etudes Francophones* 20 (1): 149–162.

Traoré, Assa, and Geoffroy de Lagasnerie. 2019. *Le Combat Adama*. Paris: Stock.

Tsai, D.F.-C. 2005. The Bioethical Principles and Confucius' Moral Philosophy. *Journal of Medical Ethics: Journal of the Institute of Medical Ethics* 31 (3): 159–163. https://doi.org/10.1136/jme.2002.002113.

Unter Ecker, Marjolaine. 2016. *Questions identitaires dans les récits afropéens de Léonora Miano*. Toulouse: PUM.

Wassink, Joshua, and Jacqueline Hagan. 2020. How Local Community Context Shapes Labour Market Re-entry and Resource Mobilization among Return Migrants: An Examination of Rural and Urban Communities in Mexico. *Journal of Ethnic and Migration Studies*. https://doi.org/10.108 0/1369183X.2020.1758552.

Weil, Patrick. 2005. *La République et sa diversité: Immigration, Integration, Discrimination*. Paris: Seuil.

Woon, Yuen-Fong. 1986. Some Adjustment Aspects of Vietnamese and Sino-Vietnamese Families in Victoria, Canada. *Journal of Comparative Family Studies* 17 (3): 349–370.

Yeager, Jack. 2004. Bach Mai and Ying Chen: Immigrant Identities in Québec. In *Textualizing the Immigrant Experience in Contemporary Québec*, ed. Susan Ireland and Patrice Proulx, 137–148. Westport: Praeger.

Yildiz, Yasemin. 2012. *Beyond the Mother Tongue: The Postmonolingual Condition*. New York: Fordham University Press and Seuil.

Youtube, INA. 2014. Fatou Diome: Le mythe de la France Eldorado. Accessed 20 November 2017. https://www.youtube.com/watch?v=xIULie9dN-A.

Yun, Chul-Ki. 2007. Aspects spatio-temporels de la migration dans Les Lettres Chinoises de Ying Chen. *Etudes québécoises: Revue internationale de l'ACEQ* 1: 137–141.

———. 2013. Migrance, sensorium et translocalité chez Ying Chen et Kim Thúy. *International Journal of Francophone Studies* 16 (3): 281–301.

Zadi, Samuel. 2010. La "Solidarité africaine" dans *Le Ventre de l'Atlantique* de Fatou Diome. *Nouvelles Études Francophones* 25 (1): 171–188.

CHAPTER 3

Reconfiguring Community and Masculinities

Some events can lead to societies radically seeking to rethink what community, belonging, inclusion and exclusion might mean. One such historical moment occurred on 25 May 2020, with the death of George Floyd, an African American man at the hands of a white Minneapolis police officer, Derek Chauvin, sparking riots across the USA for several days. Floyd's death symbolized the latest attack against the already disenfranchised African American community who are victims of racism and discrimination on a regular basis.[1] The unfair circumstances surrounding his passing singed the nation, leading to the #BlackLivesMatter movement gaining momentum and demanding redress and reform. For a number of days, the USA became fragmented, dispersed into incohesiveness and dissolution: a community contemplating its own tenuous unity.

A similar vision of community was predicted by Jean-Luc Nancy in 2001, in *La Communauté affrontée*, wherein he posits the global community as 'séparée et confrontée à elle-même' (2001: 17). Nancy envisages this as an abyss or 'béance', a community which confronts its own

---

[1] This crime occurred in the aftermath of Breonna Taylor's shooting in her own apartment by policemen, Ahmaud Arbery's demise at the hands of vigilantes, one of whom was a retired police officer, and weeks after a young New Yorker, walking her unleashed dog in a park, threatened to call the police on an African American man who had politely asked her to put the dog on the leash.

© The Author(s), under exclusive license to Springer Nature Switzerland AG 2021
A. O. Kistnareddy, *Migrant Masculinities in Women's Writing*, Global Masculinities,
https://doi.org/10.1007/978-3-030-82576-8_3

101

rupture (2001: 17). Examining this text, Ian James argues that 'community is recast not as the intimate sharing of an essence or identity but rather as the opening of an absence of an identity in the spacing of a shared finitude' (2010: 173). For the critic, this is an 'exposure to, or of, a nothing' (2010: 173). The impact of war and conflicts in the global community has prompted Nancy to rethink what community might mean when everything has ceased to matter, when those who suffer can submit no more. Floyd's demise gave impetus to anti-racist #BlackLivesMatter manifestations across the world. In France, it gave additional traction to the 'Justice pour Adama' movement, with Assa Traoré reminding her followers that her brother, Adama too, died unable to breathe at the hands of the French police. On 2 June 2020,[2] and in subsequent weeks, mass protests occurred in Paris, against the racist violence perpetrated by the police against Adama Traoré. While America's unsettled community grapples with its inequities, the commonality of experiences evoked by Floyd's and Traoré's deaths generates a community of dissenting voices who speak in the name of justice. Nancy's understanding of community and how it is shaped is crucial as it is constantly being recast by philosophers as events unfold and the world alters.

James asserts that 'this thinking of community occurs in the experience of the community of writing' (2010: 186), since Nancy interweaves his text with references, terms and reflections garnered from other philosophers who augment his theory. It is indeed through these writerly reflections on what community might mean, in a world where global mobility, societal changes and personal development call into question the notions of belonging and identities, that I explore Miano's short story 'Afropean Soul', her novel, *Tels*, while drawing on her essays, as well as Mokeddem's *Mes Hommes* and Devi's *Les Hommes*. In this chapter I evaluate what community entails for host societies, (im)migrants and migrants in their quest to redefine themselves in the wake of migration and alterity. I examine Nancy's theories for this as his elucubrations on the notion of community as something which is redefinable facilitates this plasticity.

Thus, in this chapter, in the first section I draw on Nancy's notion of 'interruption of myth' as theorized in *La Communauté désoeuvrée* to interrogate the premise of groups such as the 'Fils de Kemet' who seek to provide a foundation myth to Afrodescendants who struggle to define

---

[2] See Révolution Permanente (2020) 'Justice pour Adama: Le discours poignant d'Assa Traoré'.

who they are and their place in France, in Miano's texts. Through the lens of Sara Ahmed's notion of 'willful subjects' (2014b, 2017), I analyse Mokeddem's narrator's position as a dissident voice speaking against the patriarchal Islamic community in Algeria. I return to Nancy and his community of writing to gauge the extent to which Devi's text adumbrates a new community of writers so she can come to terms with the pressures the men in her family exert on her and, thereby, creates an ungendered writerly community. Ultimately, this chapter explores the different ways in which community might be re-imagined, through writing, and adapts to a range of needs and circumstances.

LIVING IN-BETWEEN 'COMMUNITIES': RACE AND MASCULINITIES

'Il nous faut trouver comment être ce peuple du milieu. […] le meilleur de l'un et l'autre monde' writes Miano in *Tels* (2008b: 370).[3] Miano's entreaty, through the anonymous narrator who opens and concludes the novel, unveils the profound sense of disconnection and disjuncture experienced by Afropeans in the text. For her, being Afropean in France is being a 'peuple du milieu' insofar as they were born in France to parents who were born in Sub-Saharan Africa or have Sub-Saharan African origins.[4] Thus, French by birth but visibly 'other' due to their skin colour,[5] Afropeans straddle two so-called identities. The first remains administrative, since they are French nationals by birth. The second is affective as they are categorized as second or third generation immigrants, or simply Black African, by members of the French society who do not see past their skin colour.[6] For Kinouani, this is the very definition of 'racialisation', that is 'the process by which a group of people becomes defined by their race'

[3] See also Barrett and Roedinger on immigration and feeling 'in-between' (1997).

[4] According to Hitchcott and Thomas (2014), Afropean refers to a number of people who were born in France (or Europe) but whose origins can be anywhere in the Sub-Saharan region.

[5] Beaman complexifies the concept of colour identification further by asking 'are French people white?' (2018). More recently she has worked on comparing 'colorblindness' in France and in the USA (Beaman and Petts 2020). See also Boni-Claverie's (2017) *Trop noire pour être Française*.

[6] For discussions on citizenship and belonging in France, predominantly in narratives and films featuring Muslim protagonists see Mielusel and Pruteanu (2020). See also de Montaigne's *L'Assignation* (2018) and Weil (2005).

rather than by the land of their birth (2021: 7). Here, community is based on race and appearance, so that rejection stems from divergent origins,[7] as opposed to Nancy's community as 'être-en-commun', which is based on shared finitude, as I examined in the introduction to this book.

In his recent documentary essay, entitled Afropean: *Notes from Black Europe*, Pitts underlines the liminal space occupied by Afropeans in Europe as 'an *invisible* world through which white Europe blithely passes without really seeing' (2019: 34). In the chapters dealing exclusively with France, Pitts documents his voyages into the heart of Parisian enclaves and suburbs as well as his meetings with activists who deplore the fact that 'there is no black identity here; West Africans stick together and it's the same with the Caribbeans' (2019: 76). For Almamy, Pitts's interlocutor, the French government seeks to keep them 'divided so there is no unifying voice, and no power' (2019: 77). Thus community, for activists, is equated to power and the ability to stand united against discrimination. Conversely, the absence of community, which Almamy deplores, leads to diffraction and a feeling of non-belonging.

Miano's texts, the first published as a short story in the eponymous collection Afropean *Soul*, and the second as a full-length novel, share similar concerns regarding notions of identity, community and belonging. While 'Afropean Soul' is a first-person narrative beginning *in medias res* and ending with a resolution as is typically associated with the short story form, *Tels* is a polyphonic narrative offering multiple perspectives on the experience of Black ontology in France, and on different journeys towards negotiating one's identity.[8] The texts mirror each other insofar as the anonymous narrator of 'Afropean Soul' is a telemarketer, as with Amok in *Tels*, and the 'Fils de Kemet' also have a strong presence in both narratives. However, while Amok is a socio-economic migrant, the narrator of 'Afropean Soul' was born and raised in France, as were most of the 'Fils de Kemet', thus complicating the problems of identity, community and belonging in the narratives.

In her introduction to *Marianne*, Miano explicitly decries the fact that young Black men bear the brunt of racism and stop checks in France.[9] According to the writer, they are regularly victims of 'des actes de barbarie

---

[7] See also Appiah's (2018) reflections on identity when one is at the crossroads of cultures, class, creed and even countries.

[8] See Blain (2017), Nguetse (2011, 2016).

[9] See de Maillard et al. (2017).

ayant pour objectif de blesser la masculinité de l'agressé' (2017: 9).[10]
Inevitably, it is difficult to extricate the notion of masculinities, and how
masculine identities are negotiated, from that of race in the context of
Afropeans in France. Intersectionality is crucial insofar as Black men born
in France live their masculinity through the prism of exclusion and dis-
criminatory discourses which affect their self-perception. Thus, in this section, I focus on a range of Miano's writings to investigate the ways in
which she employs both fiction and non-fiction to theorize a new form of
identity building for Afropeans.

Reframing Race, Community and Masculinities

> [..] les personnages dont je parle ne sont pas des immigrés. Ils ont grandi en
> France, contrairement à moi. Je souhaite qu'il n'y ait plus d'amalgame entre
> noir et immigré. Quand je me suis lancée dans mes projets d'écriture, j'ai
> pensé à ma fille qui est une afropéenne, née en France, de parents subsaha-
> riens. Elle a des attaches en Afrique et de la famille, mais son pays, c'est la
> France. Les Afropéens sont les Noirs d'Europe, avec leur histoire propre [...].
> —Miano, Interview *Africultures*

Discussing her essays *Ecrits pour la parole* (2012) in an interview with
Doumbia published in *Africultures* (2012), Miano unveils a direct critical
engagement with so-called second generation immigrants' negotiation of
identity in France. In her recently published essay *Afropéa,* Miano explains
ta 'pour la plupart dans l'Hexagone, le préfixe *afro* ne saurait renvoyer
qu'à un ailleurs, un hors de France essentiel plutôt qu'originel. Cela justi-
fierait que ce soit classé, dans la catégorie afropéenne, tout individu
d'ascendance subsaharienne établi dans le pays' (2020: 9). Seeking to separate the issues faced by Afropean individuals from those of first generation immigrants, Miano underlines the specificity of the dislocation, and
the history of, immigrants' children. She clearly defines an Afropean as
'une personne d'ascendance subsaharienne, née ou élevée en Europe' and
who has the lived experience of being European (2020: 10).[11] While her
daughter's birth country is France, and is by default, Afropean, Miano's
own home country is Cameroon. For her, there is a conspicuous

---

[10] Though Kinouani (2021) argues that Black individuals are regularly discriminated
against be they children, adults, men or women.
[11] See Vermeren (2014).

difference of belonging in each case. The question that is posed is whether the dominant, homogeneous, French population considers these children, who occupy a space between France and an elsewhere, as French, especially when they are visibly different. In this way, race becomes an integral aspect of the debate as it includes or excludes those who are deemed to be of a particular race, in or from, the dominant French (white) community. Miano reveals in both her fiction and non-fiction, through forms such as the novel, short stories and essays, that such social ills as racism and sexism are part of society and must be examined to facilitate the recuperation of Black masculinities. In particular, I explore the malaise experienced by male Afropeans to gauge the extent to which Miano accords importance to this 'peuple du milieu' and their role in her redefinition of masculinities and community.

Writing in *Postcolonial Poetics: Genre and Form* (2011), Jane Hiddleston understands poetics as the way in which 'texts offer multiple distinct ways of responding to political and historical questions' (2011: 1). For Hiddleston, 'the inventive use of genre and form brings about alternative ways of "referring" to the world and of reflecting political and historical context' (2011: 2). Central to the 'postcolonial poetics' articulated by the critic is the need to 'question the concept of a text's political impact and to explore rather the idiosyncratic ways in which literary works use form and genre to reflect on the world' (2011: 4). Within this framework, I want to study and underline Miano's wide use of different genres to transmit a specific political and poetic message about masculinities and notions of community, race and belonging.

To understand Miano's texts and the message that they transmit, the context within which she writes must be investigated. The short story, 'Afropean Soul', and the novel, *Tels,* were both published in 2008, at the time when President Nicolas Sarkozy brought the notion of 'identité nationale' to the forefront of government policy by establishing a ministry called 'Ministère de l'Immigration et de l'identité nationale'. Sarkozy launched a debate on national identity in 2009, fomenting a sense of dissatisfaction in both the population and in academic circles. Sarkozy's aim was to connect with the voters who would have otherwise given more clout to the Front National, whose popularity had posed a threat in the previous election. The notion of a national identity in France is not a novel concept and there have been numerous occasions in the past when this

3 RECONFIGURING COMMUNITY AND MASCULINITIES   107

was foregrounded.[12] However, the voices of those whose identity was being questioned: African (North and Sub-Saharan) immigrants and their children became a central concern.

In a special report aired by France24 in January 2010, entitled 'Identité nationale: Qui sont les vrais Français ?',[13] the Muslim inhabitants of Marseille, which is referred to as 'la ville la plus cosmopolite de France', reveals the constant racism and Islamophobia they experience. One of the speakers interrogates the existence of the 'vrai Français' and, by default, the definition of those deemed to be 'faux Français'. He further asks whether the so-called faux Français deserves to be punished for being 'faux'.[14] Thus, the report stresses the purely political discourse that this line of questioning symbolizes. Central to the inhabitants' concern is whether children of immigrants are 'vrais Français' and what their status and identity would be if they were regarded as 'faux Français', that is outside of what is perceived to be the French community. Examining the presence of former colonized peoples in France, Fiona Barclay speaks of a 'postcolonial haunting' insofar as their presence is felt even as they are not recognized as tangible people by the government and public policy. For Barclay, 'the ghosts which haunt postcolonial France may assume multiple forms, but they share a common feature, they are raised by an individual or a group whose roots lie in North Africa' (2011: xxii). This haunting is exacerbated by the disavowal of colonialism.[15] This is also the case for Black Africans and Afrodescendants,[16] whose difference is simultaneously recognized and not acknowledged. For the critic, '[t]heir identity, constantly problematized, represents a threat to the integrity of what is homely, safe and familiar, that is, to the nature of Frenchness as it has routinely been conceptualized since post 1962' (2011: xxii). Central to this assessment is the idea that immigrants' children, despite being born in France, have another identity and belong to another culture and community simultaneously.

I want to return to Kinouani here as she explains the notion of being beyond the bounds of the (French) nation well. For Kinouani, speaking about her own upbringing as an Afropean, the second generation are

[12] See Noiriel (2007b), Weil (2005), Bancel et al. (2010).

[13] For the full coverage see France 24 (2010).

[14] See also Hajjat's (2012) exploration of the frontiers of national identity. See also Nilsson (2018).

[15] See Gilroy (2005).

[16] 'Afrodescendants' refers to anyone whose parents, grandparents and ancestors originate from Sub-Saharan Africa, regardless of whether they were born in island territories or Europe.

often called '*les déracinés* or those who are uprooted', but she reminds us that these children's 'roots are more solid than they appear. They simply extend beyond the boundaries of one nation' (2021: 15). Rather than see the importance of this duality and the depth of Afropeans' appurtenances to both France and their parents' country, French society seems to reject them as others as if they were born and raised elsewhere. Competing identities render them unplaceable, in-between communities and undermine the notion of a 'French' identity which was once homogeneous and monolithic but is now publicly celebrated as diversity.[17] On a daily basis, children of immigrants are consistently victims of racial abuse, as underlined by the above report. Thus, the discrepancy between public discourse and private reactions to immigration and diversity affects a large number of people, as outlined by Noiriel (2007a) in the previous chapter, so much so that it becomes crucial to discuss race in order to understand the predicament in which Afropeans find themselves in Miano's texts.[18] Miano's fiction and non-fiction both attest to the difficult positioning of Afropeans inhabiting a space in-between France and Africa and whose belonging to France's community is perpetually questioned by others and themselves.[19] Central to Miano's work are the sexism and racism experienced by Black men in society and how deeply these affect them as they negotiate their identity as French nationals.

Examining race and masculinity in her introduction to her edited volume *Marianne*, Miano highlights the correlation between being male, being Black and being a victim of police brutality in France. In the case of Théo Luhaka who was stopped, suffered 'des injures à caractère raciste' before being violently beaten in 2016 (2017: 9), Miano emphasizes the fact that 'en France, le comportement des forces de l'ordre à l'égard des hommes noirs est hérité' from the colonial past (2017: 12). Here the essay form enables her to seize upon the socio-historical and political events

[17] See Verpeaux (2014).

[18] According to Bessone (2013; Bessone and Sabbagh 2015) it is important to speak about race as it is a social issue that must be tackled. If it is impossible to speak about it as it is disavowed, then it cannot be problematized. Bessone argues that the onus is on philosophers to change the ways in which race is conceptualized and discussed. See also Hall's discussion of race as a 'discursive construct, a sliding signifier' (2017: 32).

[19] See Guillaumin (1972) who began thinking about race in France earlier. Dorlin's *La matrice de la race* (2006) delves into the sexism experienced by 'other' women in France due to their temperament (2006: 19–33), their weak physiology (2006: 34–60) and their bodily differences (2006: 61–79).

occurring in French society and to comment on what such events emblematize for Black individuals in the wider society. Writing about the essay as a form, with specific reference to Virginia Woolf's works, Elena Gualtieri retraces the form back to its Renaissance roots and particularly to the mode of self-expression for which stalwarts such as Montaigne deployed it. Taking us through a rapid progression of the form until Woolf, via Lukacs and Adorno, Gualtieri then underlines the fact that the essay is first and foremost a form of autobiography (1998: 52), enabling an 'I' to process feelings and thoughts, combining aesthetics and social commentary. Narrative is eschewed while the writer guides the reader towards the message that s/he intends. In *Marianne* Miano highlights the fact that whilst these Black men are born and raised in France, they are considered to be from elsewhere and even dehumanized in order to justify violence against them. The affective experience of being dominated and discriminated against by virtue of being considered racially other and representing a threat to white masculinity due to their perceived 'hyper-virilité noire' becomes significant (2017: 17). Miano underscores the fact that men are targeted whilst Black women are not perceived as a threat by citing her own personal experience, as befits the essay genre: 'pour les hommes la menace est constante. Femme, jamais je ne fus contrôlée' (2017: 13).[20] She continues: 'ce sont les hommes que l'on surveille en particulier. Ce sont les hommes qui font le plus fréquemment l'objet de confrontations musclées, parfois létales, toujours dégradantes, avec les forces de l'ordre' (2017: 13–14).[21] Black men are pitted against the larger dominant community, which discriminates and perpetuates racist ideologies, and where the shared commonality is their perceived superiority. In her essay *Afropéa*, Miano compares the experiences of the first generation immigrants to that of Afropeans. She underlines the fact that being a stranger in France is not always a negative experience as she was born and raised in a Sub-Saharan society where everyone was Black and where aspirations were not 'entravées en raison de la couleur de [s]a peau' (2020: 10). By contrast, Afropeans not only suffer from a 'déficit en matière de représentation' but also a lack of a sense of belonging to a community due to French society's rejection of them (2020: 10). Afropeans are summarily deemed to be part

---

[20] Conversely, Larcher et al. (2018) have recently published an edited volume on the discrimination experienced by Black French women in French society. However, here Miano is specifically looking at physical violence and random stop checks which often target Black men.

[21] See also Traoré and de Lagasnerie (2019).

of the immigrant Black community due to their skin colour, a Black community which actually is not one at all.

In an earlier essay entitled 'COMMUNAUTÉ' published in *Ecrits pour la parole*, Miano deconstructs the very idea of a Black community in France. According to her, 'les Noirs de France[…] ils ont des origines trop diverses […] aucun soubassement commun, aucune histoire commune, aucune culture propre, partant de là, ils ne sauraient former une communauté […]' (2012: 30). Since there is no common 'souche' such as the one claimed by the French community, Miano argues that 'la communauté [noire] dont tout le monde parle n'existe pas' (2012: 36). In so doing, Miano underlines the imposition of a Black community on Afropeans and Black immigrants. Since their specificities are not recognized, they are lumped together into one overarching but inexistent Black community. Ironically, it is precisely the absence of a community, and therefore the power to resist as a collective, that Pitts's interlocutor, Almamy, identified earlier. In her analysis of Miano's texts, Natalie Etoké remarks that 'la douleur raciale entraîne des pratiques qui divisent le soi, mais dont le paradoxe est de réconcilier le sujet avec lui-même' (2017: 39). Nonetheless, Etoké acknowledges that 'ce dernier doit sans cesse négocier les tensions ontologiques à son statut de français non blanc' (2017: 39–40). She concludes that 'le Français noir se situe en contrepoint de celle du Français blanc' (2017: 43). However, the problem that Afropeans face in France is the fact that the existence of 'le Français noir' is constantly disavowed. If the Black French individual does not exist, then how do those who, like Miano's daughter, were born in France but have Sub-Saharan African parents, define themselves? It is through her fiction that Miano proposes a means of answering this question, more specifically, through her short story 'Afropean Soul'.

The choice of the form of the short story and the didactic collection of Flammarion to publish this story is not incidental. According to Mary Rohrberger, the short story usually presents an 'epiphanic moment … parenthetically enclosed by the story's beginning and end' (2004: 9). Miano targets a specific audience at the age where they are beginning to interrogate their notion of identity. The narrating 'je' is male, much as the many Black men who suffer racism on a daily basis, as delineated by Miano in *Marianne*. He is also commencing a journey of self-discovery triggered by Sarkozy's focus on 'l'identité nationale'. The young man is compelled to question his own identity and his belonging (2008a: 53), leading to doubts, in his own mind, as to whether he is French since his parents hail from the African continent and are Black. The remark about African 'bou-bous', which a patron in a café directs at him, generates an examination of what impact the national drive to define Frenchness has had since he is now imprisoned in 'la marge, ce non-lieu où le regard des autres l'enfermait maintenant en lui faisant comprendre que la couleur de sa peau n'était pas d'ici' (2008a: 54). However, while the government initiative is new at the point where the narration commences, practices demonstrate that the era-sure of colour and difference are longstanding and recurrent. Thus, the telemarketers who are Afropean see their names stripped and blended into an 'identité unisexe'—'Dominique Dumas' (2008a: 57),[22] which

> [...] effaçait la couleur. Farid et Fatou, tous deux nés en France et parlant le français sans accent, se fondaient d'un coup dans la fameuse identité natio-nale. En devenant *Dominique Dumas,* ils s'inscrivaient dans ce qui était communément considéré comme la norme. (2008a: 57)

This so-called norm is a French name with no outside origins according to the management of the company, which employs countless individuals with diverse origins, including the narrator. The specificity of each of these employees is effaced as their backgrounds are whitewashed through a French name.[23] The proper name becomes an identifier which includes the protagonist in the dominant (French) community and excludes him when it is his own. Nevertheless, the conflation of masculinity and femininity under the same asexual name is also revelatory of a more insidious project: the repression of masculine alterity. Much as Frantz Fanon felt objectified at his being referred to as a 'sale nègre' (1952: 88), creating a feeling of being an 'objet au milieu d'autres objets' (1952: 88), rather than being 'un homme parmi d'autres hommes' (1952: 91), here the non-gender specific proper name assigned to the telemarketers is symptomatic of a lack of respect towards the individual identity of those deemed to be divergent. As with Fanon, it is also a form of emasculation which is in line with

---

[22] Amok too becomes Daniel Laurent as I discussed in Chap. 2.

[23] Knox argues that *Tels* 'probes the relationship between minorities' literal (in)visibility within predominantly whitewashed mediascapes [...]' (2016: 94). However, 'far from point-ing out the absence of racial and ethnic minorities [...] the novel puts itself forth as its own Afropean mediascape' (2016: 94). Knox's article focuses on the privileged white heteronor-mative gaze and its tendency to whitewash and strip not only media but also history and memory (2016: 96).

Miano's assertion that men suffer the most at the hands of white French authority in contemporary society.

Miano's nameless first-person narrator in the short story underlines the precarious position of Afropeans. Adulthood brings the realization that Afropeans are different from the homogeneous French community, since 'pour ceux de sa génération, c'était cela, entrer dans l'âge adulte. S'apercevoir qu'on ne vous avait pas prévu au programme, qu'on vous tolérait d'extrême justesse au nombre des humains, et à condition que vous filiez doux' (2008a: 56). The fact that they were not 'prévu[s] au programme' attests to the reluctance of society in acknowledging emerging identities. The use of the verb 'tolérait' brings to bear the lack of acceptance of those who are in-between two cultures and two communities. Their precariousness is exacerbated as their invisibility ensures their survival. Yet it is difficult for them not to attract attention due to their hypervisibility as people of colour. Whilst they can be 'normalized' on the telephone, behind the white mask of a French name, to borrow Fanon's term, their appearance does not permit them to 'filer doux'.

Writing on affect and the relationship between the mind and the body, in 'Writing shame', Elspeth Probyn notes the splitting that takes place between the mind and the body in the notion of shame.[24] Using Deleuze as a point of departure, Probyn concludes that the mind judges the body for shaming it (2010: 80). In the case of Miano's narrator in 'Afropean Soul', the 'Occidental' mind judges the Black male body for placing it in an in-between position outside of community. The affective experience of being an outsider is lived on a daily basis leading to the hyperconsciousness of their bodies as other, and in many ways, creating a sense of shame, which is salient in Miano's texts. Nonetheless, while the collective experience of racism creates rifts and a 'community' of fellow sufferers, each individual experience is deeply affective. The experience of non-belonging is profound in Afropean individuals who are torn between two cultures and two countries. When the protagonist of the short story recounts his journeys to his parents' country of origin, he notes: 'chaque fois qu'il s'était rendu dans leur (his parents') pays, il avait eu conscience d'être un Occidental' (2008a: 65). Just as with the 'marmaille caramel' whose presence, colour and body signal them as in-between, out of community, in the incipit of *Tels* (2008b: 21), the narrator's disarticulation is evidenced

---

[24] Kinouani (2021) also discusses the shame that Black individuals experience due to their bodily difference.

in 'Afropean Soul'. His difference is contingent upon the body looking 'African', but the mind being 'Occidental' rendering the Afropean uncategorizable by both communities.[25] Miano's foregrounding of the narrator's suffering in 'Afropean soul' reflects her intention to unveil the violence experienced by Afropean men, due to their in-between position. It reveals a sensitive and human portrayal of circumstances changing Afropean men's perception of their own masculinities, as well as enabling the reconfiguration of the notion of belonging.

Interrupting Myth

> On ne parlait pas d'identité puisqu'elle s'indiquait par des signes. On en parle lorsqu'il n'y a plus de signes ou qu'ils ne renvoient plus à rien.
> —Nancy, *Identités: Fragments, franchises*

At this point in my analysis, I turn to Nancy and his notion of community, in particular, the interruption of myth to examine how Miano reconsiders belonging and community in her writing. Miano's texts do more than simply foreground the complex identity issues affecting Afropean men: they also discuss the different ways in which disenfranchised Black individuals attempt to create a community. However, the writer warns against going to extremes to solidify such groups as the 'Fils de Kemet', which rely on myths and create new forms of inclusion and exclusion to the detriment of Black individuals themselves. In *La Communauté désoeuvrée*, Nancy articulates the notion of the myth as the power to gather people together. Rather than a story celebrating the construction of a community, a myth is a story we tell because of a loss of foundation. As outlined by Nancy, the use of myth to create a pan-African brotherhood such as the 'Fils de Kemet' gestures to the crisis experienced by Afropeans and members of the African diaspora in France. The interruption of myth occurs at the point of realization that myth leads to the impossibility of being with, which is crucial to Nancy's idea of community, so much so that myth invalidates being-in-common. I contend that Miano uses the notion of

---

[25] In Niang's documentary *Les Mariannes noires* (Niang and Nielsen 2016), several of the interviewees also speak of the 'écartèlement' they experience between their French identity and their Sub-Saharan African origins. In *Identités françaises* (2019), she discusses the difficulty of integrating these bodies in the French Republic.

myth as represented by the 'Fils de Kemet' to challenge the position of the group as a community and shift the notions of belonging and identity, even as she questions the masculinities at play through a deconstructive approach. Thus, in both 'Afropean Soul' and *Tels*, the 'Fils de Kemet' group is emblematic of unification. Since their membership is secret and reserved to those who recognize Egyptian gods and sacred Africa as their legacy, I argue that the 'Fils de Kemet' functions as a community which includes as much as it excludes those who do not adhere to its precepts. Constructed as a brotherhood, the 'Fils de Kemet' represents a gendered entity, even as it permits some women, such as Amandla, to speak.

Miano's deployment of the 'Fils de Kemet' in each text serves distinct purposes. In the short story 'Afropean Soul', the narrator's encounter with the 'Fils de Kemet' occurs during a demonstration organized in the aftermath of the accidental killing of a Black child, Aboubakar, when a white policeman's firearm is discharged during the cleaning process. The 'Fils de Kemet' provide assistance to the family, yet their agenda is quickly revealed as political. Their discourse shifts from obtaining justice for the dead child's family to their own dispute for recognition, culminating in the child's mother 'ne comprena[nt] pas de quoi on parlait' during the group's spokesperson's address to the people assembled (2008a: 67). The compactness of the short story form generates a swift debunking (or what Rohrberger calls the 'epiphanic moment' which frames the short story form as discussed earlier (2004: 9)) of any notion that the 'Fils de Kemet' is anything less than an extremist group as the narrator declares:

> [...] tous les extrémistes étaient les mêmes. Qu'ils s'adressaient au coeur des hommes, davantage qu'à leur intelligence. Qu'ils se nourrissaient de peurs et de frustrations. Que. l'autre était leur ennemi. Qu'il était toujours plus simple de se replier sur soi que de s'ouvrir. (2008a: 67)

Here, the narrator's disambiguation of extremism unveils Miano's denunciation of such a means of regaining one's sense of identity in society.

Further critiquing the premise of a return to Africa, the narrator's remarks on the state of the African continent as he has witnessed it during his journeys with his parents are a contrast to the mythical Africa which the leaders of the group laud throughout their speech. As with every country, the rich and those who have power dominate and control the poor (2008a: 65). Against the rhetoric of vengeance and retaliation of the 'Fils de Kemet', Miano's narrator underlines the universal hierarchies underpinning the enterprise: in their revenge, the poor would be targeted and the rich would remain out of reach. For Miano's protagonist, the myth of the 'Fils de Kemet', the premise on which they have established their narrative, is flawed. Thus, Miano interrupts the myth of an African brotherhood and a mythical Africa which can alleviate the suffering of the Black diaspora in France. In the novel *Tels*, with the space which the novel form allows her, Miano takes the time to elaborate this interruption of myth further through the use of irony as well as through the deployment of fantastical elements. Shrapnel, Amandla and Amok are all associated with the 'Fils de Kemet' in the novel, but in each case, Miano uses the character's positioning in a different manner. Although Amandla and Shrapnel each have divergent experiences of negotiating identity, they both have distinct opinions as to how recuperating their Sub-Saharan African identities would lead to a sense of empowerment for all the members of the diaspora.

At this point I want to consider what the novel as a genre enables Miano to accomplish here. If the short story necessitates a central event which is elucidated by the end, the novel is a form which remains fluid and is constantly in process according to Vilashini Cooppan (2018).[26] For Cooppan, the 'heterogeneity and the heterochronicity' of the genre itself is significant (2018: 34). Building upon Mikhail Bakhtin's notion of the novel as emerging considerations of time and history, and 'from certain regimes of space (nationalism, imperialism, transnationalism, globalization)', Cooppan then goes on to caution us that 'its history reminds us that such spaces, no less than the genres that mirror them, are always also forms of time' (2018: 35). Miano's novel, *Tels*, is interesting as it features four narrators who are recounting their experiences from the first-person perspective, and not only going through a see-saw backward, forward movement as they recall their own experiences of living in their homeland and in France, but also innovative in the ways that history and space are deployed.

In Amandla's case, the recuperation of identities takes the shape of an actual return to Africa for all Afrodescendants. In her examination of Miano's oeuvre, Marjolaine Unter Ecker draws on Etoké's notion of *Melancholia Africana* (2010) to discuss the nostalgic obsession with Africa in this text. The melancholia depicted is Freudian and particular to descendants of slaves, and those who have left Africa, and cannot return.

---

[26] See Bakhtin (1981).

Amandla's personal quest for identity translates into her universalizing this to the rest of the group. Nonetheless, Amandla needs a Bantu man to effect this return as she was born in a DOM-TOM and has never been to Africa. The fact that the only militant woman in the novel cannot independently negotiate her identity is paradoxical. Equally the fear of the 'Fils de Kemet' group 'de se retrouver parmi des gens qui ne les attendaient pas, qui ne les connaissaient pas' is poignant. Caught between the slavery and colonial past and a future 'return' which might be problematic, the group inhabits a form of limbo of their own making (2008b: 87). The genealogy which they claim is far removed from the reality of living in Africa. Pretending to be sons of gods or princes does not equate to (re)constructing a life they never had. Finally, as Amandla underlines, 'aucun patrimoine ne se transmettait par mimétisme' (2008b: 91). Writing about colonial mimicry, Homi Bhabha sees the phenomenon as a form of lack or lagging. By definition, mimicry is 'partial' or 'incomplete', or as Bhabha would have it, 'almost the same *but not quite*' (1994: 86). In this case, the 'Fils de Kemet' attempt to emulate an 'African culture' from which they are far removed and cannot fully assimilate which is the reverse of the colonial trope. In fact, there are a range of cultures, urban and rural spaces, religions, histories and societies on the African continent and one single group 'myth' cannot possibly encompass the heterogeneity present on the continent. Thus, outside of the French dominant community and outside of Africa, the 'Fils de Kemet' belong in a no man's land, which further destabilizes them. Whilst Amandla's personal negotiation of identity involves a return to Africa, which she effectuates in the sequel to the novel, not all Afrodescendants can or should negotiate identity in the same way.

This disparity is exemplified with Shrapnel, who presents another conceptualization of identity for the 'Fils de Kemet'. Black masculinity and its relationship with community are foregrounded as Shrapnel emphasizes belonging and shared values. For Shrapnel, 'La Communauté était un prolongement de soi. Une famille' (2008b: 281). Kathryn Kleppinger perceives Shrapnel as 'a form of liaison between Amok and Amandla's respective positions' towards Black identity (2018: 119). While Shrapnel's death is a catalyst for both protagonists to make a decision about their futures, I argue that Shrapnel does have an important role to play in terms of representing an alternative perception of Black identity, despite the failure of this endeavour. Envisaging Black French identity from an outsider perspective, Shrapnel proposes that Afropean history must be reinscribed in collective history since:

Qui étaient-ils? ils se posaient depuis longtemps cette question dont la réponse n'était écrite nulle part. Personne ne leur avait raconté l'histoire de leur naissance. Personne n'avait cru bon faire figurer leur ascendance sur l'inventaire des constituants humains de ce territoire. Ils s'étaient donc trouvés là, comme surgis de nulle part, devant s'inventer à partir de rien. (2008b: 56)

As outlined by Barclay, this is a form of 'postcolonial haunting' which stems from the inability to reconcile the colonial past and the presence of former colonized peoples in France.[27] For Afropeans whose history has been disavowed, Miano's Shrapnel promulgates the formation of what he calls 'le Noir du Nord [...] [qui] n'existait toujours pas. Il ne s'était pas créé' (2008b: 72). Shrapnel believes in a form of self-determination for Black individuals. Nevertheless, for him, French Black identity is a collective project and subsumes both masculinities and femininities. The alliteration of 'n' in the identity that Shrapnel hypothesizes, the capitalization of the 'N' in 'Noir' and the use of the definite article 'le' are significant as they imply the existence of only one type of universal Blackness in France for Shrapnel. However, this notion is undermined by the fact that Miano has underlined the absence of cohesion and commonality amongst Black individuals in France in the text 'COMMUNAUTÉ' quoted earlier. Shrapnel mirrors the very act of the dominant community in grouping all Black individuals together without understanding their singular experiences.

Miano disputes the notion of a mythical collective Black identity further through fantastical elements. Shrapnel's unexpected demise on a train, prior to achieving any of his plans, leads to him occupying a limbo space where Martin Luther King and Malcolm X, stalwarts of Black collective projects, are condemned to hear the cries of those who keep chanting their names. This liminal space was generated by their inability to forego the past during their lifetime. Thus, Miano sets up these leaders as examples not to be followed as their collective projects impeded their passing on after death, and, ultimately, have failed. In so doing, the writer demonstrates the need for an individual negotiation of identity as each person has their own experiences and singularities.

---

[27] See Gilroy's discussion of this in *Postcolonial Melancholia* (2005). See also Hannoum's (2019) notion of 'colonial forgetting in postcolonial France'.

Miano's novel and short story foreground the human landscape and the affective experience of community as something coveted by the majority due to the need for a connection to others who share the same experiences, in this case, of racism and exclusion. While they may not have a common history or common culture, as Miano underscores in her essay 'COMMUNAUTÉ' (2012: 30), they do form a makeshift community of those who suffer from racial discrimination. Racial difference is not effected through a simple recognition that anyone who is not 'I' is automatically other, regardless of gender, race, class, as outlined in Nancy's theory, but through a set of criteria which determine whether the person can belong or not. This is exacerbated by the fact that the principal criterion is whiteness, and 'other' is synonymous to Blackness in Miano's works. For the 'Fils de Kemet', the other is white and cannot differentiate between migrant and immigrant Sub-Saharan Africans and Afropeans: 'ils étaient semblables au regard des autres' (2008b: 143), thereby inducing a deep-seated sense of malaise. Termed illegitimate sons of France due to their skin colour (2008b: 190), they become disenfranchised. Once again, the focus remains on the dislocation experienced by Black masculinities since the 'sons' are emphasized.

Nonetheless, the experience of exclusion from community is lived in a range of ways as each Afropean is singular: 'la douleur se manifestait différemment en chacun d'eux' (2008b: 197). Thus, while there is a collective project of belonging, each Afropean individual does have specific experiences of being outside of community. Miano's text allows us to perceive the individual as singular while experiencing similar problems to others, thereby engaging with the concept of singularity within plurality as linked with belonging.

Belonging and the Community of Humanity

> I belong to the country whose membership I share with others, this is my country as well as other people's country, our shared membership makes us part of it as it also makes us its co-owners, as it were.
>   —Balibar, 'Toward a Diasporic Citizen'

> Un Français avant tout, parce qu'on appartient à la terre de son enfance.
>   —Miano, 'Afropean Soul'

Since all Afropeans form part of the African diaspora,[28] Etienne Balibar's statement on the notion of belonging with regard to members of the diaspora is salient as it brings the focus on the singular 'I' who experiences mobility and the sense of disarticulation it entails. For Balibar, the question of where 'I' belong is moot due to the fact that 'I' have the same right as any other person who has 'membership' of the country 'I' call my own. The ownership at stake is a shared one but it is an affective belonging to a country and a common space enabling each of us to feel at home and be the master of our home. Miano's narrator in 'Afropean Soul' is more precise: he is French because he belongs to the land of his childhood. Yet, in *Tels*, the protagonists have a different rapport to their country of origin, and most of them disavow this country as home. Members of the 'Fils de Kemet' reclaim their African ancestry, albeit idealized, since they do not feel they are 'Français avant tout', as the country where they were born, France, rejects them in their alterity. In fact, only the narrator of 'Afropean Soul' disentangles himself from both the French national identity ideals and the 'Fils de Kemet' to find a middle path, which is the first step towards what Miano calls being 'ce people du milieu' (2008b: 372). I argue that Miano's notions of identity and belonging ultimately efface the differences she focuses on in her texts and empower her protagonists to make their own choices.

Miano herself ultimately considers race and alterity to be superficial differences in the quest for equality she foregrounds in these texts. Ayo Coly argues that 'Miano is less interested in a process of transformation than she is in a condition of transformed identities' (2014: 160). For Coly, this relies on the concept of bricolage, which is reflected in 'Amok's nondescript sartorial choices', which 'effectively amounts to a counter performance of masculinity and denotes a major shift in his practice of identity, but most importantly in the audience of his masculine performance' (2014: 162). In the previous chapter, I discussed the extent to which Amok represents an alternative masculinity through his suffering and love for Mabel. In terms of identity, rather than Amok's 'sartorial choices', his philosophy is most relevant here. For Coly, *Tels* represents a

---

[28] Pursuant to Cohen's definition (1997), there are two types of diasporas, the first compelled, as in the case of the Jews and African slaves, the second willed, as is the case of socio-economic migrants. Afropeans can encompass both children born to descendants of former slaves living in the Caribbean who have moved to France and have families there, as well as children born in France of migrants from Sub-Saharan Africa.

'Post-identitarian Afropeanism' (2014: 163). However, the very epigraph to the novel declares 'pour les identités frontalières'.[29] Through Amok, this notion is explored further in the text:

> les identités ne seraient pas nationales mais frontalières. Les frontières seraient un long côte-à-côte. Plutôt qu'une cicatrice barrant l'unité du genre humain. Les hommes sauraient leur destin commun. Leurs différences superficielles les divertiraient. Les enrichiraient. Si le racisme disparaissait, il n'y aurait plus à valoriser la couleur. (2008b: 117)

In *Tels*, Miano argues for a commonality linking all human beings, irrespective of gender, race and class. However, Miano does not identify this 'destin commun'. Differences, such as skin colour in her concept, are 'superficial' to the extent that if they were to be discounted, racism itself would disappear. There would be no otherness outside of the fact that whatever is not 'I' must perforce be the other. This idea is developed further in 'Afropean Soul':

> Le racisme, qu'il soit le fait de Blancs ou de Noirs, était irrationnel et sans fondement à ses yeux. On ne pouvait haïr les gens parce qu'ils étaient au monde, et qu'ils ne vous ressemblaient pas. Ils vous ressemblaient toujours au-delà de la surface, sous ce corps dont le jeune homme avait jusque-là négligé l'apparence, pour toucher l'humain au-dedans. (2008a: 59)

In stressing the humanity at the core of all human beings, Miano shifts the focus from race and gender to the human condition. Much as Fanon advocated for a new type of humanism after being objectified as a Black man,[30] Miano deconstructs the body as a vessel, the skin as a surface and the soul as a universalizing principle common to all mankind.

In the short story 'Afropean Soul' Miano's narrator asserts that 'l'identité était un processus, un mouvement constant' (2008a: 60). He interrogates the very notion of a reified Afropean, and indeed, a European identity: 'il y avait autant de manières d'être un Afropéen, que de façons d'être un Européen de souche' (2008a: 60). If there is no set definition for an Afropean nor for an 'Européen de souche', if they are by definition plural, and divergent, then how do these communities decide who is to be included and who is to be excluded? If the criteria for inclusion are broad

---

[29] See also Lefilleul (2014).
[30] See Gagiano's (2018) examination of Fanon's humanism.

enough to encompass a range of individuals who identify as Afropean or 'Européen de souche', then who draws the line of belonging, or not belonging, to either group? Do Afropeans and 'Européens de souche' choose these communities themselves or are they arbitrarily categorized as such? In the essay 'COMMUNAUTÉ', published four years later, Miano proclaims that the dominant discourse chooses to ghettoize Afropeans and African immigrants into one community, thereby subsuming their inherent differences, as examined earlier. Thus, be it in her essays or through her fiction, Miano clearly explores the same ideas. Where the fictional short texts such as 'Afropean Soul' appeal to a younger audience, the longer novel *Tels* might garner interest from a different tranche of readers, and the essays ultimately target those who are specifically interested in her conceptualizations of identities and belonging as an intellectual. Each form, has its own aesthetics, and as Hiddleston underlines, 'Particular genres invite readers to read in particular ways' (2011: 6), but they can also work in tandem too, as Miano's texts demonstrate.

Ultimately, in 'Afropean Soul', Miano advocates a form of self-determination, with the individual identifying where they would like to belong and who they would like to be. Thus, the narrator of 'Afropean Soul' quickly realizes that 'ce pays (France) était le sien. Il était sa seule terre' (2008a: 60), and that he would not let mainstream French society decide whether he belongs or not. Further expatiating his differences, the narrator positions himself against the collective 'Fils de Kemet' community, since 'il ne partageait pas leurs opinions. Il ne se posait pas les questions qui semblaient les obséder' (2008a: 61). For Miano's narrator, Fanon's need to feel 'un homme parmi les hommes' in the face of his objectification as a Black man (1952: 91) is significant here as Miano brings the focus back to basic shared humanity. While Fanon's primary objective was to be recognized as a human in his subjectivity, the choice of 'homme' instead of 'humain" is significant here as it does bring to bear the emasculation of the Black man, or wounded masculinity that Miano perceives in policemen's treatment of Black men in French streets.

In her introductory essay to *Marianne*, Miano asserts that 'pour l'individu blessé aussi bien dans sa chair que sur le plan psychologique, pour le groupe humain qu'il incarne par métonymie sans le vouloir, les choses ne s'arrêtent pas là' (2017: 10). Miano's message is not to counter violence with more violence.[31] The objective is to change the way in which Black masculinities are perceived and to recuperate them through resistance. However, her ultimate goal is that of promulgating 'cette humanité invaincue' (2017: 34). Thus, regardless of origins, humanity should shine through and triumph over racial prejudice and overbearing nationalism. The lucidity with which the narrator of 'Afropean Soul' observes the political ulterior motives of the 'Fils de Kemet' in the short story, as well as the political discourse on national identity, is crucial as it is emblematic of the Afropean individual's ability to objectively observe society from a liminal position. The liminal gaze permits an unequivocal declaration that 'les hommes étaient bien tous les mêmes' (Miano 2008a: 68) and that France is a wounded country which is struggling to attain its ideals of '*liberté, égalité, fraternité*' (2008a: 68).

In Miano's short story, the physical and emotional dislocation engendered by being outside of both the French dominant community and the 'Fils de Kemet' community creates a new resolution that is instituted upon the individual's own concept of belonging. In this narrative, identity does not reside in collective and exclusionary practices, but in an inward turn. Whilst this might redact out some of the real-life issues that are at stake, Miano's vision is one that sees individuals re-appropriate their own sense of identity on their own terms. Miano's texts allow for an interrogation of the current state of affairs in France regarding Afropeans who were born and raised in France but appear different. The characters' experience of community in and as displacement, in which any togetherness is configured as a common experience of spacing or distance, or an encounter with finitude or mortality remains ungraspable. In both her fiction and nonfiction, Miano invites us to rethink differences and what identities mean for the individual and for the collective. Since opening the country's borders inevitably leads to a shifting definition of one's 'identity' as a people, more than ever, the need to recognize that otherness is part of each society is becoming crucial.[32]

[31] In light of the skirmishes and acts of violence in the USA in the aftermath of George Floyd's death, the institutionalized racism in both countries is flagrant. Assa Traoré was certain that it is to avoid the same reactions in the streets of France that Adama's case is not elucidated. See BFMTV (2020).

[32] In Morrison's words: 'There are no strangers. There are only versions of ourselves, many of which we have not embraced, most of which we wish to protect ourselves from. For the stranger is not foreign, she is random; not alien but remembered; and it is the randomness of the encounter with our already known—although unacknowledged—selves that summons a

It is from this perspective that she moves towards what she calls a 'utopie post-occidentale et post-raciale' in her latest essay *Afropéa*. Though the term Afropean itself was coined by a Westerner,[33] Miano argues that it is actually 'post-national' (2020: 69). Rather than focusing on colour, for Miano, 'Afropéa' necessarily implies that 'l'identité n'est pas dans la couleur, elle est dans la culture et le vécu' (2020: 98). Self-determination becomes a significant aspect of this as the power to decide what is Afropean resides with the individual who claims it, rather than the charge of Blackness which is imposed by colonialism and its afterlives. In its newness, 'Afropéa' 'vise l'union' rather than fragmentation and segregation (2020: 102). Although she recognizes the ambivalence felt by Afropeans towards Africa and what the continent represents for them, Miano also believes that 'Afropéa' allows a form of malleability and becoming which will enable individuals to reconceptualize culture and identity on their own terms. There is much work to be done before such an enterprise can come to fruition, including changing the discourse according to which 'l'Histoire glorifie les bourreaux' (2020: 215). Miano ends her essay on the notion that it is indeed from the individual that change must originate as 'chacun est invité à oeuvrer pour transformer son monde', but for this to happen, 'il convient d'habiter pleinement sa demeure' (2020: 218), and rethink what home and belonging means for them.

By contrast, when community is affected by patriarchy Mokeddem demonstrates that a different form of power and love are crucial to recuperating masculinities.

WILLFULNESS AND (ISLAMIC) MASCULINITIES

'Mon père, mon premier homme, c'est par toi que j'ai appris à mesurer l'amour à l'aune des blessures et des manques', writes Mokeddem at the inception of *Mes hommes* (2005: 11). The incipit underscores the father's importance in the narrator's life, as well as the complex relationship she maintains with him, as a woman. The nasal sounds with the recurrent 'm' and occasional 'n' and the plosives produce an effect of lament and nostalgia, which is reflected in the narrative at large. The first sentence reads as an elegy to the father, but critically, it emphasizes the possessive adjective,

ripple of alarm' (2017: 38–9). Morrison's words echo Kristeva's notion of 'étrangers du dedans' which I explored in the first chapter in relation to hospitality.

[33] See Hitchcott and Thomas (2014).

'mon', repeated twice. It represents Malika's re-appropriation of her father on her own terms, as her property, as her first man, thereby reversing tropes of women as men's possessions. The play on the (Freudian) father-daughter relationship comes as a shock as the inference of 'mon premier homme' is sexual.[34] Yet the 'blessures' and the 'manques' designate another, more profound, understanding of the consequences of the father's misogyny. This is especially true of the effects of patriarchal values shared by the Islamic community, to which they belong, on her as a daughter, and later, as a woman, in her relationships. In this section I explore the relationship between community and love and how these affect masculinities in Mokeddem's *Mes hommes*.

Mokeddem was born in the late 1940s in Algeria, to nomad parents who settled into a sedentary life in a village near the Sahel Desert. Growing up at a time of change in Algeria, in the aftermath of the Algerian war of Independence, Mokeddem was the only girl to complete her education in her family and, indeed, her town.[35] She subsequently finished a medical degree in Oran and emigrated to France, where she specialized in Nephrology, much like the narrator of *Mes hommes*. The text is a first-person narrative which begins *in medias res* and describes Malika's relationships, both sexual and non-sexual, with several men. From the overbearing and controlling father, to the many lovers who have had a fleeting presence in her life, via her brother and male best friend, Malika takes the reader through a life narrative not structured chronologically but through the influence these men have had on her at particular points in her life.[36] While in earlier texts, Mokeddem's first name is not mentioned, in *Mes hommes*, the narrator is referred to as 'Malika' during a conversation involving a family friend and her mother.[37] The shift to using her own first name is significant as it allows for a more personal and poignant reading of the text as autobiographical.

---

[34] According to Biller and Weiss, the father has a role to play in determining how the girl's sexuality and her own relationships with men will develop (1970: 79).

[35] See Helm (2000) and Le Sueur (2007).

[36] However, this does not, of course, mean that Mokeddem does not change or choose which aspects are included and how the text is constructed. The plotting is itself carried out with specific events highlighted more than others and certain men garnering more interest than others.

[37] Critics such as McNee (2005) and Green (2008) have examined the extent to which Mokkedem's texts are largely autobiographical, even though her name is not explicitly mentioned in the earlier texts.

Taking as point of departure the Islamic community from which she hails as a disempowering community that privileges men, Mokeddem delineates a mode of rethinking female empowerment through a re-evaluation of masculinities. It is from this perspective that I turn to Ahmed whose notions of willfulness and dissent are of paramount importance in this section. She argues that the will must be understood as 'as experiential, not as something we already have, but as something we come to experience ourselves as having' (2014a: 24). It entails the suspension of belief that something called a will as a faculty exists (2014a: 24–25), in order to 'describe willing as a mode of experience' (2014a: 25). In essence, 'willfulness' is a charge made by some against those who do not go with the flow, who work and live against the grain. This charge, rather than being a blemish, as patriarchal society would perceive it, is deemed to be an empowering facet as 'willful subjects' dare to fight for their beliefs and their individuality. Rather than accepting the role that others impose on them, 'willful subjects' work against the grain of the majority to be who they wish to be.[38] Ahmed's theories allow us to contextualize Mokeddem's positioning in and against the Islamic community. In countering the dominant patriarchal and religious discourse, I also ask whether willfulness and dissent result in the destabilization and subversion of gender norms, thereby re-inscribing masculinities on Mokeddem's terms.[39]

Central to the dissident voice at play in this text are the notions of power and hegemony and the struggle against Islamic patriarchy. I draw on Kristeva's concept of power in 'Women's Time' and her recent discussion of faith in *Cet incroyable besoin de croire* to gauge the extent to which Mokeddem chooses a non-conforming lifestyle to obtain the power she requires to attain freedom. Equally, the specificity of the locale, the particular experiences of love in a postcolonial Islamic community are significant in Mokeddem's narrative. Thus, sociologist Amal Treacher Kabesh's *Postcolonial Masculinities: Emotions, Histories and Ethics* (2013) offers a final perspective to demonstrate the sensitive and humble way in which Mokeddem writes a love poem to all the men who have aided her in her emancipation and ultimate independence, and which she can only actualize when she obtains love from, and forgives, her father.

---

[38] Downing offers the notion of 'self-ful' as a means of countering dominant paradigms of women as 'selfless' beings and as a 'value-judgement-free alternative to selfishness' (2019: 3).

[39] See also Kistnareddy (Forthcoming 2022).

Malika's Emancipatory Dissent

Mokeddem's title, *Mes hommes*, alludes to the title of the French singer Barbara's song 'Mes hommes', in which men follow the singer for her beauty and fame, placing the woman as the focal point of so many men's attention. It also enables Mokeddem's narratorial 'je' to assert herself as the centripetal force of the narrative as the numerous men form a small community whose only link is Malika. The plurality of the possessive 'mes' reinforces the multiplicity of experiences, while simultaneously highlighting the number of ways in which she has attempted to negotiate her identity through these experiences.

The ability to enunciate, and subjectivation itself, are not a given for women in the Islamic community where Mokeddem situates the text. Set in the period following independence, contemporaneous with changes in politics and society occurring in Algeria, the text's treatment of gender relations unveils a tension between the conservative patriarchal values that privilege men at the expense of women, and transformations occurring in the society, especially with regard to women's education. During the Algerian war, France offered Algerian women the opportunity for emancipation and to fight for their own rights as a means of inveigling them to fight on their side against their own men.[40] Ultimately the women fought for their own country, hoping that the new Algerian state would recognize their role in winning the war and enable their emancipation. Nonetheless, although they fought as equals during the war,[41] in the aftermath of independence, they were expected to return to the domestic space. In Mokeddem's text, the narration begins after the war of independence and demonstrates that in the villages, communities remain strongly patriarchal, with fathers representing dominant masculinity and women occupying the domestic space, as Pierre Bourdieu evokes in *La domination masculine* (1998). Indeed, writing forty years later, Bourdieu underlines the fact that there is a 'division sexuelle du travail' as well as the public space occupied by men 'et la maison réservée aux femmes' (1998: 23).[42] Virility is expected as 'point d'honneur' and presupposes that anyone with a penis is dominant while women are subordinated (1998: 25, 36).

[40] See Leonarhdt (2013), Moussa (2016).

[41] See Vince (2010).

[42] This is also similar to the inside/outside gender division I identified with Confucian values in my examination of *Vi* in the previous chapter, lending credence to Bourdieu's premise that most patriarchal societies operate in the same fashion.

Similarly, the Algerian society depicted by Mokeddem's oppresses both through women who perpetuate gender divisions by aiding and abetting patriarchal values and men who are brought up to value sons. Since women seemingly have no worth until they bear a male child, they also bring up their sons to not accord importance to their wives until a son is born (2005: 12), a practice which is decried by the narrator in the text.[43]

According to Amanullah De Sondy, men play a dominant role in Islamic communities, wherein women are deemed to require protection. Women are perceived as 'the other, the abject, the foil' (2013: 11). De Sondy explores the work of women who are attempting to create their own paths by proving that they can be good wives and mothers while working. However, the women whose work the critic discusses 'have to tread carefully in order to demonstrate that they can be pro-family and in support of women's agency, both critical of masculinity and submissive to God' (2013: 56), thereby playing to the tune of prevalent discourses seeking to control their empowerment. Engaged in feminist scholarship, these women defy patriarchal order but within the limits imposed by the Quran. I contend that Malika's dissent in *Mes hommes* distinguishes her as a unique voice, at a time of great transition, that retaliates against not only patriarchal Islamic values, but also against gendered roles and choices. Her wilfulness insofar as it is perceived as otherness in a society where behaviour is coded and common leads to a form of rupture.

The title of the text, *Mes hommes*, is a subtle play on the 'mes fils' whom the father privileges. Foregrounding an inequitable value system where daughters are their mother's property as they hold very little value, whereas sons are their father's possessions as the source of lineage and posterity, Mokeddem calls into question the edicts of patriarchal society. The pride involved in the utterance 'mes fils' is unequivocal in the text. According to Ahmed, 'willing is thus what a subject does—or even must do—when a command has not been obeyed. A command is when a subject wills itself to will' (2014a: 29). Not obeying creates 'willfulness' as much as the command itself is a will at play. The clash of wills allows for a subjectivity to form even as it is perceived as negative by the person whose command is being disobeyed. Thus, 'being unwilling to obey' (2014a: 137) underpins the very nature of subjectivity as one's disobedience underlines one's

---

[43] This is in line with Connell's (1995) notion of hegemonic masculinity wherein such hegemony is facilitated by both men and women who perpetuate the hierarchy as I discuss in the introduction to the present study.

power over one's own life and choices. In her story of her childhood and her tense relationship with her father, Malika, the narrator, asserts that: 'La colère c'était quand je désobéissais. [...] Par rébellion et parce que c'était ma seule façon de t'atteindre' (Mokeddem 2005: 11). From the inception, her father's anger erupts as a reaction to her non-conformity. The clash of wills here allows for the realization that recognition of her individuality occurs with disobedience, much as Ahmed argues. Even as a child, the narrator is conscious of the fact that being disobedient would elicit an emotional response, a reaction which the other daughters never evoked in their father. Disobedience leads to an emergent subjectivity which is only felt in opposition to the other silent and conforming daughters who significantly remain nameless and voiceless in the narration. Transgressive behaviour is edulcorated as Malika is finally referred to as 'ta fille' in a conversation between her parents (2005: 16), signalling that even as she is rebellious and a problematic personality in the traditional society she inhabits, she is also the only daughter who speaks her truth and gains undeniable subjectivity. Her dissidence finally gives her a 'voix' (2005: 16). This culminates in the father's single utterance of 'ma fille' leading to her jubilation, 'j'ai bu. le ciel mon père' (2005: 16). Rather than faith in Islam and the God she must obey, she claims 'c'est d'abord en toi que j'avais besoin d'avoir foi, mon père' (2005: 13).

Nevertheless, the happiness experienced by the girl whose subjectivity has been acknowledged through the possessive 'ma' is marred by the fact that the father regrets 'qu['elle] ne soi[t] pas un garçon' (2005: 13), since strength of character is deemed to be within the remit of masculinity. The quest for paternal recognition is conducive to empowerment as every setback is a means of fighting for her rights. As Malika demonstrates her 'willfulness', she is seen as a 'having an obstinate and unyielding nature', which must be 'disciplined or straightened out as Ahmed discusses in *Living a Feminist Life* (2017: 66), and this is seen through her father's constant punishments. In her 'willfulness', Malika destabilizes the gender divide and the carefully constructed role of women as supporting the men in her society. Minor victories notwithstanding (for instance, her father buys her a bicycle in acknowledgment of her hard work and sheer determination), the overbearing values of the society are decried as there are multiple attempts to compel her to conform by threatening to marry her off at a young age and putting an end to her schooling. Mokeddem's text exemplifies the tensions that might prevail in father-daughter relationships during a time of societal changes and when girls are being educated in post-war Algeria.

Crucially, an important comparison can be drawn between Malika's father and Assia Djebar's narrator's father in *Nulle part*, which was published two years after *Mes hommes*, in 2007. It is important to note that the cover explicitly states 'roman' in Djebar's case, whereas Mokeddem plays with the genre of the text by not saying whether it is autobiographical or a novel. However, Djebar's 'roman' is highly autobiographical in nature as a number of critics have pointed out.[44] Notably, there is a revealing contrast in the way that the two girls are brought up. *Nulle part* is a clear and deeply intimate story of a little girl brought up in colonial Algeria wearing Western clothes and speaking French. Nevertheless, the very first scene sets up the traditional domestic space where the mother's ubiquitous Islamic veil is given a significant role in siting the patriarchal values at play in the Islamic community represented.

Djebar's narrator declares from the outset: 'je me sens "la fille de mon père"' (2007: 18). The double quotation marks signal the words are borrowed from the old ladies whom the narrator's mother visits. By the visible signs of her acculturation, her dress and her language, she *belongs* to her father since he is a French teacher. Contrary to Malika who fights to be acknowledged as her father's daughter, Djebar's narrator cannot be anything but her father's daughter in this context. The sustained complicity between the narrator and her father creates an environment which fosters a thirst for knowledge and reading. The father's insistence on educating his daughter creates a different life for her and he allows her to achieve her full potential as I explore in Chap. 4. Yet Djebar's narrator is also reminded that she belongs to a patriarchal Islamic community in the chapter entitled 'La bicyclette' in the narrative. The narrator recounts her father's anger at the sight of his daughter's thighs as she rides a bicycle: 'je ne veux pas que ma fille montre ses jambes en montant à bicyclette' (2007: 55). There is a jarring contrast between Western upbringing he has provided for his daughter and the Islamic patriarchal values wherein the female body must remain covered. While it was fully instantiated in the veil scene with the mother in the first chapter of the text, the little girl thought herself different due to her father allowing her to enjoy a Western upbringing and education. Djebar's narrator describes this particular episode with palpable shock, as her father's face becomes 'pas tout à fait humaine, pas

---

[44] See for instance Meddahi-Bereksi (2015) and Guendouzi (2017).

exactement bestiale; plutôt une matière brute entrevue, une boue' (2007: 56). The particularly Islamic patriarchal identity it betrays is significant as Djebar describes it as another identity, someone else masquerading as her father, since the reaction is at odds with her father's usual behaviour towards her. Thus, despite being very encouraging towards his daughter, Djebar's male protagonist is also at times limited by Islamic values, much like Malika's father. Both fathers, in different ways, have provided the impetus for their daughter's success: one succeeds through adversity and the other one through constant encouragement, although the latter does demonstrate that her father too can be conservative in his outlook. In Malika's case, the father is torn between his values and the admiration which his daughter's impropriety and tenacity evoke in him.

Irony is employed to establish Malika's father's admiration for his daughter's determination as her earning money to pay for her own tuition fees and education prompts the proud statement 'ma fille, maintenant tu es un homme' (2005: 17). Earning is deemed to be a masculine accomplishment, in line with De Sondy's argument that Islamic masculinities' first duty is to provide and protect. However, the language deployed by members of this community to congratulate their sons reaching manhood through financial gain cannot reflect the reality of a woman earning and providing for herself, representing a temporal and linguistic lag in a changing society. In Malika's case improper femininity is at play and jars with traditions, as outlined by Ahmed. The 'promotion' to masculinity is depicted with derision and laughter. Yet, whilst the father is perceived as an oppressor, his actions and reactions serve as a spur to the daughter to challenge accepted gendered roles and adopt the mantle of masculinity, through what she calls 'le refus de l'oppression, de la médiocrité et de la résignation' (2005: 19).[45] In *Mes hommes*, masculinity is associated with a girl's ability to earn money, a property usually assigned to a male, thus fostering disjuncture. However, rather than acknowledging her equality, the father accentuates the transformation into a man through the performance of a 'masculine' act.

The displacement of the woman into the realm and space of the masculine further echoes Ahmed's notion of willfulness. The conflictual

---

[45] This is reminiscent of Halberstam's notion of 'female masculinity' (2002). Halberstam's theory is based on the fact that masculinity is not the property of men alone. Whilst it is not 'an imitation of maleness, female masculinity actually affords us a glimpse of how masculinity is constructed as masculinity' (2002: 355).

relationship between the father and daughter becomes a political act, which is further reinforced by the movement from the domestic space, in line with Bourdieu's observation earlier, where the girl is forced to clean and take care of her siblings, to the public sphere where she is among the very few to go to secondary school, and the only one who completes her education fully. Malika's 'willfulness' creates a space for a new voice to emerge as she breaks the rules and creates a new subject which defies established order. In the text, Malika's resistance is not only instantiated through verbal and intellectual rebellion, but also through a corporeal disaffection.

Ahmed notes that the willful subject is a political one as she is disobedient (2014b: 2). Ahmed argues that 'to be identified as willful is to become a problem' (2014b: 2). The stubbornness that marks the political act is present in Ahmed's "willful subject" and is constantly reiterated. Ahmed extends it to the corporeal. Examining the unwillingness to obey as a trait which a body might 'come to acquire' in a chapter entitled 'Willfulness as a style of politics', Ahmed argues that in a Foucauldian sense that 'there is power because there is disobedience' (2014a: 138). Nonetheless, this resistance is often accomplished through the body. The refusal of a tyranny is accomplished by the rejection of becoming the corporeal instrument of tyranny since 'to become subject to the will of the tyrant is to provide him with the very organs of this power: you become his feet, his arms, his eyes. Becoming the limbs of the tyrant means becoming *the agent of your own harm*' (2014a: 139). Thus, following Ahmed, resisting patriarchy begins with disobedience but also a recuperation of one's own body. This willful subjectivity was already present in Malika as a child even as she asserts her control over her own body. In her quest for subjectivation, Malika makes some very significant choices that mark her will to defy the values imposed on her by her society through a re-appropriation of her body and choice. Contrary to the feminist scholars De Sondy examines, Mokeddem contests the image of the dutiful Muslim woman as wife and mother. Faced with an unwanted pregnancy, she undergoes an abortion, following which she makes the decision to remain childless. This 'willful' act goes against the principles inculcated by the dominant discourse, be they enforced by her father, her mother, or the Islamic community. If the mother is perpetually in the kitchen, representing food and eating, Malika uses anorexia as a form of resistance. The girl's 'willfulness' is here seen both as an act of defiance and as a desperate need to claim her own subjectivity. That the young girl feels the need to 'bander [se]s seins' so as not to be objectified and desired as a woman (2005: 42) testifies to a society which polices the female body. Malika's recuperation of her own body is thus a political act insofar as it disrupts the order and is emancipatory.

Nonetheless, Malika's concern is not purely feminist in purport. Rather, the author does not want to be in the 'ghetto' of feminist writing (2005: 161). Her main concern is emphasizing the inhumanity of the community towards both men and women. While the text presents the struggle of a woman in the face of Islamic patriarchal values, it is also the story of the many suffering men who have been part of her life.

Women's Power

Malika's 'wilfulness' stems from her inability to comply with her father's authority, and by extension, the Islamic community's demands on her as a young girl. The father is portrayed as an obstacle to freedom, repeatedly hampering Malika's emancipation. His obduracy is emblematic of stasis at a pivotal time in the wake of Algerian independence. He becomes the starting point of Malika's rebellion against Islam and patriarchy, and her subsequent relationships with men. Consequently, Malika disowns Islam as her religion: 'Je suis athée depuis mes quinze ans' (2005: 55). However, this precocious rebellion is not translated into action until after she has left her father's house. The narrator recounts the ways in which she deploys her counter-Islamic values through her transgressions, such as eating on her balcony during Ramadan and smoking in public, while she is at university in the city (2005: 56). The public defiance against religious precepts is revelatory as she exhibits no fear of repercussions. However, her discordant behaviour does not foment revolt in others, nor does it change the course of the lives of other women around her. Malika's political act is an individual one, aimed at her own self-determination and positioning as a marginal figure. In her dissidence, she exercizes her political right to choice, fostering a decentring of dominant masculine Islamic discourses through the displacement of power from the male protagonists to herself. Nonetheless, this power does not replicate dominant masculine patriarchal discourses. Instead, it allows for a re-conceptualization of men as equal by foregrounding their vulnerabilities.

From this perspective, I argue that Kristeva's notion of power as set out in 'Women's Time' lends itself to an examination of Mokeddem's text in many ways. Combatting exclusion due to gendered roles, fighting against the functions which ask women to fulfil what she calls a 'sociosymbolic contract (*sic*)', Kristeva underlines the means of transforming women's position in society, and specifically, how power is wielded. She raises important questions: 'What happens when women come into power and identify with it? What happens when on the contrary, they refuse power and create a parallel society [...]?' (1981: 26). The danger, for Kristeva, is replicating 'the old ruts of the initially combated archetypes' (1981: 28). For the theorist, thus, acquiring power is not the be-all and the end-all of feminism. Rather, it is the decision to wield this power and, in particular, *how* to wield it that becomes a central concern.

Power in Malika's case comes through knowledge, education, love and the reclaiming of her right to choice: 'le droit à l'amour, à l'amitié d'un homme, au savoir' (2005: 55). Education brings an openness and a shift of perspective as it works against the grain of Islamic femininity. According to Siobhan McIlvanney, the Algerian War of Independence is seen as 'incarnating distinct aspirations for Algerian women who desired to play a more egalitarian role in their country's new political era' (2016: 135). In line with my earlier discussion of women's role during the Algerian war of independence, for the critic, Algerian women 'were key beneficiaries of this educational drive' (2016: 135). While Mokeddem's aim is to take the advantage represented by education to escape her community and its constraints, her endeavour remains very personal at this point. Faced with the choice between Jamil, her first lover's emotional blackmail and her studies, Malika states: 'moi c'est de ne pas poursuivre mes études, de rester ici qui me tuerait. [...] Je ne marcherai pas à ce chantage' (2005: 31). Intertwined with this is the idea of eschewing patriarchal male control. Having wrested power over her destiny away from her father, Malika cannot bear to hand it over to Jamil. She cannot perpetuate the cycle of 'sociosymbolic contract' which she has inherited, to borrow Kristeva's words. Belonging to Jamil is tantamount to conceding to her father and Islamic patriarchy. Instead, Malika's attitude towards men places her in the dominant position in this narrative.

If power and dominion are exercised over society and a group of people so that hegemonic masculinity is performed, as I discussed with Connell (1995) in the introduction to this book, Malika wields power over a group of men who love and admire her. In a beautiful poetic prose Malika creates a world where the men have feminine attributes, in a reversal of roles. Jamil venerates her and is 'en adoration' (2005: 26). This image is juxtaposed with a portrayal of his feminine 'yeux de biche' (2005: 28).[46] Mokeddem's re-appropriation of feminine stereotypes demonstrates the power she now commands over her own sexuality and men. Men are depicted as constantly emotionally needy, with Jamil attempting 'chantage' (2005: 31), to convince her to stay in their village. Later, with her second lover, Saïd, at university, she is faced with traditional Kabyle upbringing and the dogmatic way in which he approaches sex. Again, in a paradigmatic shift, Saïd resists pre-marital sex, leading Malika to observe 'à quel point les hommes peuvent être aussi inhibés par le carcan de la tradition' (2005: 57). Examining 'Postcolonial masculinities', Elahe Yekani argues that by the end of the twentieth century, 'the hegemonic status of masculinity is clearly more strongly contested and the crises of men in fiction become more pronounced and exposed' (2011: 154). While hegemonic masculinity is certainly undermined in Mokeddem's text, it is juxtaposed with a willingness to understand and sensitively depict the transformations which postcoloniality and societal changes are bringing to masculinities.

In *Mes hommes*, Islamic masculinities have an equal burden of responsibility and values that they are charged with upholding. Nonetheless, Mokeddem never uses this opportunity to combat or reduce this role reversal to a challenge against masculinities. As Saïd and Malika lose their virginity, the latter states that claiming control over their own sexuality can 'faire pleurer les hommes' due to the 'carcan' of patriarchy (2005: 58). Here, rather than asserting her power in a negative way, as Kristeva exhorts feminists not to do, Malika is deeply respectful and empathetic in her depiction of the affectivity of the Muslim man who loves her and suffers as he relinquishes his community's values in so doing. Sexuality as power is redemptive, but it is also lived as a necessity, as Malika claims: 'j'ai besoin des bras d'un homme. J'ai besoin de cette force de vie. C'est tout' (2005: 63). Ironically, the anaphoric repetition of 'j'ai besoin' underscores Malika's dependence even as she exerts her power over men. Power is fragile since it relies on the complicity of those who give the power and those who wield it. Those who have power are always dependent on those who are dominated.[47]

[46] See Szymanski et al. (2011).

[47] Female libido is set up as one of the significant aspects of Malika's power here. Freud famously stated that there was only one libido, the masculine one, in *Three Essays on the Theory of Sexuality* (1905). Mokeddem evidently focuses on the equality of female sexuality,

Crucially, in order to 'bafouer la religion' (2005: 63), non-Algerian men are used as the means of resisting her Algerian sexual repression, but also in many ways as a rebellion against her own father. Even as she has left him behind in Béchar, he is constantly at the forefront of Malika's rebellion. The imagery that Mokeddem deploys is that of a form of slavery from which she needs to be liberated, with the word 'affranchie' (2005: 64). Sexual intercourse with a European man becomes an experience undertaken to counter the 'simulacre du collectif' or 'communautés' (2005: 64), that is countering the precepts of her Islamic community. The French men possess what Algerian men in her text cannot have due to their religion and culture: the freedom to have sex and the freedom to choose who they marry contrary to Saïd, whose Kabyle family rejects her. Needing *a man* is eventually replaced with "j'ai besoin d'un homme libre" (2005: 67).

Moreover, men are depicted in what used to be domestic spaces, thus disrupting traditional notions of dominant masculinity as depicted by Bourdieu. In France c'est 'le Français qui [lui] fait la cuisine' (2005: 67). While Bourdieu underlines the distinct division between the kitchen as a feminine space where the woman holds sway in Algeria, in contemporary France as represented in the text, such a distinction is not present. Rather, the French man attempts to woo the narrator through his culinary prowess. An overt feminization of the men is instantiated as his body becomes a continent to be colonized: 'son corps est devenu mon continent' (2005: 73). Mokeddem here reverses the trope that a woman's body is to be conquered by a man by positing herself as the hegemonic power reigning over the man's body. The masculine body is both desired and colonized as 'c'est exotique et érotique' (2005: 67).[48] Nevertheless, while Malika remarks: 'J'ai un comportement de macho' (2005: 69), she does not brandish such an attribute as a coveted power. Rather, it is highlighted as a pure discovery of unrepressed sexuality as she moves to France. Though this might seem to play upon stereotypes of French women being more liberal, with the French feminists reclaiming the right to sexuality,[49] it nevertheless does not come across as a negative aspect here as Malika navigates her new life with confidence and aplomb.

but when she describes her behaviour as 'macho' (2005: 69), it attenuates the effect as the focus is on the masculine rather than her own femininity.

[48] This evokes orientalist tropes as discussed by Said in *Orientalism* (1978) wherein the West always seeks to conquer the feminine East, which is deemed to be exotic. Here Mokeddem once again reverses another masculine trope.

[49] See Downing's discussion of this notion in *Selfish Women* (2019).

However, the question that Mokeddem raises is whether religion and the attendant notion of 'faith' are both problematic. Kristeva, in *Cet incroyable besoin de croire*, underlines the need to have faith, which she sees as 'prépolitique et préreligieux' (2007: 21). For Kristeva, faith underpins the need for knowledge which is highly secular and spurs us to better ourselves. Earlier I briefly mentioned Malika's use of the word 'foi' to displace it from religion to her father as a means of shifting towards secularity and love, but in the child's case, it is a simple need to trust and have faith in her father as a paternal and protective figure rather than an oppressive representative of Islamic patriarchy. For Kristeva, any 'être parlant est un être croyant' (2007: 23). *Logos* then belongs to those who have faith, but it is not necessarily religious faith. Kristeva's faith relies on the fact that one needs to 'tenir pour vrai' or else 'apprentissages, convictions, amours et actes tout simplement ne tiennent pas' (2007: 27). Nevertheless, Kristeva insists that this necessity for believing should be 'incroyable' as it must not become an absolute. Instead, faith should be a 'soutien, une condition optimale pour le débat démocratique' (2007: 27). Kristeva's faith is not a collective experience but a basis for 'individuation' (2007: 39), which goes against the grain of institutionalized religion. Kristeva's secular faith is crucial to understanding Malika's power over the men in her life insofar as she needs to have faith in her own individual path and her own way of life. While she moves from an Islamic community to a secular lifestyle, she also in tandem moves from Algerian men to European men. These conscious choices are not perceived as acts of rebellion, rather, they become acts of individuation as a woman. Whether it be in 'Women's Time' or in *Cet incroyable besoin de croire*, Kristeva's primary focus is on 'the singularity of each person' (1981: 35), which is crucial for this analysis of Mokeddem's text as it is not the story of every Algerian woman's struggle for independence and individuation; it is a single woman's combat to find her own voice and fashion her own place in the world.

In *Mes hommes*, power is both demonized and instrumentalized and questioned to the point that it disintegrates, allowing for a perception of the men, and Malika herself, through the affective experiences which they undergo and leading to a re-conceptualization of gender through the concept of love.

Re-appropriating Love and Reframing Masculinities

Mokeddem inscribes her recuperation of her position in her family as not simply rebellion, but as an act of love. The depiction of the little girl spying on her father's movements from the dunes where she hides, unveils poetry and admiration, from the sibilant description of 'la souplesse de [s]on saroual', to the rolling, rumbling 'rs' of the 'rondeurs de caresses autour de ton torse', culminating in her admission that she would have liked to 'courir vers' her father (2005: 13). Rather than an outright rejection of the father and his values, Mokeddem stresses the innocence of the child who wishes to gain love and recognition from her father: 'moi je voulais de l'amour, de la joie. A essayer de les conquérir, c'est la liberté que j'ai gagnée' (2005: 15). Malika demonstrates that, as a woman, she is outside of community. By claiming her subjectivation and flaunting her voice, she attains freedom, but there is no sense of triumph as the objective was simply being loved. Thus, rather than a struggle for the collective of women who are repressed by the patriarchy, *Mes hommes* is, first and foremost, an individual woman's struggle for paternal recognition and love.

Love itself takes on different guises in the text. The first type of love is indubitably the love of the little girl for her father. This love, or lack of love, as I underlined earlier, does have a psychological aspect insofar as it casts a shadow over Malika's subsequent relationships: 'Je t'ai quitté pour apprendre la liberté, la liberté jusque dans l'amour des hommes. Et je te dois d'avoir toujours su me séparer d'eux aussi. Même quand je les avais dans la peau' (2005: 18). Where love is perceived as control, Malika's automatic reaction is resistance, which, in turn, translates into resistance to love. The psychological dimension to her relationships with men cannot be eschewed here, especially when Malika asserts: 'je ne t'ai pas cherché en d'autres hommes. Je les ai aimés différents pour te garder absent' (2005: 19). However, deliberately seeking men who do not resemble her father is also inadvertently indicating the extent to which she is perpetually impacted by her relationship with him and foregrounds the impossibility of loving.[50]

---

[50] In *La Communauté inavouable*, Blanchot speaks of the impossibility of loving and the community of those who do not belong elsewhere. For Blanchot, love is 'jamais sûr' and can take the form of 'l'impossibilité d'aimer' (1983: 58). According to Blanchot, examining Duras's *La Maladie de la mort* (1982), love brings about community in its absence rather than in its presence. Malika begins her journey back to her father when she encounters unrequited love for the first time as well.

Nonetheless, love in *Mes hommes* is not limited to romantic love or to the lack of love from the father. Perhaps one of the most important types of love that Mokeddem showcases in her text is that of Malika's love for her brother, Tayeb. Significantly, Mokeddem does not discuss this 'man' in her life until the second half of the text. The chapter is written in a prose that is remarkable due to its simplicity and the repetition of the possessive 'mon frère', which reveals the deep affection which Malika feels for her brother. With awe and surprise Malika observes: 'mon frère est un garçon' (2005: 139), 'un jour il sera un homme mon frère' (2005: 145). Having fought her way thus far against all the boys at school and in the neighbourhood, the fact that the person she is closest to is a boy is jarring but fascinating. Malika's love for her brother, the complicity that links them, permits a different way of seeing masculinity, not as oppressive towards her, but as restrictive for the brother. Malika sensitively writes: 'il est un peu plus démuni mon frère parce que c'est un garçon' (2005: 147). Thus, her brother's masculinity is the root of additional responsibilities and restrictions marring his life, such as compulsory military service.

Tayeb's need for freedom translates into fleeing for Europe, much as Malika. Nonetheless, the text emphasizes the difficulty of being a man of colour in Europe. Where Malika is perceived as exotic, Tayeb 'fait partie des basanés' (2005: 149). While Malika is oppressed by patriarchy in her home community, men such as Tayeb are racially targeted in predominantly white societies in Europe. In *Sexagon: Muslims, France, and the Sexualisation of National Culture* (2017) Amadeus Mack identifies the different stereotypes that are associated with the Arab boy in France. This includes the fear of the Arab, but also the emasculation of the man who cannot work to provide for his family (2017: 168). In some ways, Tayeb's inability to succeed as a writer is a form of emasculation insofar as it posits him as lesser than his sister. Ironically, it perpetuates the De Sondian notion of Islamic men as providers for women, which he sought to escape. Malika's brother represents her strongest love and her most important heartbreak since he eventually cuts off all communication between them, which, compounded with her father's rejection of her, creates a series of 'manques d'amour' (2005: 152), which devastate Malika.

According to Treacher Kabesh, it is imperative to understand that postcolonial men do not simply avoid intimacy. For the critic, it is crucial 'to posit masculinities as free of bonds, and the notion that men can and do operate in a landscape of freedom and independence' (2013: 44). Speaking of postcolonial families in Islam, Treacher Kabesh states that:

families are formed within the political and social spheres and yet they can have their own idiosyncratic way of forging a family life. Lives are made out of family narratives and histories and involve connections, bonds, disappointments, joys, hurts, and pleasures. (2013: 46)

Power and love operate on the same level in families and these are constantly renegotiated. It is not completely surprising that Tayeb cuts communication with Malika when his own writing career does not garner the success he hoped for. Alongside the sentiment of failure is the feeling of shame at not succeeding, unlike her. Malika does not lay blame on Tayeb as much as reinforce the sensitive nature of the young man who then returns to the desert but in another part of the country. The gesture of not acknowledging that it might be a gendered feeling of quashed superiority, which he internalized as a coveted son, is emblematic of the sister's own understanding of his ailing ego and masculinity here. In this, too, she remains a loving sister.

Mokeddem's discussion of love culminates in an important end of a cycle. According to Treacher Kabesh, 'fathers, whether we are sons or daughters, are inevitably folded into our most profound psychic investments and desires for reparation' (2013: 148). While 'l'écriture redevient l'espace de toutes les résistances' (Mokeddem 2005: 201), it also becomes a journey to the past and towards redemption. Treacher Kabesh further underlines that 'these ghosts of the past whisper, they have presence—demanding love, justice, healing' (2013: 148–9). For Malika, learning to love truly begins with reconciliation with the father, going back home to relearn love and forgiveness. The power of the affect is reinforced here as the experience of unrequited love, leads to the desire to reconcile with herself, her father and reconstruct the love through his 'bénédiction' after he asks for her 'pardon' (2005: 218). Discussing Mokeddem's position vis-à-vis her father in *Mes hommes*, Abdelkader Cheref asserts that Mokeddem 'seems to forget that her father's behaviour is conditioned by a patriarchal structure over which he has no control' (2010: 55–56). For Cheref, Mokeddem is wrong in blaming 'a victim for being an executioner' (2010: 56). I read *Mes hommes* as part of the process through which Mokeddem recognizes the oppression of patriarchal Islam on masculinities, be they the father, the brother or the Algerian lovers. The text is an ode to their suffering, which culminates in the return to the paternal home. The father asking for her pardon and the act of forgiving restores Malika's ability to love. However, she must first reconcile with her childhood self and acquire self-love and thus, she comes to the conclusion that: 'à ce point des rébellions, des ruptures, des départs, des exils, seule notre enfance peut nous réconcilier avec nous-mêmes' (2005: 218). Malika's awareness of her father's position and inability to speak of love towards a daughter is underscored in this text. Just as, as a daughter, she suffers from this masculine impossibility of expressing one's love, so too does her father since he must negotiate the shifting position of women in postcolonial society and how to address his daughter's subjectivation in this new paradigm.

It is from this perspective that I contend that comparisons may be drawn with bell hooks and her relationship with her father as she resituates love in their relationship. hooks states: 'Understanding him, I understand myself better. To claim my power as a woman, I have to claim him. We belong together' (2004: xvii). For hooks, one cannot speak of women without speaking of men. Recuperating the woman she is can only occur if she understands and reclaims her father simultaneously. Mokeddem's recovery of her own power as a woman, of her life and her different relationships begins with a return to the father and the act of forgiveness. When hooks writes that 'every female wants to be loved by a male. Every woman wants to love and be loved by the males in her life' (2004: 1), she is not speaking of normative heterosexual romantic relationships. Her focus is simply on the fact that women do not exist in a world exclusive to women. To ground themselves and accept the different sides of themselves, women should also understand and respect men in the same way that they wish to be respected. Criticizing the wave of feminism she calls 'manbashing', hooks calls for attention to be paid to 'the depth of male suffering' (2004: 4), and the negative impact of 'emotional stoicism' as imposed on men in patriarchal society (2004: 5). In making men 'emotional cripples' (2004: 27), patriarchal societies create such men as Malika's father, who admires tenacity but has no words to express it to a daughter, who loves but cannot demonstrate his love, and who perpetuates this cycle with all his children. Love is only possible if men and women are given the chance to fully love, to be loved and to understand one another.

Similarly, in *Les Hommes*, Devi explores the anguish of men under patriarchy while giving space to love, both towards herself and towards the men in her life. In finding herself, she creates a new community through the writers who inspire her.

Patriarchal Masculinities and Writing Community

Je suis offerte à la parole des hommes. Parce que je suis femme.

—Devi, *Les Hommes*

Les hommes disent "les femmes" et elles reprennent ces mots pour se désigner elles-mêmes; mais elles ne se posent pas authentiquement comme Sujet.

—de Beauvoir, *Le deuxième sexe*

Devi's incipit to her autobiographical text, *Les Hommes*, unveils a poetic but stark representation of femininity as subjugated by the dominant power of masculinity. The verb 'offerte' evokes a passivity despite the enunciation of a distinct subject 'je'. The syntax creates a jarring effect, a pause before the causal phrase signalling her as female and, therefore, secondary, much as Simone de Beauvoir argues women internalize masculine discourses of women as occupying an inferior position. The opening lines announce a terse text within which is situated the deconstruction of Devi's multifocal relationships with the 'fils, mari, père, amis, écrivains morts et vivants' (2011: 11), who have influenced her, and continue to do so. It is also a linear prefiguration of the male voices who speak to her in their varying capacities and judge her apparent failure to successfully accomplish the different roles she plays.

As with Mokeddem's *Mes hommes*, the title evokes masculinity and the focus on binary gender division. However, whilst Mokeddem's possessive 'mes' indicates her will to re-appropriate her men, the definite article and a short sentence place the men at a distance from the narrative 'je' in Devi's title. The passive pronoun 'me' shifts the attention to the men and the narrative voice becomes secondary, thereby announcing masculinity as overbearing and oppressive. Nevertheless, contrary to de Beauvoir's premise that women do not authentically position themselves as subject, I contend that Devi's writing enables her to redefine her subjectivity through a recuperation of the different roles she plays in the text. The ways in which writing affects female-male relationships become central to this section as they highlight men's interrogation of women's priorities. They also permit Devi to probe, dissect and take stock of her husband's and son's reactions through the lens of the 'carcan' of patriarchy (2011: 47), as explored in the first part of this section.

The text is a first-person autobiographical narrative written by A.D.N, Ananda Devi Nirsimooloo, under her pen name, Ananda Devi. Born in Mauritius, Devi completed her studies in the UK before moving to France with her husband and working in Geneva. She lives in Ferney-Voltaire, near the Franco-Swiss border. Written over a period of a few days which are traced to an upheaval in her life, the text blurs past and present to recount the writer's journey to find herself, culminating in a postscript written a few months later. Devi's narrative stems from her son's accusations that she has failed as a mother. Suffering from severe depression, he is prone to violence and is suicidal. In the midst of this family crisis, her husband, instead of being supportive, accuses her of failing both as a wife and as a mother. Oppressed by the diktats of patriarchal community, Devi in her marginal position interrogates patriarchy's nefarious impact on both men and women. Since she writes primarily from the perspective of her roles as a mother and as a wife, the first part of this section underlines the ways in which her position and disposition temper her views on masculinities and the men in her life. Writing becomes a centripetal impetus for Devi as she renegotiates her relationship with her son and her husband, and the role which love plays in her portrayal of them, as I discuss through Ahmed's *The Cultural Politics of Emotion*. The scission she experiences between her identity as a writer and her roles as wife and mother lead to a discussion of autofiction as a means of enabling her to renegotiate her self in the second part.

In her text, Devi weaves together intertextual references to a number of writers from the Anglophone, Francophone and Indian literary canons. Given the importance accorded to these multiple writers, I draw on Kristeva's notion of intertextuality as a critical way of interpreting the text. Thus, the final segment of this section evaluates the role played by such textual practices in placing the text in the context of writing beyond the self. Ultimately, the multiple voices with whom Devi creates a dialogue engenders a form of writing community which empowers Devi to ground herself in her writing. From this perspective, I explore the concept of the writing community as Nancy discusses it in *La Communauté désoeuvrée* to gauge the extent to which the writer, regardless of gender, belongs to a community of like-minded individuals, who enable her to create a new community on her own terms.

Suffering Men

Je ne peux pas parler. Seulement écrire.

—Devi, *Les Hommes*

Ecrire c'est aussi ne pas parler. C'est se taire.

—Duras, *Ecrire*

In *Les Hommes*, the narrator underlines the place of writing in her life. Since men constantly silence her through speech, writing becomes her only means of unveiling the matters that preoccupy her. Yet the negation of the modal verb 'peux' in the quote above highlights her powerlessness. Its elision in the second phrase emphasizes the adverb 'seulement', which is ironic as Devi is a prolific and well-known writer in the Francophone world. Devi's incipit sets her up as a victim to patriarchal values. Oppressed by the demands of men, she feels the need to 'changer de sexe et de corps' (2011: 11). Deeply marked by masculine expectations and rejecting male desire, the narrator wonders if she can become 'androgyne, asexuée, débarrassée de ses propres besoins et du désir des autres' (2011: 11). The term 'androgyne' implies being of both genders simultaneously. Conversely, the adjective 'asexuée', which follows, refers to the absence of gender. The narrator's disarticulation is evident here as she navigates the possibilities between multiplicity and lack, both bringing to bear the problematic nature of gendered expectations. Central to this text is the need to efface oneself, or as Duras puts it 'se taire', withholding language or stopping its flow. Writing is thus seen as the tool for communication even as it permits the writer to not physically speak. From 'femme', 'amante', 'mère' to 'proie inaccessible' or 'être de faiblesse et de fragilité', Devi is constantly held up to patriarchal standards which lead her to think of destroying her subjectivity and silencing herself. The absence of speech is related to a loss of humanity and devolution to the status of 'monstre' (2011: 11). However, as she enunciates, she can never be devoid of emotion, and especially, love, for the men who speak to her. This text is thus a voyage through her life and choices, as well as her sentiments as she grasps the reality of both her son's and husband's suffering under patriarchy.

Indeed, from the second page Devi quickly shifts the narration to one of the men who speaks to her, 'celui qui me juge' (2011: 12), that is one of her sons. Devi does not reveal his name to her readership, presumably to maintain a degree of privacy for the young man in his suffering. Employing the metaphor of reading and writing, Devi declares that 'le cadet est celui qui en ce moment ouvre le livre de sa mère et la force à se lire' (2011: 47). The image is apt since she is an avid reader and a writer. The son's harsh words, calling her a 'charmeuse' recalls the fact that she concocts stories and creates a world which is far from reality, as it is 'facile pour [elle] d'être triste' (2011: 12) and 'l'écriture est l'habit qu'[elle] porte pour justifier son existence' (2011: 15). Devi's son feels emotionally and physically disenfranchised on two levels: firstly, he is ill at ease in Ferney-Voltaire, since it is a small village with no immigrants aside from themselves. In keeping with the issues examined earlier in this chapter, as a dark-skinned man living in a predominantly homogeneous white society, the son is constantly made to question where he belongs.[51]

Devi is cognizant of the fact that that 'il est aussi entouré d'un carcan qui l'empêche de vivre et dont il n'arrive à se défaire' (2011: 47). This 'carcan' is the patriarchal values that his father has transmitted to him and of which he cannot bear the charge. Equally problematic in this case is the model of masculinity represented by the father, who is stoic. Incapable of expressing emotions save through anger,[52] the son's only outlet is violence as he destroys appliances in their house, and attempts suicide on several occasions, ultimately asking his mother to euthanize him. This focus on affectivity enables Devi to interrogate different types of masculinities in her text. The first type of masculinity, hegemonic masculinity, as outlined by Connell, is the notion that masculinity uses power hierarchies to assert its dominion over women (1995: 77). It is usually accompanied by the oppression of weaker and lesser men.

Hegemonic masculinity is at the root of the lack of comprehension but also the malaise experienced by Devi's husband. Since virility and stoicism are characteristics of the model of masculinity he emblematizes,[53] he is set up as a contrast to her own father who was from a line of men who were 'doux, secrets, artistes' (2011: 48), and who had a 'rare capacité d'amour et de générosité' (2011: 50). Yet Devi's mother also suffered because her father was antisocial and did not speak. Devi's son, an artist, is portrayed as the heir to this type of masculinity, which is at odds with his father's

---

[51] See also Kistnareddy (2015b).

[52] See Jakupcak et al. (2005).

[53] This is similar to the notion of masculinity that Bourdieu (1998) finds in Algerian society as discussed earlier.

model. Nevertheless, Devi's text does not vilify nor aggrandize either model of masculinity. Both present difficulties for the women who are in their lives. Similarly, neither the 'weak' masculinities represented by Devi's father and her son, nor the virile, stoic, hegemonic masculinity exemplified by her husband, is empowering for the men themselves. Rather, Devi's aim in this text is to rethink outdated notions of masculinities and the danger posed by patriarchy on men and their emotional well-being. Accordingly, the suffering of men is not perceived as vindication but as a sensitive realization that men are just as vulnerable, if not more vulnerable, due to their so-called superior positioning against women. Indeed, of her husband who cannot admit that he will cry when she dies, Devi says:

> Il cherchera toujours à se déguiser, comme si cela pouvait le protéger de je ne sais quelle vulnérabilité. En jouant aux hommes forts, il s'est rendu plus vulnérable. C'est quand il laisse entrevoir à son insu sa fragilité, c'est là que nous l'aimons le plus et sommes prêts à lui pardonner. (2011: 103)

The notion of 'jouer aux hommes forts' gestures towards performative virile masculinity which is counter-productive if the man is to be understood in his humanity.

While there is resentment present from the son, dissatisfaction and unhappiness from all three, hate does not occur as it is countered by recognition and love. In *The Cultural Politics of Emotion*, Ahmed argues that 'it is through emotions, or how we respond to objects and others, that surfaces or boundaries are made: the "I" and the "we" are shaped by, and even take the shape of contact with others' (2014b: 10). For Ahmed, affect is relational and an emotion such as hate is economic: 'it circulates between signifiers in relationships of difference and displacement' (2014b: 44). Since affects are relational, they are either moving towards or away from the object of emotion (2014b: 8). Thus, Devi's escape from the family home, from the 'carcan' of femininity imposed upon her by both her son and her husband, is not conducive to her feeling vindicated at her husband's sense of loss due to her discordant behaviour. A sense of victory is absent as she does not posit him as an oppressor but as an equal victim to the values with which patriarchy has burdened him. Devi recognizes that he, too, must 'dépasser le carcan du mâle pour arriver à sa propre vérité' (2011: 67). For those whose lives have been dictated by patriarchy, the only way forward is to find their own voice and path, as she has, and to refuse to surrender to negative affect.

In lieu of privileging a denunciation of patriarchy's oppression of women solely, Devi acknowledges and underscores the difficult positioning of men who uphold patriarchal values and cannot love freely. Vulnerability to women, to their own feelings, to love, is thus set up as a means of finding their truth, their humanity. This text is a way of understanding this process of becoming vulnerable, of learning how to love as a way out of the prison of patriarchy for men. Judith Butler argues that vulnerability can become a means of resisting against dominant factions (2016: 14). The theorist focuses on the vulnerability of 'women or minorities' (2016: 22) and foregrounds the 'power of those who are oppressed' and the 'vulnerability of paternalistic institutions themselves (2016: 23). For Butler, 'the very meaning of vulnerability changes when it becomes understood as part of the very practice of political resistance' (2016: 24). She argues that vulnerability is 'operating in a middle region [...] both affected and acting' and can emerge as a 'deliberate mobilization of bodily exposure' (2016: 26). In Devi's text, the men are not even acknowledging their vulnerability. It is only when they become more self-aware and mobilize this that they might resist it. However, there is an overwhelming feeling that it will take a long time for this realization to take place. Devi pre-empts their initial reaction to her book, as she surmises they will be offended:

> Enveloppés de leur ego d'hommes, ils se sentiront bafoués, fustigés, m'accuseront de révéler des choses qui doivent rester privées, et ce qu'ils me reprocheront par-dessus tout, c'est de mettre à nu leurs faiblesses. Ce qu'ils ne comprendront pas, c'est que ce ne sont pas leurs faiblesses que je mets à nu, mais les miennes. (2011: 68)

The 'faiblesses' here refer to both their vulnerabilities as humans but also her own incapacity to comprehend them from their perspective until now. It is only through a clear, unequivocal analysis of their motivations, of their words and her own actions in the past that she is able to draw her conclusions about men's suffering.

As I discussed in the previous section, in 'Women's Time', Kristeva argues that it is not just the fact that a woman gains power that is important, but how she chooses to wield it. For Kristeva, it is important that women should not replicate patriarchal values. As the writer of this text, Devi has the power to influence her reader, to make us like or dislike the men. Being the sole narrator, she decides whose voice she will include, who she will vilify and who she will exonerate. Although the text is entitled 'Les hommes qui me parlent' neither man is quoted in direct speech. She controls the positioning and logos of the men who have attempted to rein her in, and her own power is seen in this respect. In so doing, Devi silences the men who do speak to her, even as she reflects on their words. Their silence is exacerbated as there are writers who are given ample space to 'speak' in her writing through extensive quotations as I examine later in this section. Thus, to a certain extent, Devi does reclaim her right to speech, to her own space, by writing about the men who speak to her without giving them a voice. Nevertheless, this is carried out subtly and not as a means of completely undermining them. In fact, the love she has for both her son and her husband is tangible in the text.

While Devi highlights her husband's failures, she forgives him and expresses her own love for him: 'je ne t'en veux pas. Tu as été élevé ainsi, conditionné ainsi. [...] Toujours j'aimerai ce qu'il y a de toi d'entier. Toi aussi tu es prisonnier de ta nature d'homme' (2011: 93). The blame for his treatment of her is laid at the feet of patriarchal society and the values with which he was brought up. Nonetheless, rather than her own victimhood, it is the equivalent victimhood of men which is underscored here. As a woman, she has the capacity to see this fact, acknowledge it, comprehend it and conclude that men, too, must flee the prison of patriarchy or endure suffering. However, this shift in her conceptualization of masculinity has only been possible due to an interrogation of her own identity. The irony of Devi using the medium of writing to understand her son's accusation that she has lived in the bubble of her writing is not lost on the reader. Significantly, coming to terms with the men who speak to her is only possible as she reconciles the two identities which she has kept separate: herself as a woman and as a writer.

Autofiction: Negotiating Identities Through Writing

Personne n'a jamais écrit à deux voix.

—Duras, *Ecrire*

Throughout her autobiographical text, Devi underlines the duality at play within herself. Between the writer self and the woman who is questioning her roles as mother and wife, the narrative 'je' is constantly grappling with what she perceives as two identities which she wishes to reconcile. As

Marguerite Duras underlines in *Ecrire* a writer does not write in two voices, each time they write, it is a distinct voice which comes through. Writing is also problematized in this text as, while it is an outlet, it is also a way of creating an alternative world to eschew reality. In penning *Les Hommes*, Devi underlines that she is creating autofiction. The role autofiction plays in aiding Devi in grounding herself and negotiating her dual identities is significant as it permits her to use her own analytical skills to navigate between the two selves and thereby construct an in-between space which empowers her.

According to Serge Doubrovsky, in his famous cover to *Fils* (1977), the term 'autofiction' is based on a 'je', which is the author, but the work is fictional in its content. Conversely, in *Le Pacte autobiographique* (1975), Philippe Lejeune highlights the fact that if the narrator and the author are the same person and s/he is the main protagonist, then the autobiographical pact is signed. Doubrovsky's term in essence negates this pact as the author does not fulfil this pact in autofiction. Indeed, for Doubrovsky, in 'Autobiographie/vérité/analyse', 'l'autofiction c'est la fiction que j'ai décidée, en tant qu'écrivain, de me donner de moi-même, en y incorporant, au sens plein du terme, l'expérience de l'analyse, non point seulement dans la thématique mais dans la production du texte' (1980: 77). Later, in *Le Monstre* (2014), Doubrovsky states that the objective in both autobiography and autofiction is the same: 'ressaisir sa vie et la raconter mais pas de la même manière [...] de la manière fictionnelle'.[54] For Doubrovsky, thus autofiction is fictional life writing.[55]

However, Devi in a way posits her understanding of autofiction as different insofar as whatever is written is automatically fiction simply by being written: 'toute écriture n'est peut-être que cela (l'autofiction), déguisée de mille et une façons. Même en faisant la vaine tentative de la révélation on se transforme en fiction' (2011: 68). For Devi, writing about herself and her family automatically fictionalizes their experiences in the sense that writing is contrived and a process. This notion is significant in Devi's case as she explicitly says that she has split herself into two since the age of fifteen, when she experienced her first heartbreak. It is from this moment

---

[54] See also Grell's (2014) extended discussion of the different forms of autofiction.

[55] For Gasparini, 'autofiction' is a 'lieu d'incertitude et de réflexion' (2016: 7). It can mean different concepts to a range of theorists: for instance, for Genette in *Fiction et diction*, autofiction was pure fiction, in the sense that all details are inventions even though the writer's name is real.

that she sees herself as distinct from the writer who 'ne ressentait rien' and instead was looking and writing about her suffering as if she were a 'cobaye' (2011: 31). This initial split allows her to separate her feelings from the material she writes. It later permits her to completely remove herself from situations and to write about the darkest subjects.

In his 'Note de lecture' to *Les Hommes*, Sami Tchak states that 'C'est Ananda Devi qui parle d'Ananda Devi, cette fois-ci sans le recours aux masques dont elle a toujours su habilement user, en dansant, perverse, et surtout moqueuse du lecteur qui la cherche en vain' (Tchak 2011: no pag.). Devi admits that she hid behind her characters in an attempt to deflect from her own identity issues in the text. However, her finally speaking about herself allows her to navigate the difficulties she experiences. Splitting opens up the possibility of a writerly identity that allows her the freedom she was denied as a woman: 'Je me suis toujours conformée à un mode de vie [...] intérieurement je suis autre' (Devi 2011: 96). While this division was initially a coping mechanism, the son's illness leads to the need to come to terms with herself fully. For this to occur, Devi must face both the person she is and the writer in her, for she finally realizes: 'ce n'était pas moi. Je le sais aujourd'hui, elle n'a jamais été moi. Elle m'abandonnait dès qu'elle avait fini d'utiliser ma main pour écrire' (2011: 31). In an interview given at the time *Les Hommes* was published, Devi explains her scission thus: 'je me sentais un peu dans ce dédoublement entre la personne et l'écrivain. Je me disais j'aimerais bien rejoindre cette personne qui écrit' (Schuin 2011: no pag.).[56] This 'dédoublement' proves to be problematic as it does not enable her to claim a part of herself: 'je n'en pouvais plus d'être dédoublée, démantelée, remise en question' (2011: 24). It created an inner tension between the person who was writing and the one who enunciated 'je' on a daily basis. Devi herself remarks in her text: 'ce n'est plus de la littérature, c'est de la pathologie' (2011: 197).

Yet there is also a dimension of self-reflexivity as the writer self is constantly observing and analysing the woman who fulfils the roles of daughter, wife and mother and who inhabits the society. What is at stake could equally be the writer discussing herself as an 'other', as Paul Ricoeur discusses it in *Soi-même comme un autre* (1990). For Ricoeur, the self and the other are intimately linked (1990: 2). The theorist argues that 'je ne peux pas parler de façon significative de mes pensées si je ne peux en même

---

[56] This is akin to what psychiatrist R.D. Laing calls the 'divided self' in his work of the same name (1969).

temps les attribuer potentiellement à quelqu'un d'autre' (1990: 2). Nevertheless, Ricoeur highlights the fact that if it is something that is attributable to oneself, it is 'ressenti', whereas if it is attributable to someone else, it is 'observé' (1990: 53). Thus, reflexivity and alterity are simultaneously needed. Significantly, Devi underlines the writer self as the observer and the woman with multiple roles as the feeling self. The choice to write about herself is seen as the writer identity finally deciding that 'je suis matière à écriture enfin' (Devi 2011: 32). The act of writing about herself permits the writer to give voice to the other within, which for long has been silenced. In writing about herself, the writer creates a new space where the two selves merge and where the opportunity for the writer to feel and for the woman to analyse and dissect her own life.

In creating this space between her two selves, Devi creates a new mode of thinking identity and belonging for herself, through the imaginary.[57] Devi explores another way of conceptualizing identity through the space of fiction by negotiating multiple 'je' through the gaps they contain. As the 'je' come together on the page, they gain each other's attributes or abilities. This represents a means of unifying divided selves within a safe space without creating one single identity. This concept of plural possibilities is evoked with the image of shedding skins,[58] even as the author turns a new page in the metaphorical book of her life (2011: 208). This new ability is lived humorously as Devi uses the conditional tense to explore what she would do if she were devilish instead of the angel she currently is: 'je serais aussi inaccessible qu'avant, mais cette fois je jouerais avec les cœurs. Je me moquerais des états d'âme' (2011: 208).[59] Whoever she chooses to become, she concludes that language and ultimately writing will always triumph.

[57] I explore this further in Kistnareddy (2015a).

[58] Darrieussecq also echoes this idea of other skins in her address "Je est unE autre" (2007). While Darrieussecq describes herself wearing fictional identities as skins in her texts, here Devi sees her own multiplicity as skins she wears and sheds through writing as she reflects on her own life.

[59] In his discussion of the self and morality in *Sources of the Self: The Making of Modern Identity*, Taylor emphasizes the fact that the imperative to do good is a craving that marks humanity (Taylor: 2004: 44). When one fails to achieve this one chastises oneself as having a sense of 'being evil' (2004: 44). In this case, Devi is toying with the notion that the new space where her quest for identity has taken her could take away the need to police herself morally. Ironically, being able to lie could lead to positive outcomes in her novels. In this way, she complexifies the relationship between good and evil both within herself and in the world of writing.

Devi's use of the autofiction genre is emblematic of postcolonial migrant women writers' ability to use a genre which is associated with contemporary women's writing in France order to create new paradigms. According to Sarah Brouillette,[60] postcolonial literatures in the Anglo-American market present both a 'niche fragmentation' and 'market expansion' (2011: 56). With regard to authorship, Brouillette remarks on the close links between 'the author's name and attached personae' as being 'the key focal points for the marketing of literary texts' (2011: 65). Since the authors are irrelevant to the actual publishing process, Brouillette, following Barthes's *La mort de l'auteur*, signals authors' use of metacommentary to re-insert themselves into the writing: often by commenting on the act of writing itself for instance (2011: 69). With respect to postcolonial writers, Brouillette underlines that the publishing industry demands that they 'act as interpreters of locations they are connected to through personal biography' (2011: 70). While Brouillette's focus is on the status and demands placed on postcolonial writers of the English-speaking world, Devi's positioning is different insofar as she is published in the NRF Gallimard collection in France. While *Les Hommes* does allude to her native Mauritius through comments relating to the fractures at play between communities in the society, the text remains a self-reflexive one and a running commentary on the act of writing itself. It becomes an autofiction, or as she puts it herself, the story of her life, which thus recounted turns it into autofiction. Unlike other writers of the genre, such as Annie Ernaux or Marie Darrieussecq,[61] for instance, the focus is not on the playfulness or ability to fictionalize oneself (autofiction) but to emphasize the fact that any writing is fiction, even when the story itself is the truth.

For Odile Cazenave, discussing Devi's writing in *Les Hommes*: 'l'écriture n'est plus simplement perçue comme substitut de vie, mais aussi dans un dépassement de la qualité physique du geste d'écrire, [...] de regarder l'écran, d'avoir l'écran devenir son propre miroir, d'arriver à un point de non-retour, ne plus écrire' (2013: 47). For Devi, writing about herself, writing her self becomes a journey to finding her own position, her own space, which she calls an 'espace blanc' (Devi 2011: 118). This blank space is perceived as a *tabula rasa*, where she can now inscribe her story and her

---

[60] Brouillette herself constructs her argument on Huggan's notion of the "postcolonial exotic" (Huggan 2001).

[61] See Darrieussecq (1996) "L'Autofiction, un genre pas sérieux".

life anew, with the help of all the writers who have helped her on her journey to finding herself. Devi reclaims the power of writing as that which enables her to move beyond the constraints of finding a unified 'je' which is forever elusive. Thus, writing becomes a space of possibilities for Devi and it is this writing space which enables her to create a community, a new family consisting of writers in order to ground herself, even as her own family falls apart.

Writing Beyond the Self: Writing Community

> Le mot (le texte) est un croisement de mots (de textes) où on lit au moins un autre mot (texte).
>
> —Kristeva, *Semeiotikè*

During the act of writing about the men in her life, their struggles with masculinity and the values imposed upon them, Devi creates a web of intertextuality in *Les Hommes*. While her son and husband have silenced her in many ways, she writes about the other men who have allowed her to reconsider her own identity: male writers. In reading them, and in including them in her text, Devi creates a new community, which in turn generates a new space of belonging for her as a writer. In her often-cited essay, 'Word, Dialogue and Novel', Kristeva claims that the literary text is 'an intersection of textual surfaces rather than a point (a fixed meaning), as a dialogue among several writings' (1980: 65). In her initial publication *Semeiotikè*, she argues that both a word and a text always contain references to other words that have been used before. No original text exists since every word we use has been employed before. Similarly, when we write we always refer to what we have read or to other writers on the subject. Every text is inherently intertextual.[62] Kristeva's intertextuality amalgamates both the word and the text, allowing for a more holistic

---

[62] The concept of intertextuality has been proffered in different guises by a few theorists: notably Bakhtin's notion of heteroglossia in *The Dialogic Imagination* (1981) or Genette's 'trans-textualité' (1982). While Bakhtin's heteroglossia explored the ways in which languages and words from different languages are present in enunciations, Genette's 'trans-textualité' which he develops in *Palimpsestes* (1982) argues that poetics must go beyond the text to the other texts to which it refers. It is due to this multiplicity in the terms that such a concept takes that Gignoux calls it a 'flou terminologique' (2006: 1).

approach to interpreting the text, not only through the words utilized but also by grasping the socio-historic-cultural context.

For Maria Alfaro, discussing Kristeva's intertextuality, 'The concept of intertextuality requires, therefore, that we understand texts not as self-contained systems but as differential and historical, as traces and tracings of otherness, since they are shaped by the repetition and transformation of other textual structures' (1996: 268). According to Kristeva, 'À la place de la notion d'intersubjectivité s'installe celle d'intertextualité' (1969: 146). The space of writing becomes a dialogue between different languages, diverse cultures and a range of writers whose works are constantly transforming and adding to the text. However, as with every concept, intertextuality has its flaws: notably that interpretation is subjective, and it varies from reader to reader. The onus is on the reader to understand those references and not every reader will be able to comprehend the full extent to which intertextuality is at play. Kristeva's deployment of intertextuality lays emphasis on the power of the text itself since it refers to texts within and others without. It is in this that every text creates a world, a community of its own.

My interpretation of Kristeva's intertextuality as a form of community allows me to return to Nancy, and particularly to his concept of writing community or community of writing, in *La Communauté désoeuvrée*. For Nancy, the community of writing is made up of 'textes intercalés, alternés, partagés, comme tous les textes, offrant ce qui n'appartient à personne et qui revient à tous: la communauté de l'écriture, l'écriture de la communauté' (1999: 104). The philosopher, who has spent most of the first half of his text speaking of the dangerous nature of absolutism, of the importance of the lack of difference and of finitude as that which is shared by those who are in community, underlines the community of writing as constantly evolving. Writing is never complete as texts are always in the process of being written as authors dialogue with each other and build upon what others have penned. It is also from this perspective that Nancy's community weaves together existing concepts and builds upon Heidegger, Bataille and his conversations with Blanchot as I explore in the introduction to this book. While Kristeva's intertextuality underlines the word and the references as constituting the text and its own world, Nancy foregrounds the actual dialogue unravelling between the writers and the extent to which the writer overtly relies on these other writers in the process of writing the text.

According to Odile Cazenave, in *Les Hommes*,

> Devi renouvelle son rapport au texte et au lectorat et propose de nouveaux espaces d'écriture où s'inscrivent et s'entremêlent le soi, l'intime et le littéraire; où l'auteure renégocierait donc la proposition de (s')écrire entre soi et les autres lorsque soi devient Ananda Devi elle-même. (2013: 40)

Much as with Nancy's community of writing, Devi's *Les Hommes* ascribes unprecedented space to many writers with whom she dialogues or references or simply reads and quotes on her journey to finding her identity. Firstly, we encounter Bret Easton Ellis whom she criticizes for saying that only men can get physical pleasure from seeing. Then come a plethora of male writers: Albert Camus, Boris Vian, François Quevedo, Georges Bataille, Samuel T. Coleridge, William Faulkner, Albert Cohen, James Joyce, J.M. Coetzee, Louis-Ferdinand Céline, Joseph Conrad, Rabindranath Tagore, Henry James, Gustave Flaubert, Romain Gary, T. S Eliot, whom she quotes at different points. All play with heteronyms in their texts, thereby reinforcing the playful nature of language, and all belong to a range of cultures and nationalities. These writers are woven into the narration as Devi navigates her way to the answers to her questions about herself. Belonging to both Anglophone and Francophone canons, they exemplify her bilingualism. There are also texts in Urdu, *The Sufi Message*, which is quoted in English and song lyrics in Bengali, thereby underlining her Indian origins. The intertextual references to multiple canons bring to bear the importance of reading and dialoguing between cultures as well as across the ages, much in keeping with Kristeva's intertextuality and Nancy's notion of the community of writing. Since Devi's writing is postcolonial and her position at the confluence of cultures and languages is directly linked with her notion of identities, the fact that her intertextual references move beyond Kristeva's and Nancy's Western European philosophical references is significant here. The ease with which the postcolonial Franco-Mauritian writer interweaves these transcultural, transnational and translingual references is dizzying,[63] but also testifies to the complexity of her writing.[64]

Moreover, Devi gives voice to an anonymous male writer with whom she has shared correspondence for a decade at the time of writing. The fact

---

[63] Kellman (2001) underlines that being translingual is either writing in another language which is not one's mother tongue or writing between different languages. Devi in this case reads, quotes and listens to music in different languages.

[64] See Ramazani (2009).

that her husband and son are silenced whilst the male writer is quoted extensively attests to the significance of the male writer in her negotiation of her own identity as a writer. Discussing this male writer in an online interview on *Les Hommes*, Devi asserts: 'Ce qui était important pour moi c'est que le miroir qu'il est me renvoie l'écrivain' (Schuin 2011: no pag.). In her quest to recuperate the writer in herself, her exchanges with the male writer allow her to gain perspective. He is the voice of reason who pushes her to see her own role in her son's illness. In the introduction to this study, I discussed the ways in which Nancy's notion of community was augmented through his exchanges with Blanchot's *La Communauté inavouable* and the questions it raised, allowed for different modifications to community in *Être singulier pluriel*, *La Communauté affrontée* and more recently, in *La Communauté désavouée* (2014). Significantly, Devi also underscores the fact that her dialogue with this male writer 's'est entremêlé à [leurs] livres qui créaient des échanges étonnants les uns avec les autres, comme si les livres eux-mêmes s'étaient rencontrés dans une dimension autre et esquissaient leur propre danse' (2011: 98). This dance and exchange that Devi underlines is akin to the writing community which creates a space for creativity and a continuation of writing analogous to Nancy's own process.

With the exceptions of Toni Morrison, Virginia Woolf and Marguerite Duras, all the writers Devi refers to are male. Devi compares herself to Woolf in needing to find a room of her own and admires Morrison in how she articulates discrimination in her texts. She sees herself in Duras with the incipit of the latter's novel *L'Amant* and the description of ageing, which speaks to her as a fifty-three year old woman. However, her references and utmost admiration is directed towards the male writers. For instance, Flaubert's *Madame Bovary* is referenced on several occasions and Gary's *Pseudo* offers the perfect comparison to her own feeling of being in-between two identities. Direct intertextual references are employed here to generate a writerly space where she is able to speak to other writers, irrespective of gender and bring their perspectives to bear on her own situation. Thus, while Kristeva underlines the fact that every text is by nature intertextual, Devi takes this notion further by overtly creating this space for dialogues across genders, ages and cultures to underscore their empowering nature. In including the names of authors, along with so many quotations and intertextual references, she sublimates the need for the reader to attempt to find out who she is quoting. Nonetheless, removing this step does not diminish the reader's pleasure or desire to find the books and read them just as Devi did. In fact, it might encourage them to read these writers too.

According to Devi, the writing community is 'cette famille qui n'exige rien des uns des autres que de poursuivre ce travail d'écriture, chacun dans son lieu, chacun dans son temps' (2011: 157). It becomes a space of belonging that is not contrived and does not impose its rules save for the very act of writing. Feeling emotionally and physically discombobulated due to her family situation, Devi can only recuperate her identity through writing and through a different family which will not oppress nor repress her. As James states in his analysis of community in Nancy, community is literary, since 'literature is where the sharing of human voices and community occurs; it is where the new and the different can be affirmed' (James 2010: 201). Thus, I contend that it is through this unequivocal sharing within the writing community that gender loses its importance. As Devi herself asserts, 'quand je dis hommes, je parle d'humains, bien sûr, puisque les écrivains sont au-delà du genre' (2011: 154). The un-gendering of the writing community is significant here as it allows her to listen to the many voices speaking to her without feeling that they are judging her or categorizing her according to her femininity. It is also a means of writing back and writing over male voices which have dominated the Western and Eastern canon. Thus, while she has already silenced her husband and her son in not giving them a voice in the text, even as she engages with what they express, Devi's own voice soars above all other writers as she brings them together in her text. The pleasure of writing, the will to subsume all the texts to which she refers within her text, is evident here as Devi brings them all into her world and into her writing space.

The un-gendering of writing enables the ideas to come through more prominently as opposed to being regimented by the concerns of male or female writers being different. As Duras reminds us in her text on writing, *Ecrire*: '[les livres] sont fabriqués, ils sont organisés, réglementés [...] une fonction de révision que l'écrivain a très souvent envers lui-même' (1993: 42). In a recent interview with Emmanuel Bruno Jean-François, Devi describes what writing can do for a writer explicitly:

> [...] writing is a way of shifting the building-blocks of the real world to create as convincing an alternate world as possible. This is the power of literature, in the end, that it reflects the world in a distorted mirror, or in a different dimension, in which we both recognize ourselves and don't; which is precisely what it intends to do: show the reader what could be and make

them believe wholly in it. It is a world built on possibles, but by setting it in writing, we make these possibles become real. (Jean-François 2018: 143)

Devi's text is her own creative means of fashioning a world which empowers her to be herself and to recuperate her own agency, her creativity, her femininity, her authorial voice, and rise above any other voice. While she acknowledges the vulnerability of the men in her life under patriarchy, their liberation is seen as being their own path which they need to find. Her own freedom is gained through writing.

Speaking of her need to write *Les Hommes*, Devi states: 'j'ai un peu besoin d'être enracinée puisque j'ai été déracinée toute ma vie' (in Schuin 2011). Although the wish to lay down roots, mooring herself, is identified as a reason for writing this text, the fact that she never finds these roots but instead finds the pleasure of writing and the triumph of language is significant here. The writing community provides a space of belonging to Devi and the many others who are part of it. Nonetheless, writing also allows her the freedom not to belong, and instead, explore the space of writing as an empowering one which permits her to be who she wishes to be and change as she pleases.

Writing Love, Righting Men

In this chapter, I have argued that Miano, Mokeddem and Devi foreground different forms of community in their texts. In a range of ways, I have examined these texts through Nancy's theories; with Miano, the interruption of myth, which Nancy evokes in his notion of community, effaces difference, giving space to the community of humanity to come to the fore. Ahmed's notions of willfulness and dissent permit a reconfiguration of gender as well as an understanding of postcolonial Islamic masculinities as equal victims of patriarchal community in Mokeddem's text. Devi's autobiographical text brings to bear the effects of patriarchy on both men and women and creates a new community which is not reliant on gender. Her new space of belonging is constructed as a writing community which Nancy identifies as a very important part of new conceptualizations of community.

In their endeavour to explore exclusion and the role that race, religion and gender play in their life and texts, Miano, Mokeddem and Devi all speak of writing as the means through which their narrators or themselves are able to deal with their exclusion from communities. For all three women writers, finding a place to belong in their texts begins with the act of writing, which itself is born out of a need to understand and demonstrate love when it is least expected. Amok's avowal of his love for a transgender woman only comes in *Crépuscule 2* after a voyage of self-discovery back to Africa leads to him beginning his new life as a writer. The narrator of the short story 'Afropean Soul' in many ways demonstrates a new awareness and self-love, which occurs swiftly due to constraints of the form. Malika's love for her father, her brother and the men who have been part of her life, creates a redemptive space in her writing, where masculinities are recuperated and understood for the oppression they experience. Devi writes out of the love she feels for the men who speak to her, be they victims of patriarchal values who repressed her in turn or the writers who dialogue with her across ages and countries. All three texts demonstrate a growing sensitivity towards masculinity and an innate understanding that men suffer too, and perhaps, it is writing about their love for these men that will make a difference.

Writing becomes a form of being-in-common which allows for creativity to supersede social considerations and leads to a more empowering vision of oneself. The act of writing itself is beyond borders and beyond languages, leading to a new form of a home for writers, regardless of their gender, creed, religion or indeed, race.

References

Primary Texts

Devi, Ananda. 2011. *Les Hommes qui me parlent*. Paris: Gallimard.
Miano, Léonora. 2008a. *Afropean Soul et autres nouvelles*. Paris: Garnier Flammarion.
———. 2008b. *Tels des astres éteints*. Paris: Poche.
———. 2012. *Ecrits pour la parole*. Paris: Plon.
———. 2017. *Marianne et le garçon noir*. Paris: Pauvert.
———. 2020. *Afropéa: Utopie post-occidentale et post-raciste*. Paris: Grasset.
Mokeddem, Malika. 2005. *Mes hommes*. Paris: Poche.

Secondary Material

Ahmed, Sara. 2014a. *Willful Subjects*. Durham: Duke University Press.
———. 2014b. *The Cultural Politics of Emotion*. Duke University Press.

————. 2017. *Living a Feminist Life*. Durham: Duke University Press.

Alfaro, Maria Jesús. 1996. Intertextuality: Origins and Development of the Concept. *Atlantis* 18 (1–2): 268–285.

Appiah, Kwame Anthony. 2018. *The Lies that Bind, Rethinking Identity: Creed, Country Colour, Class, Culture*. London: Profile Books.

Bakhtin, Mikhail. 1981. *The Dialogic Imagination: Four Essays*. Trans. Michael Holquist and Cary Emerson. Austin: University of Texas Press.

Balibar, Etienne. 2011. Toward a Diasporic Citizen? From Internationalism to Cosmopolitics. In *The Creolization of Theory*, ed. Françoise Lionnet and Shu-Mei Shih, 207–225. Durham: Duke University Press.

Bancel, Nicolas, Florence Berneault, et al. 2010. *Ruptures postcoloniales: Les nouveaux visages de la société française*. Paris: La Découverte.

Barclay, Fiona. 2011. *Writing Postcolonial France: Haunting, Literature and the Maghreb*. Lanham: Lexington Books.

Barrett, James, and David Roedinger. 1997. Inbetween peoples: Race, Nationality and the 'New Immigrant' Working Class. *Journal of American Ethnic History* 16: 3–44.

Beaman, Jean. 2018. Are French People White?: Towards an Understanding of Whiteness in Republican France. *Identities* 26 (5): 1–17.

Beaman, Jean, and Amy Petts. 2020. Towards a Global Theory of Colorblindness: Comparing Colorblind Racial Ideology in France and the United States. *Sociology Compass* 14 (4): 1–11.

Bessone, Magali. 2013. *Sans distinction de Race*. Paris: Vrin.

Bessone, Magali, and Daniel Sabbagh. 2015. *Race, Racismes, Discriminations: Anthologie de textes fondamentaux*. Paris: Hermann.

BFMTV. 2020. La Justice française a peur de la verité sur l'affaire Adama. 2 June 2020. Accessed 2 June 2020. https://rmc.bfmtv.com/emission/la-justice-francaize-a-peur-de-la-verite-sur-l-affaire-adama-traore-assure-sa-soeur-qui-appelle-a-la-mobilization-1925471.html.

Bhabha, Homi. 1994. *Locating Culture*. London and New York: Routledge.

Biller, Henry, and Stephan Weiss. 1970. The Father-Daughter Relationship and the Personality Development of the Female. *The Journal of Genetic Psychology: Research and Theory on Human Development* 116 (1): 79–93.

Blain, Arsène K. 2017. L'afropéanisme dans *Tels des astres éteints* de Léonora Miano: Une scription rhématique de la transmigration des identités. *e-scripta Romanica* 4: 16–26.

Blanchot, Maurice. 1983. *La Communauté inavouable*. Paris: Editions de Minuit.

Boni-Claverie, Isabelle. 2017. *Trop noire pour être Française*. Paris: Tallandier.

Bourdieu, Pierre. 1998. *La domination masculine*. Paris: Seuil.

Brouillette, Sarah. 2011. *Postcolonial Writers in the Global Literary Marketplace*. Basingstoke: Palgrave Macmillan.

Butler, Judith. 2016. Rethinking Vulnerability and Resistance. In *Vulnerability and Resistance*, ed. Judith Butler, Zeynap Gambetti, and Leticia Sasay, 12–27. Durham: Duke University Press.

Cazenave, Odile. 2013. *Les Hommes qui me parlent* d'Ananda Devi: Un nouvel espace pour se dire? *Nouvelles Etudes Francophones* 28 (2): 39–52.

Cheref, Abdelkader. 2010. Assia Djebar and Malika Mokeddem: Neo-colonial Agents or Post- Colonial Subjects? In *Women in the Middle East and North Africa: Agents of Change*, ed. Fatima Sadiqi and Moha Naji, 48–61. London and New York: Routledge.

Cohen, Robin. 1997. *Global Diasporas: An Introduction*. Seattle: University of Washington Press.

Coly, Ayo. 2014. Postcolonial Masculinity as Bricolage. In *Francophone Afropean Literatures*, ed. Nicki Hitchcott and Dominic Thomas, 155–170. Liverpool: Liverpool University Press.

Connell, Raewyn. 1995. *Masculinities*. Cambridge: Polity Press.

Cooppan, Vilashini. 2018. The Novel as Genre. In *The Cambridge Companion to the Novel*, ed. Eric Bulson. Cambridge: Cambridge University Press.

Darrieussecq, Marie. 1996. L'Autofiction: Un genre pas sérieux. *Poétiques* 107: 372–373.

———. 2007. Je est UnE autre ou pour qui elle se prend. In *Ecrire l'histoire d'une vie*, ed. Anne Olivier, 105–121. Rome: Edizioni Spartaco.

De Beauvoir, Simone. 2011. *Le Deuxième sexe, I*. Paris: Folio.

De Maillard, Jacques, Daniela Hunold, et al. 2017. Different Styles of Policing: Discretionary Power in Street Controls by the Public Police in France and Germany. *Policing and Society* 28 (2): 175–188.

De Montaigne, Tania. 2018. *L'Assignation: Les Noirs n'existent pas*. Paris: Grasset.

De Sondy, Amanullah. 2013. *The Crisis of Islamic Masculinities*. London: Bloomsbury.

Djebar, Assia. 2007. *Nulle part dans la maison de mon père*. Paris: Babel.

Dorlin, Elsa. 2006. *La matrice de la race: Généalogie sexuelle et coloniale de la Nation française*. Paris: La Découverte.

Doubrovsky, Serge. 1977. *Fils: Roman*. Paris: Galilée.

———. 1980. Autobiographie/Verité/Psychanalyse. *L'Esprit Créateur* 20 (3): 87–97.

———. 2014. *Le Monstre*. Paris: Grasset.

Doumbia, Eva, and Léonora Miano. 2012. *Écrits pour la parole* et *Blues pour Élise* Pour la première fois sur scène! Accessed 12 January 2019. http://africultures.com/ecrits-pour-la-parole-et-blues-pour-elize-11060/.

Downing, Lisa. 2019. *Selfish Women*. London: Routledge.

Duras, Marguerite. 1982. *La Maladie de la mort*. Paris: Editions de Minuit.

———. 1993. *Ecrire*. Paris: Gallimard.

Etoké, Natalie. 2010. *Melancholia Africana: L'indispensable dépassement de la condition noire*. Paris: Le Cygne.

———. 2017. 'COULEUR' et 'COMMUNAUTÉ' de Léonora Miano: Du noir dans le bleu-blanc-rouge'. *Nouvelles Etudes Francophones* 32 (1): 27–42.

Fanon, Frantz. 1952. *Peau noire, masques blancs*. Paris: Seuil.

France 24. 2010. Identité nationale: Qui sont les 'vrais' Français? Accessed 10 January 2019. https://www.france24.com/fr/20100122-identit-nationale-sont-vrais-fran-ais.

Freud, Sigmund. 1905. *Three Essays on the Theory of Sexuality*. London: Verso.

Gagiano, Annie. 2018. Frantz Fanon: Toward a Revolutionary Humanism. *Journal of Postcolonial Writing* 54 (1): 130–131.

Gasparini, Philippe. 2016. *Poétique du 'je': Du roman autobiographique à l'autofiction*. Lyon: Presses Universitaires de Lyon.

Genette, Gérard. 1982. *Palimpsestes: La littérature au second degré*. Paris: Seuil.

Gignoux, Anne-Claire. 2006. De l'intertextualité à la récriture. *Cahiers de Narratologie*, 13. Accessed 4 December 2018. http://journals.openedition.org/narratologie/329.

Gilroy, Paul. 2005. *Postcolonial Melancholia*. New York: Columbia University Press.

Green, Mary Jean. 2008. Reworking Autobiography: Malika Mokeddem's Double Life. *The French Review* 81 (3): 530–541.

Grell, Isabelle. 2014. *L'autofiction*. Paris: Armand Colin.

Gualtieri, Elena. 1998. The Essay as Form: Virginia Woolf and the literary tradition. *Textual Practice* 12 (1): 49–67.

Guendouzi, Amar. 2017. Assia Djebar and the Legacy of French Colonialism in Algeria: Mimicry and Subalternity in *Nowhere in My Father's House*. *The Journal of North African Studies* 22 (2): 205–219.

Guillaumin, Colette. 1972. *L'idéologie raciste: Genèse et langage actuel*. La Haye: Mouton.

Hajjat, Abdellali. 2012. *'Les frontières de l' 'identité nationale': L'injonction à l'assimilation en France métropolitaine et coloniale*. Paris: La Découverte.

Halberstam, Jack. 2002. An Introduction to Female Masculinity. In *The Masculinities Reader*, ed. Rachel Adams and David Savran, 355–374. Oxford: Blackwell.

Hall, Stuart. 2017. *The Fateful Triangle: Race, Ethnicity, Nation*. Cambridge, MA: Harvard University Press.

Hannoum, Abdelmajid. 2019. Memory at the Surface: Colonial Forgetting in Postcolonial France. *Interventions* 21 (3): 367–391.

Helm, Yolande. 2000. *Malika Mokeddem envers et contre tout*. Paris: l'Harmattan.

Hiddleston, Jane. 2011. *Introduction. Postcolonial Poetics: Genre and Form*, Eds. Patrick Crowley and Jane Hiddleston. Liverpool: Liverpool University Press.

Hitchcott, Nicki, and Dominic Thomas. 2014. *Francophone Afropean Literatures*. Liverpool: Liverpool University Press.

hooks, bell. 2004. *The Will to Change: Men, Masculinity and Love*. New York: Washington Square Press.

Huggan, Graham. 2001. *The Postcolonial Exotic*. London and New York: Routledge.

Jakupcak, Matthew, Matthew Tull, et al. 2005. Masculinity, Shame, and Fear of Emotions as Predictors of Men's Expressions of Anger and Hostility. *Psychology of Men & Masculinity* 6 (4): 275–284.

James, Ian. 2010. Naming the Nothing: Nancy and Blanchot on Community. *Culture, Theory and Critique* 51 (2): 171–187.

Jean-François, Emmanuel Bruno. 2018. An Interview with Ananda Devi. Beyond Façade and Grotesque Spluttering: The Worlds and Work of Literature. *Contemporary French and Francophone Studies* 22 (2): 142–151.

Kellman, Steven. 2001. *The Translingual Imagination*. Lincoln: University of Nebraska Press.

Kinouani, Guilaine. 2021. *Living While Black: The Essential Guide to Overcoming Trauma*. London: Ebury Press.

Kistnareddy, Ashwiny O. 2015a. *Locating Hybridity: Creole, Identities and Body Politics in the Novels of Ananda Devi*. Berg: Peter Lang.

———. 2015b. Victimes ou bourreaux?: Ecrire les hommes dans *Le Sari vert*, *Blue Bay Palace* et *Les Hommes qui me parlent*. *Interculturel Francophonie* 28: 135–156.

———. Forthcoming 2022. 'Against the Flow': Exile and Willful Subjects in Malika Mokeddem's *My Men* and Kim Thúy's *Vi'*. *Journal of Contemporary Women's Writing*.

Kleppinger, Kathryn. 2018. Relighting Stars and Bazaars of Voices: Exchange and Dialogue in Léonora Miano's *Tels des astres éteints* and Alain Mabanckou's *Black Bazar*. In *Post-Migratory Cultures in Postcolonial France*, ed. Kathryn Kleppinger and Laura Reeck, 110–123. Liverpool: Liverpool University Press.

Knox, Katelyn E. 2016. *Race on Display in 20th and 21st Century France*. Liverpool: Liverpool University Press.

Kristeva, Julia. 1969. *Semiotiké: recherche pour une semanalyse*. Paris: Seuil.

———. 1980. Word, Dialogue, and Novel. In *Desire in Language: A Semiotic Approach to Literature and Art*, ed. Leon S. Roudiez, Thomas Gora, et al., 64–91. New York: Columbia University Press.

———. 2007. *Cet incroyable besoin de croire*. Paris: Bayard.

Kristeva, Julia, Alice Jardine, and Harry Blake. 1981. Women's Time. *Signs* 7 (1): 13–35.

Laing, R.D. 1969. *The Divided Self: An Existential Study in Sanity*. London: Tavistock.

Larcher, Silyane, François Germain, et al. 2018. *Black French Women and the Struggle for Equality 1848–2016*. Lincoln: University of Nebraska Press.

Le Sueur, James Dean. 2007. James Dean Interviews Malika Mokeddem about Her Writings and Life in Exile in France. Accessed 20 January 2019. http://vimeo.com/22664871.

Lefilleul, Alice. 2014. Afropéanisme, Identités frontalières et Afropolitanisme: Penser les nouvelles circulations. *Africultures* 99–100 (3): 84–91.

Lejeune, Philippe. 1975. *Le pacte autobiographique*. Paris: Seuil.

Leonarhdt, Adrienne. 2013. Between Two Jailers: Women's Experience During Colonialism, War, and Independence in Algeria. *Anthós* 5 (1): 7–16.

Mack, Mehammed Amadeus. 2017. Sexagon: Muslims, France and the Sexualization of National Culture. In *Modern Language Initiative*. New York: Fordham University Press.

McIlvanney, Siobhan. 2016. Education and Exile in the Writings of Maïssa Bey and Malika Mokeddem. In *Exiles, Travellers and Vagabonds: Rethinking Mobility in Francophone Women's Writing*, ed. Kate Averis and Isabel Hollis-Touré, 131–152. Cardiff: University of Wales Press.

McNee, Lisa. 2005. Fantasmes du réel: le discours autobiographique chez les écrivaines francophones. *Dalhousie French Studies* 70: 129–144.

Meddahi-Bereksi, Lamia. 2015. *Nulle part dans la maison de mon père* ou la recherche des points d'ancrage. Accessed 18 November 2018. http://revue.ummto.dz/index.php/khitab/article/viewFile/1229/1030.

Mielusel, Ramona, and Simona Emilia Pruteanu. 2020. *Citizenship and Belonging in France and North America*. Cham: Palgrave Macmillan.

Morrison, Tony. 2017. *The Origins of Others*. Cambridge: Harvard University Press.

Moussa, Nedjib Sid. 2016. Algerian Feminism and the Long Struggle for Women's Equality. Accessed 10 January 2020. https://theconversation.com/algerian-feminism-and-the-long-struggle-for-womens-equality-65130.

Nancy, Jean-Luc. 1983, rep 1999. *La Communauté désoeuvrée*. Paris: Christian Bourgois.

———. 2001. *La Communauté affrontée*. Paris: Galilée.

———. 1996, rep. 2004. *Être singulier pluriel*. Paris: Galilée.

———. 2014. *La Communauté désavouée*. Paris: Galilée.

———. 2015. *Identités: Fragments, franchises*. Paris: Galilée.

Nguetse, Paul Kana. 2011. Ecriture romanesque, musique et (re)construction identitaire dans *Tels des astres éteints de Léonora Miano*. Le Blog de Mondes Francophones. Accessed 30 April 2019. https://mondesfrancophones.com/espaces/creolizations/ecriture-romanesque-musique-et-reconstruction-identitaire-dans-tels-des-astres-eteints-de-leonora-miano/.

———. 2016. Hybridité artistique et hybridité littéraire dans *Tels des astres éteints de Léonora Miano*. *Quêtes Littéraires* 16: 147–156.

Niang, Mame-Fatou. 2019. *Identités françaises: Banlieues, féminités et universalisme*. Leiden and Boston: Brill Rodopi.

Niang, Mame-Fatou, and Katie Nielsen. 2016. *Les Mariannes noires*. USA: Round Room Image.

Nilsson, Per-Erik. 2018. *Unveiling the French Republic: National Identity, Secularism, and Islam in Contemporary France*. Leiden and Boston: Brill.

Noiriel, Gérard. 2007a. *Immigration, antisémitisme et racisme en France (XIXe-XXe siècle)*. Paris: Fayard.

———. 2007b. *A quoi sert l'identité nationale?* Paris: Agone.

Pitts, Johnny. 2019. *Afropean: Notes from Black Europe*. London: Penguin Random House.

Probyn, Elspeth. 2010. Writing Shame. In *The Affect Theory Reader*, ed. Melissa Gregg and Gregory Seigworth, 71–92. Durham: Duke University Press.

Ramazani, Jahan. 2009. *Transnational Poetics*. Chicago: University of Chicago Press.

Révolution Permanente. 2020. Justice pour Adama: Le discours poignant d'Assa Traoré. Accessed 2 June 2020. https://www.revolutionpermanente.fr/Justice-pour-Adama-Le-discours-poignant-d-Assa-Traore.

Ricoeur, Paul. 1990. *Soi-même comme un autre*. Paris: Seuil.

Rohrberger, Mary. 2004. Origins, Development, Substance, and Design of the Short Story: How I Got Hooked on the Short Story and Where It Led Me. In *The Art of Brevity: Excursions in Short Fiction Theory and Analysis*, ed. Per Winther et al., 1–13. Los Angeles: University of Southern California Press.

Said, Edward. 1978. *Orientalism*. London: Penguin.

Schuin, Annick. 2011. Babylone: Le Grand Entretien avec Ananda Devi. Accessed 10 December 2013. http://www.rts.ch/la-1ere/programmes/babylone/3609388-babylone-le-grand-entretien-du-11-12-2011.html.

Szymanski, Dawn M., Lauren B. Moffitt, and Erika R. Carr. 2011. Sexual Objectification of Women: Advances to Theory and Research 1ψ7. *The Counseling Psychologist* 39: 6–38.

Taylor, Charles. 2004. *Sources of the Self: The Making of Modern Identity*. Cambridge: Cambridge University Press.

Tchak, Sami. 2011. À propos du dernier récit d'Ananda Devi, *Les Hommes qui me parlent*. *Cultures Sud*. 29 November 2011.

Traoré, Assa, and Geoffroy de Lagasnerie. 2019. *Le Combat Adama*. Paris: Stock.

Treacher Kabesh, Amal. 2013. *Postcolonial Masculinities: Emotions, Histories and Ethics*. London: Ashgate.

Vermeren, Pauline. 2014. Identité nouvelle: une approche philosophique de la notion Afropéa. *Africultures* 99–100 (3): 66–75.

Verpeaux, Michel.2014. L'unité et la diversité dans la République. Accessed 10 January 2019. https://www.cairn.info/revue-les-nouveaux-cahiers-du-conseil-constitutionnel-2014-1-page-7.htm?contenu=resume.

Vince, Natalya. 2010. Transgressing Boundaries: Gender, Race, Religion, and 'Françaises Musulmanes' during the Algerian War of Independence. *French Historical Studies* 33 (3): 445–474.

Weil, Patrick. 2005. *La République et sa diversité: Immigration, integration, discrimination.* Paris: Seuil.

Yekani, Elahe H. 2011. *The Privilege of Crisis: Narratives of Masculinities in Colonial and Postcolonial Literature, Photography and Film.* Chicago: Chicago University Press.

CHAPTER 4

Writing Vulnerability: Instructing, Conversing, Silencing

In *Le* Masculin *dans les œuvres d'écrivaines françaises,* Françoise Rétif claims that women who write are not only interrogating masculine creation but also the masculine world itself. The critic asserts that for women writers, 'la littérature est tout autant un moyen qu'un but en soi', which is conducive to 'des visions différentes du monde' (2016: 8). The women writers whose texts I explore are in a unique position since they all originate from non-Western countries and, through education and migration, have been able to achieve a different social status in France or in Canada. This shift fosters the need to consider what their changed circumstances permit. By extension, this new social position is equally apt for observing the transformations occurring in men as they negotiate changes within the family unit, as well as in extra-familial relationships. Andrea Grewe, discussing masculinity in Yasmina Reza's plays, asserts that 'le masculin n'est pas uniquement une histoire d'hommes', as it is closely linked to alterations in society for women as well (2016: 12). Grewe underlines the propensity of women who write about men to modify 'la masculinité à travers des qualités dites féminines ou des compétences sociales (notamment l'empathie) opposées à l'affirmation masculine de soi' (2016: 12). I argue that the women writers whose works I examine reshape masculinities as feeling, as vulnerable in their texts. This chapter investigates modes of communication, such as instructing, letter writing, telephone conversations and the absence of speech itself, to gauge the ways in which

A. O. Kistnareddy, *Migrant Masculinities in Women's Writing,* Global Masculinities, https://doi.org/10.1007/978-3-030-82576-8_4

167

immigrant women writers reconsider masculinities and foreground equality in vulnerability between masculinities and femininities.

From this viewpoint, it is important to understand what it means to speak to and with another person without hierarchical imperatives. As I discussed in the introduction to this book, one particular theorist who has examined the power of speech is Gayatri Spivak, for whom beyond speaking for, or representing the subaltern, it is important to 'speak with' the individual whose voice has not been heard (1988: 91). Indeed, as I analyzed earlier, often cast outside the dominant paradigms, subalterns are individuals whose opinions are overlooked. Spivak's 'speaking with' engenders a mutual exchange between the intellectual who recognizes the fact that the subaltern's role has been elided, as has the subaltern herself. In this dialogic relationship, in the context of which Spivak sets her examination of who is allowed to speak, it is often women who are the subalterns. For instance, this is evident in the practice of *sati* in India, where women were expected to jump on their dead husband's pyre to follow him in the afterlife since it was deemed that their own lives ended with their husband's. The women committing *sati* were perceived as victims to Indian men's torturous ways and underlining their predicament was often viewed as 'white men saving brown women from brown men' according to Spivak (1988: 93). The theorist decries the fact that from their saviour position, white colonialists in India never queried whether the women performing *sati* were doing so against their will, assuming that no one would wish to die in such a fashion (1988: 93). Deliberating Spivak's denunciation of 'the imperial project' in this essay in an online interview in *Guernica Magazine*, Ahmed states that Spivak's 'diagnosis [...] remains precise' in the contemporary world (in Mehra 2017). For Ahmed, both white men and white women share culpability in this project and adopt a hierarchically superior position to people of colour. Thus, equality and, especially agency, become crucial to the recuperation of those deemed to be in an inferior position. Spivak does not advocate the practice of *sati*, but she promulgates the notion that these women or 'subalterns' have a say in decisions and judgments made on their behalf, that is they should have agency, for 'one never encounters the testimony of the women's voice-consciousness' (1988: 93). In this chapter I develop the notion of 'speaking with' in several ways as I contend this notion takes on the guise of equal say, of sharing and mutual understanding through teaching, letters and telephone conversations. Throughout this chapter, 'speaking with' will serve as a thread linking the texts together as women writers negotiate writing (about) men.

Drawing on Hélène Cixous's *Coming to Writing*, I consider the notion of instructing as a means of creating a different form of filiation between fathers and daughters with Djebar's *Nulle part* and Diome's *Ventre*. With reference to Chen's *Lettres chinoises*, I then explore the epistolary form as a way of inhabiting both male and female characters and thereby allowing for a range of perceptions to emerge. I introduce *Lenteur* as a point of comparison as an immigrant mother writes to her son and solidifies the temporal lag between writing and response. In my subsequent discussion of telephone conversations in Diome's narrative, I delve into the ways in which the conversation, through a reading of bell hooks's and Stuart Hall's *Uncut Funk* (2018), permits a reframing of the gender narrative as balanced and equal. Finally, I examine the silences which pervade Miano's *Crépuscule 2*, Djebar's *Ventre* and Thúy's *Ru*, while referring to theorists of silence and Blanchot's disaster writing. I demonstrate the need to understand men and women who have undergone traumatic experiences, which lead to their equal vulnerabilities. In so doing, I explore the various ways in which women writers speak with (and through) men and attempt to break silences.

WRITING FATHERS

Je me sens "la fille de mon père".
Une forme d'exclusion – ou une grâce?

—Djebar, *Nulle part*

Il (Ndétare) m'a tout donné: la lettre, le chiffre, la clé du monde.

—Diome, *Ventre*

Djebar's and Diome's texts, written five years apart by two writers at different ends of their writing career, Diome at the beginning and Djebar at the end, attest to the prominence and ineluctable importance of fathers and father figures in transmitting knowledge to their daughters. While Djebar questions whether being her father's daughter excludes her from the guarded world of Algerian women and the rest of the society she inhabits, Diome unequivocally evokes the role played by Ndétare as an enabler in her journey to France, to writing and to discovery of the world at large. Both writers' texts interrogate the role played by the father (figure) in shaping their protagonists' writing as well as their perception of life.

Djebar (born Fatima-Zohra Imalhayène) wrote *Nulle part* as an autobiographical text which recounts Fatima's life from her early years in Césarée, in Algeria, to parts of her experience of boarding schools in neighbouring towns and elements of her years abroad.[1] The narrative focuses on her close relationship with her father, Tahar, a teacher, who allows his daughter the freedom to attend both the French school, where he works, and the Quran school where the local children learn verses in Arabic to pray. As with Djebar's Fatima, Diome's Salie also leaves Niodior through schooling and eventually migrates to France. Both protagonists are aided in their education and eventual emancipation by their father (figure) and it is this nurturing masculinity that I explore in this section of the chapter.

Intimating Father-Daughter Love

> L'image idéale du père que malgré moi – sans doute parce qu'il est irréversiblement absent – je compose.
>
> —Djebar, *Nulle part*

According to Katarzyna Kotowska, Djebar's text is 'un hommage à la figure du père' (2017: 211). After having written a number of texts on the female world of Algeria, of which *L'Amour, la fantasia* (1985) is perhaps one of the most celebrated, and dabbled in her first theoretical work, *Ces Voix*, Djebar writes texts which are political such as *La disparition de la langue française* (2003).[2] *Nulle part*, her last text, marks a departure from the rest of her oeuvre insofar as it is an intimate narrative of childhood and evolution, during the colonial period and in the years immediately following independence in Algeria. The narrative is distinctive due to a deliberate focus on the father from the very title, along with a desire to

---

[1] The inclusion of the word 'roman' on the cover adds to an element of doubt as to the text's genre, as I mentioned in my discussion of *Nulle part* in conjunction with Mokeddem's text in the previous chapter. Brisley calls the text an 'auto-analyse' (2016).

[2] Harrison deems it to be 'a departure into more adventurous forms of writing' (2009: 69).

unveil emotions and aspects of her life which have heretofore not been revealed.[3] Written in the aftermath of the father's death, the text becomes a way of piecing together his life as seen through her eyes as a child.

In the introduction to this analysis, I examined Cixous's notion of writing as avoiding the reality of death: 'I write and you are not dead. The other is safe if I write' (1991: 4).[4] Cixous's premise is that writing occurs when there is nothing left to lose, in this case, when there is death and annihilation. The absence of a loved one, the mourning involved, is alleviated by the act of writing since the other lives through what one writes. The narrative space breathes life into even those who are being mourned, as with Tahar in this case. Djebar's text, from the very outset, ascribes the context to a death: the title itself refers to the Prophet Mohammed's daughter, also named Fatima, who outlives her father, thereby having lost the protection of her father's house. Examining the text, Amar Guendouzi expands on this further:

> At the literal level, in Algerian popular customs, the father's house is often the girls' only share after the decease of the father, the other parts of the inheritance (money, proprieties, etc.) going exclusively to the boys. Underlying this social practice which, it should be noted, runs against Islamic law, is the popular belief that the girl's only need after the loss of her father is a dwelling which would shelter her. Thus, the father's house is seen well before his eventual death as the only part of inheritance of his daughters, their ultimate property. (2017: 208)

Fatima is thus bereft and dispossessed. I contend that dispossession in *Nulle part* is lived not on the material level, but on the spiritual and emotional level as her father is a loving man who has always cherished her and treated her as well as he would a son.[5]

The work of memory represented by Djebar's text offers an account of colonial Algeria, the tensions between the teacher for indigenous boys, Fatima's father, and the authority in school, as well as the gradual evolution of the education system and society as Algeria enters through a transitional phase of independence. Djebar's reconstruction of her childhood

---

[3] See Matu (2015) and El Guabli (2019).

[4] See also Juncker's (1988) reflections on Cixous's writing.

[5] In line with my earlier discussion of Algerian society with Mokeddem, sons are valued more, but here Tahar does not treat her as secondary and gives her all the love and support she needs to thrive both academically and generally.

and her relationship with her father is set amidst a background of political upheavals, as suggested by the episode of her winning a prize and being awarded a book on Maréchal Pétain. This gift is a deliberate gesture on the part of the administration, since her father has not aligned himself with the Pétainistes. Amar Guendouzi goes as far as calling Tahar 'a mere mimic, subaltern subject without a positive legacy' (2017: 208), since he submits to such subtle antagonism without resistance. The child experiencing this event is blissfully unaware of the pressures on her father and is overjoyed at winning a prize. Conversely, the adult narrator relives the experience and sees the ironic smile on her father's face as he glances at the book cover. Djebar's commitment to her father and his memory is evident in this text as all events and conversations ultimately return to him. Thus, although the first episode depicts the mother's veil and her walk in her neighbourhood, it is a sustained reflection on her relationship with her father and ends emphatically on her special relationship with her father, 'la fille de mon père', as quoted at the beginning of this section. This relationship is illuminating in a range of ways as the narrator slips from her child-like eyes and memories to the adult welcoming those flurries of memories back into her life. This process of remembering occurs on various levels: through a meditation on the place of the French language in her life as cementing the relationship with her father, the conversations with him, the notions of loyalty and obedience, and finally, writing as mourning.

As I mentioned earlier, Tahar demonstrates his unequivocal love for his daughter by allowing her to be educated in the French system. The local Quran schools are mostly attended by boys whereas girls are not often educated as I examined with Mokeddem's text in Chap. 3. This very fact places him in a different position from the rest of the Algerian men. As Anne Marie Miraglia indicates, 'ce père [...] permet à ses filles d'échapper à l'ignorance et à la claustration, bref au destin de la grande majorité des filles algériennes de leur époque' (2016: 45). Tahar is a proto-feminist, in the sense that he does not perceive any difference between his daughter and boys with regard to education. He accords Fatima all the opportunities that Algerian fathers do not offer their daughters since their society dictates that men are the earners and who should be the ones educated to provide for the family, as I examine with Mokeddem in the previous chapter. In Fatima's case, Tahar never entertains the idea that his daughter should be denied the freedom of learning. Fatima is aware that 'comparée à celles de [s]a communauté, [elle] devai[t] faire figure de privilégiée', yet she perceives as much of a difference with the 'Européennes de [s]on village' (2007: 145). While she does have the luxury of education, she does not have all the liberties or the lifestyle of the European girls. As I demonstrated in the previous chapter, Tahar does have limits to what he will allow Fatima to do and he is at times quite conservative in his outlook. Nevertheless, this is not deemed to be problematic at the beginning of the narration. In fact, the acquisition of the French language establishes another level of intimacy between father and daughter.

According to Claudia Gronemann, in writing about her father, Djebar 'profite de la possibilité d'éclairer le modèle de masculinité que son géniteur présente et son impact sur la vie intime et professionnelle de sa fille' (2010: 243). This impact is related to the opportunities Tahar gives Fatima in allowing her to learn French. The linguistic bond between father and daughter is evidenced when Fatima's mother loses her son and Tahar converses with Fatima, in French, about the need to never speak of the son's demise again. In this moment, the narrator transcribes this conversation as an immediate dialogue with her father, unusually using the familiar pronoun 'tu' for effect: 'voici, père que tu me prends à témoin' (Djebar 2007: 83). The adult narrator qualifies this sudden bond which is created through language: 'je dois m'étonner que tu me parles soudain comme à une adulte' (2007: 83). The adult narrator can comprehend the extent to which Tahar is unable to share his grief with anyone else since he uses French as a means of restraint, for his affective language remains Arabic: 'à moi seule, tu peux parler, pour l'instant en français, tu te livres—oh à demi... Me parler en arabe, cet arabe qui te fait bégayer quand l'émotion t'étreint aurait été inefficace' (2007: 84). In silencing the deceased son in that instant and taking his daughter as an accomplice in alleviating his wife's agony, the father creates a deep connection with his daughter, which is solidified through the years.

The deployment of French enables the father to emotionally detach himself from the situation. The narrator's revelation that 'c'est pourtant la langue, celle des "Autres", qui reste son armure' is set in opposition to Tahar's own death (2007: 97), and Fatima's mother's utilization of the Arabic dialect, '*bla didates*', to express her grief (2007: 107). The rawness of her emotions emerges in her mother tongue, while Tahar cannot mourn his son openly. The daughter becomes an intermediary between them, and she eventually emblematizes her father in her mother's eyes when he dies: 'je devenais un peu l'ombre de son mari non enterré' (2007: 107), since she was the 'fille aînée, celle justement, dit-on, qui ressemble le plus au père' (2007: 104). According to Kenneth Doka and Terry Martin, who examine masculine responses to loss, 'Since men are perceived as less likely to show their feelings, share their reactions to the loss, and accept help from others, they are seen as having more difficulty in adjusting to loss' (1998: 143). In a society, which as I discussed through de Sondy in the previous chapter, looks at men as protectors, masculine grieving is disallowed in Tahar's case, leading to the man using French as a crutch to communicate without emoting. By contrast, his wife can give full rein to her anguish. But as Doka and Martin assert, 'the expression or behavioural manifestation of the grief experience can be quite varied', and this grief can also include avoiding reminders of the lost person, as is the case with Tahar here (1998: 145). Here the mode of grieving is closely linked to the affective experiences of language. In this way, Djebar illustrates the difference between her bonds with each parent through the use of language as a mode of grieving and mourning loss. In writing about her father's silenced sorrow, she also brings to bear the vulnerable masculinities at play in the society from which she hails. Writing here recreates the pain and the emotions experienced by the man who was not allowed to be openly vulnerable.

According to Françoise Lionnet, 'l'écrivain francophone postcolonial est lui aussi pris dans les rets du langage et du savoir occidental: plus il essaie de s'en débarrasser et plus il semble s'y enfermer, puisque ce savoir est partie prenante de son identité' (1998: 14). Critics have had conflicting interpretations of Djebar's relationship with the French language over the years.[6] In *Ces Voix*, as I articulated in the introduction to this book, Djebar does reveal the fact that she does not feel that French enables her to write her full identity. It is through 'tangage des langages' or the 'entre-langues' (1999: 23), that is re-inscribing Arabic, Berber and the language of the body into her writing that she can recreate her linguistic reality. For Mireille Calle-Gruber, 'tout témoignage est pour Assia Djebar d'abord scène de langues. Et jamais une seule: toujours deux, et plus qui se disent, qui s'entre-disent' (2001: 252). In this text, the project of writing about the father is undertaken in French, to mirror the father's own deployment of French to speak with his daughter. While Arabic and dialects are present

---

[6] While some, have called it 'a poisoned gift', an 'ambivalent gift' (Connell 2013: 292), or simply 'ambigu' (Kotowska 2017: 213), others, such as Harrison, have underlined the fact that: 'she considers [...] her access not just to literacy and literature in general, but to the French language in particular—to have been of enormous benefit to her' (2009: 70).

in other parts of the text, for instance when she recounts her relationship with Tarik, with her mother and in the epigraphs to the different segments of the text (2007: 113, 271), French remains the language predominantly utilized to write about Tahar and her love for him.

Nonetheless, tension remains present in the narrator as she regrets not knowing classical Arabic: 'je suis hélas médiocre en arabe classique! Je n'ai jamais pu apprendre ma langue maternelle comme je l'aurais désiré' (2007: 315). The term 'langue maternelle' is ironic here as she does not speak Arabic. According to Rosi Braidotti in *Nomadic Subjects*, the very notion of a 'mother tongue' is erroneous as 'all tongues carry the name of the father and are stamped by its register' (1994: 11). Discussing Braidotti's work in *Beyond the Mother Tongue*, Yildiz states that for Braidotti, '"mother" resides within the law of the father, but nonetheless it still carries within it the notions of "affection and proximity"' (2012: 11). In this case, rather than the 'mother tongue', Djebar means 'mother's tongue' and refers explicitly to her regret at not having the same proximity with her mother through Arabic as she did with her father, through French. There is a rupture between mother and daughter due to intimacy and close bonding with the father in French, to the extent that sometimes French and Arabic 's'entrechoqu[e]nt dans [s]a tête' (2007: 324). Her mother's dialect cannot be her 'langue-peau' (2007: 340). While it is her 'langue de lait' (2007: 340), it is her father who has nourished her and cultivated her love for French literature and learning in general. At this point, comparisons may be drawn with Cixous's notion of writing as mothering and nourishing. While Cixous explicitly uses the imagery for the creation of a feminine genealogy and filiation, I argue that Djebar's text posits the father as the giver and nurturer. In creating such a strong connection between himself and Fatima, Tahar creates a new genealogy, which Fatima deals with in different ways, the first of which is to 'comprendre, de [s]e comprendre' (2007: 397). Nonetheless, this understanding cannot crystallize without piecing together several episodes in her life which she has never revealed, beginning with the feeling of betrayal towards her father when reading itself takes her away from him.

Jane Hiddleston asserts that 'the multiple reading experiences that punctuate *Nulle part dans la maison de mon père* indicate that this autobiographical memoir is also the narrative of the formation of a reader' (2017: 250). Tahar, indeed, introduces Fatima to the pleasures of reading classic texts, but it is with Mag, her 'sœur en littérature' (2007: 152), that she discovers the pleasures of *Le Grand Meaulnes* by Alain-Fournier and coming-of-age narratives (2007: 147), André Gide, Charles Péguy, Arthur Rimbaud and so on. Mag becomes 'un double d['elle]-même' (2007: 149), thus rupturing the extraordinary bond with her father. Her claim that 'cela n'altérait en rien [s]a loyauté envers [s]on père' precisely stresses the fact that she believes she has betrayed him (2007: 155). Her friendship with Mag, and her discoveries, are perceived as small disloyalties against her religion and her father's recommendations, which she justifies. The text is transformed into a veiled confession as well as an account of her relationship with her father, which I demonstrate later in this chapter.

Fatima is 'sa fille aussi excessive que lui, aussi contestataire que lui' (2007: 66), and yet, while Tahar has paved her way and is also a rebel in many ways, he still expects his daughter to obey his edicts. That she is gradually escaping from his protective embrace is viewed as a process of evolution but also an affective period. In the aftermath of her first kiss, Fatima's initial reaction is 'je n'en parlerai pas à ma mère, ni surtout à mon père' (2007: 197). Fatima's experimentations with love and romantic intimacy read as a betrayal of her father as she envisions him both as a liberator and as a custodian of patriarchal values. Her allegiance is tested every time she queries whether she is betraying her father, as the loving man he is, or what he represents: conservative values and culture. Nonetheless, Fatima's gratitude towards his having authorized her living away from home for her studies and indulging in a life not accorded to other Algerian girls at the time is evident: 'il me sait "loyale" mais à quoi donc, au fait: à lui, le père-gardien, le père-censeur, le père intransigeant? Non, le père qui m'a résolument accordé ma liberté' (2007: 198). Nevertheless, the need to attend basketball matches in secrecy (2007: 286), and to embark upon a love affair without paternal approval, for instance, testify to her emerging sense of identity and subjectivity, independent of her father. It is also felt as a form of unfaithfulness since she has closely associated herself with him since her childhood.

Yet Fatima is not blind to her father's faults. As I demonstrated in the previous chapter in my comparison of this text with Mokeddem's *Mes hommes*, as a child riding a bike, Fatima' is shocked by her father's reaction to her bare legs, demonstrating his extant conservative values. This discrepant behaviour has led to Guendouzi seeing it as emblematic of Tahar's 'divided loyalties' between French culture and Algerian values (2017: 215). Similarly, on discovering Fatima's love letter from Tarik, his extreme anger is palpable as Fatima depicts 'le visage convulsé de [s]on père' (2007: 279). Here the father-daughter bond is tense and such episodes nuance the narrator's own feelings towards her father. The fact that he cannot hold her hand once she reaches a certain age (2007: 100), instead having to walk behind her, highlights the limits of Tahar's ability to contravene their society's rules about a father's relationship with his children, especially daughters. The sadness expressed by the daughter at this fissure in their close relationship is profound in the text. Significantly, it is not Tahar who is blamed for this but Algerian society, insofar as it establishes such boundaries.

Ultimately Tahar's death triggers her need for atonement: 'Voici que l'auteur se met à nu... Seulement parce que le père est mort? Le père aimé et sublimé?' (2007: 384). The images of nakedness and revelation are crucial here as the entire narrative is a form of confession of guilt as I examine further later. However, the narrator understands that this culpability is of her own making and that her 'écriture en fuite' can be simultaneously a form of modesty and a form of vanity (2007: 451). Thus, her conversations with, and reminiscences of, her father in the text bridge the gap which has been gradually created as she grows up and distances herself from him: 'C'est étrange que je me mette à parler de toi au passé! Est-ce parce que tu es vraiment mort?' (2007: 89). If, as Djebar herself says, fiction is a 'moyen de penser' (1999: 233–234), in re-writing her father's life through her recollections, Fatima has been able to make sense of both her father's role in shaping who she is as well as her perspective on life. As she claims, 'de mon nom je suis Fatima, "la fille de mon père"' (2007: 245). Here, writing recreates the father in the blank space of the page, the only space where she can speak to her father in a 'tu' which remains in the present tense, even as the father has died. Much as Cixous writes so that the other can live, in writing *Nulle part*, the daughter restores the rightful place of the father in her life. Unlike Spivak, who recommends 'speaking with', that is conversing with the other to understand them better and to be able to hear their side of the story, Djebar's Fatima is 'nowhere in her father's house'. It is only echoes of her own voice and memories that she hears. The father's voice is never heard as the 'tu' remains silent and never responds to the 'je'. Nonetheless, it is through writing her childhood and her relationship with him that she can restore his magnanimity, his love and his vulnerabilities.

Conversely, where the father figure is created within the space of writing, as with Diome's narrative, the mode of 'speaking' which is deployed is revelatory of a deeper will to change society from within.

Extraordinary Filiations

Je lui dois Descartes, je lui dois Montesquieu, je lui dois Victor Hugo, je lui dois Molière, je lui dois Balzac, je lui dois Marx, je lui dois Dostoïevski, je lui dois Hemingway, je luis dois Léopold Sédar Senghor, je lui dois Aimé Césaire, je lui dois Simone de Beauvoir, Marguerite Yourcenar, Mariama Bâ et les autres.

—Diome, *Ventre*

The enumeration of French writers, those who have been translated into French, those who write from former French colonies and, finally women writers, is vital here as they represent a treasure trove of literature which has only been rendered accessible to Salie through Ndétare's French classes and her relationship with her teacher. Diome's narrator's introduction of Ndétare to her readership is edifying in many ways. On the page preceding his first formal appearance in the narrative, anticipation is created through the deployment of words such as 'étranger' in 'au fond d'eux, il n'était que l'étranger' (2003: 63). This preliminary introduction is reinforced by the insistence that Salie remembers him: 'bien sûr que je me souviens de lui' (2003: 63). The use of palilogy with 'je lui dois' underscores the debt of gratitude that Salie has towards her teacher, without whom her life as she knows it, her studies and doctorate, and especially this narrative, would not have been conceivable. Salie dedicates a great number of pages of the narration to Ndétare, including the story of his life in Niodior, and his relationships with a range of people in the village. In writing about Ndétare, Diome's protagonist creates a new filiation for herself through French and through the shared experience of exile which they both undergo in different ways.

Beginning her physical description of Ndétare to readers, Salie underlines his distinctive attributes: 'Ndétare se distingue des autres habitants de l'île par sa silhouette, ses manières, son air citadin, sa mise européenne, son français académique et sa foi absolue en Karl Marx' (2003: 65). A 'syndicaliste', Ndétare is a political exile on the small island, which he can never leave (2003: 135). In Djebar's text, Fatima's father offers her the opportunity to learn French but does not teach her himself. Conversely, Ndétare is Salie's first teacher and her only father figure, to the extent that her grandmother treats Ndétare like a son (2003: 76), thereby fashioning a unique form of filiation in the narrative. This is of particular significance due to Salie's status as an illegitimate child, whom her mother begot with a man from another village, and whose stepfather deems her to be 'l'incarnation du péché, la fille du diable' (2003: 75). Given her muddied heritage, Salie is ostracized by her village. Salie and Ndétare's shared marginality is underscored in the latter's words: 'comme moi tu resteras toujours une étrangère dans ce village' (2003: 78), as Salie becomes the family that Ndétare does not have, and he, her literary father.

As with Djebar's *Nulle part*, in this text too, the father figure redefines the notion of mother tongue since he teaches the daughter figure everything she knows:

> Je lui dois mon premier poème d'amour écrit en cachette, je lui dois la première chanson française que j'ai murmurée, parce que je lui dois mon premier phonème, mon premier monème, ma première phrase française lue, entendue et comprise. Je lui dois ma première lettre française écrite de travers sur mon morceau d'ardoise cassée. Je lui dois l'école. Je lui dois l'instruction. Bref, je luis dois mon *Aventure ambiguë*. (2003: 66)

Situating her list of debts in a litany devolving from the aesthetics of poetry to the precarity of the 'ardoise cassée' on which she etched her first letter, Salie attributes the very origins of language for her to Ndétare. Rather than perceiving the French language and the father figure giving it as a mark of imposition, as Braidotti sees it in *Nomadic Subjects*, here it is a means of creating ties between the teacher and his student, between a stand-in father and his stand-in daughter. In this series of firsts Salie delineates, the poetry of the palilogy creates an ode to Ndétare as the father-instructor, purveyor of words and power. The reference to Cheikh Amidou Kane's (1961) famous text, which won the Grand Prix Littéraire d'Afrique noire in 1962, is also pertinent here as Samba Diallo, the protagonist, through education, also gains access to France, and to a completely different lifestyle, leading him to feel torn between cultures. Thus, Salie inscribes herself in a long line of men who have been able to achieve prestige but, in so doing, have been estranged from their own culture.

Unlike Djebar, Salie does not seem have an ambivalent relationship with the French language. For the narrator, listening to the students learning French, 'leurs chansons mélodieuses […] n'étaient pas celle de [s]a langue, mais d'une autre qu'[elle] trouvai[t] tout aussi douce à entendre' (2003: 66). Accordingly, Ndétare was 'le génie' who could teach her this language. Salie's playfulness in asking God for forgiveness for having learnt French, instead of the language of the Quran also highlights the fact that it is due to her learning French that she can speak of 'Dieu' and read sacred texts: 'Pardon, bon Dieu, pardonnez-moi, mais c'était pour la bonne cause, sinon je n'aurais jamais pu lire votre nom dans tous les livres saints. Merci!' (2003: 66). Ndétare's influence is perspicuous as he accepts her in his classroom, while persuading her grandmother to register her officially (2003: 68). In a village where 'l'arbre généalogique' is 'une carte d'identité' (2003: 79), the knowledge he transmits to her empowers her to dream beyond the confines of the village, and later, of the country itself. Though he may not be her biological father, he is the father figure whose hand accompanies and steadies her on her path to knowledge and to socio-economic betterment. Salie's thoughts on the place Ndétare occupies in her life belie the emotional and affective experience which learning and his presence represent for her:

> Il arrive qu'un individu devienne le centre de votre vie, sans que vous ne soyez lié à lui ni par le sang ni par l'amour, mais simplement parce qu'il vous tient la main, vous aide à marcher sur le fil de l'espoir, sur la ligne tremblante de l'existence. (2003: 80)

Importantly, Madické's decision to learn French from Ndétare leads to his understanding the idiomatic expressions his sister uses,[7] and this gradually evolves into a bond, thereby completing the makeshift family which Ndétare has created through teaching French to the siblings.

Salie's debt towards Ndétare engenders a text where Ndétare's voice is heard throughout the narrative, be it through the use of metanarrative,[8] when Salie recounts Ndétare's life story, or when she foregrounds his ideals and his voice. Ndétare's love story with Sankèle epitomizes the way in which outsiders are treated in their society, thus reinforcing Salie's own precarious position as an illegitimate child. The exclusionary practices in the villages are such that Sankèle's only solution to being forcefully betrothed to another man when she is in love with Ndétare is to have an illegitimate child with the latter, so that the other man would reject her (2003: 130). The child's brutal death at the hands of Sankèle's father leads

---

[7] Madické attends Quran school. According to Bello, 'Islamic education was introduced [...] with the introduction of Islam itself' in Sub-Saharan African countries (2018: 28). In the aftermath of decolonization, the community could decide which schools to send their sons to, while girls often remained uneducated. Salie was very lucky to have Ndétare on her side, enabling her to have a French education that led to her current life.

[8] See Diouf (2010).

Ndétare to aid her in fleeing from the village on her own by disguising herself and leaving by boat.[9] Ndétare never marries nor does he father other children. In telling his story, Salie foregrounds both masculine and feminine vulnerability in the face of societal edicts. Ndétare sacrifices himself for his lover's happiness, giving her the opportunity to leave when he himself is effectively imprisoned in Niodior. While Boukary Sawadogo only underlines the 'wounds of exile' in Salie herself in this narrative (2016: 160), these 'wounds' are equally present in Ndétare who is rejected from his home and marginalized in the village where he is exiled. In these shared 'wounds', Salie and Ndétare's bonds of kinship are underscored.

Diome's narrator also creates a different space for 'speaking with' in this narrative. Through Salie, Ndétare's theories about emigration find not only a conduit but also an echo. Ndétare's enjoinder to the many boys in the village who dream of becoming rich in France, that 'la France ce n'est pas le paradis' (2003: 114) might fall on deaf ears since they persist in thinking that they will not fail, unlike Moussa, as I discussed in Chap. 2. Yet Salie's own words at the end take over from Ndétare. From the oral remonstrances to writing the message in the space of the text, Salie allows Ndétare's warnings to be heard not only by the Niodior boys but also by anyone who reads the text. Nonetheless, Salie herself cannot return to the village due to her status as an outsider. Writing about the concept of expatriation Delphine Marteau asserts that 'il serait illusoire de penser que les hommes et les femmes vivent cette expérience de la même façon' (2013: 16). For Salie leaving is also a question of survival, as explored in the second section of this chapter. The act of leaving one's home is deeply dislocating even though the individual might have chosen this displacement, in Salie's case. Her illegitimacy already displaced her to the margins of her own village. Since she shares the experience of being an outsider with Ndétare, she understands the pain of not belonging.

The power to write about this exilic experience is felt deeply in her writing: 'je n'ai qu'un stylo qui tente de frayer un chemin qu'il lui est impossible d'emprunter' (2003: 211). To her realization that she is split between two continents and two modes of living, Diome's protagonist perceives writing as the only means of coalescing the two sides which are rent: 'l'écriture est la cire chaude qui je coule entre les sillons creusés par les

---

[9] Goldblatt sees this as one of the many ways in which 'The Atlantic receives the human evidence of unacceptable desire' in this text (2019: 90). See also Eubank's analysis of Diome as an 'Atlantic woman' (2015).

bâtisseurs de cloisons des deux bords' (2003: 254). As Sawadogo argues, 'the act of writing, and creative work in a more general sense, serves as the cement of a hybrid identity' (2016: 165).[10] Diome's narrator discerns writing as the only means of piecing together the realities of life both in Niodior and in France. In inscribing her story within the text, and weaving in the stories of Ndétare, and other protagonists who serve as examples to the reader, Diome's main narrator creates a panoramic view of (im)migration issues. In employing French and in permitting Ndétare's words to reach people beyond the confines of Niodior, Salie allows the exile's voice to be heard where political powers cannot silence him. In this perhaps lies the most important tribute that Salie pays to Ndétare, who has given her 'la lettre, la clé' to speak for herself and with others around her on thorny subjects (2003: 66).

Thus, both Djebar and Diome foreground a father (figure) without whom the narrator would not be the writer they have become. The act of defying one's culture to enable a young girl to obtain the freedom that she would otherwise be denied is commendable in both men. Nonetheless, there are limits to what both men can do. Indeed, Tahar is still influenced by the Islamic patriarchal values with which he was brought up, and Ndétare is not Salie's biological father. Yet it is valuable to highlight the ways in which these men have played a role in changing Fatima's and Salie's lives. At this juncture, I return to Cixous and her discussion of the walls within which she finds herself imprisoned in *Coming to Writing*. She identifies these walls as emanating from patriarchy, from the society which dictates what is allowed and disallowed for women.[11] Nevertheless Cixous was permitted schooling and a pied-noir education. Her restraints were fashioned by the men who prescribed what she as a girl was authorized to do, but they did not impede her from learning how to read or write. Conversely, Fatima and Salie were born and educated in societies where

[10] For a critique of the notion of hybrid identities in the postcolonial diasporic context see Kistnareddy (2015). Most of the protagonists who should be able to take advantage of what Bhabha calls a 'third space' or hybrid identity in *The Location of Culture* (1994) find it impossible to reconcile the two reified identities at stake. It is only the writer who is able to do so, within the space of l'*écriture*, a notion which is echoed here in Diome's text and earlier in Miano's. See also Brown (2017) for a discussion of hybrid identities in this text.

[11] In *Living a Feminist Life* (2017) Ahmed also uses the image of a brick wall to discuss the obstructions that feminists find on their path. In this context, Ahmed speaks of the daily obstacles that people who wish to speak out and be different face at work or in the home (2017: 135–137).

female literacy itself was not a given and where boys, too, only had access to limited and segregated education, depending on their family's socio-economic and cultural position. The role played by Tahar and Ndétare is of utmost importance here. They not only had the sensitivity to give more than equal rights to Fatima and Salie, but also empower them to take a path which inspires them to go over the walls erected by patriarchal society and actually destroy them. Thus, Djebar and Diome recast men as enablers for their daughter (figure) and create a new paradigm for both shared vulnerabilities and potent possibilities for change from within traditional patriarchal societies.

OF LETTERS AND TELEPHONE CONVERSATIONS

In the other texts I explore in this study, 'speaking with' acquires many guises and serves diverse purposes. In Chen's epistolary novel, *Lettres chinoises*, the exchanges of letters between Yuan and Sassa and between Sassa and Da Li, enable an understanding of the thought processes of the protagonists as a dialogue is established. This exchange allows us to gauge whether the epistolary form, conversing through writing, as dual and interlinked processes, empowers the immigrant woman writer in rethinking masculinities through a different lens. In *Lenteur*, the immigrant mother's extended missive to her son highlights the importance of speaking with sons about the realities of life in a society which perceives them as other. In Diome's *Ventre*, the only medium of communication between Salie and her brother, Madické, is the telephone. Here, conversing takes on a different significance as the male and female voices are depicted as mutually dependent: a connection to the past for Salie and a means of attaining the future he hopes for, in Madické's case. Telephone conversations unveil Madické's voice as the siblings' relationship unfolds in the text. This section explores the range of ways in which immigrant women writers use their new positioning to 'speak with' men on an equal level, giving space for their voices to create a space for equality in the text.

Epistolary Form as Affect

Mon enfant, ma vie,
Depuis longtemps déjà je souhaite t'écrire.

—Chen, *Lenteur*

Chen's autobiographical narrative, *Lenteur*, written in the form of a letter to her son, is revelatory insofar as it enables us to delve into the inner workings of the author's mind as she speaks to her son about her position as an immigrant mother with a son who is born and educated in a different country and culture. The focus on the love and intricate relationship between mother and son is emphasized here as Chen regrets not being able to create comic books for her son and can only write an essay in the form of an extended letter. This medium expresses her feelings towards him, and especially towards her writing and her choices as an immigrant writer. As with *Lettres chinoises*, the epistolary form empowers the reader to probe the mind of the narrative 'je'. I contend that it enables women to speak with men, in a dialogue which unveils a deep vulnerability on the part of both the women and men at the centre of the narrative. Letter writing also gives rise to a questioning of the positioning of the woman writing *as* a man in *Lettres chinoises* and the absence of a male voice in response to Chen's own interrogations in *Lenteur*. The author utilizes the epistolary form as a means of not only 'speaking with' Yuan, as Sassa converses with Yuan in her letters, but also speaking *as* Yuan when she creates his letters, and especially about his inner turmoil and vulnerabilities from his perspective. This is particularly compelling since Rétif argues that 'représenter les personnages masculins, cela consiste pour elles (women writers) dans un premier temps à transgresser les frontières pour s'interroger sur un genre en quelque sorte inconnu' (2016: 8). Whether writing as a man is transgressive for Chen is cogent here since she has to inhabit a Chinese man's mind and heart as he elucidates his singular experiences of migration.

I want to take a moment here to discuss the epistolary form itself as a mode of communication. According to Katherine Ann Jensen, the figure of the 'Epistolary Woman' was a 'male creation' (1995: 2), which ascertained that women writing letters would be marginalized and the epistolary would be perceived as a lesser form of writing (1995: 10). Often the themes that were adopted were those of betrayal and abandonment. For Elizabeth Campbell, 'in open epistolary fiction, writing, the attempt to be heard, is more important toward an ending, than imposing closure' (1995: 333). She claims that 'if epistolary writing [...] is a revolt against the dominant culture, it is not surprising that most epistolary literature from Ovid's *Heroides* to present-day novels has been written in a woman's voice and by women writers' (1995: 334). Concomitantly, Campbell argues that 'women's writing and the epistolary style are generally the responses of those who have been oppressed and silenced. This writing is emotional, angry, radical, and markedly different in style and form from that of the dominant culture' (1995: 335). I contend that whilst Chen has selected this form, the content itself is not subversive and instead reveals a deep concern for (im)migrants, and especially men who cannot relinquish their attachments. Though Sassa and Yuan are separated, and in that respect, the content is emotional, from the outset in *Lettres chinoises*, Yuan's words are not marked by anger or resentment, but by his love for Sassa and '[s]a souffrance de [la] quitter' as her smile 'est imprimé dans [s]a mémoire et engendrera des douleurs qui [l]'accompagneront désormais sur le nouveau chemin de [s]a vie' (1993: 9). In focusing on Yuan's feelings, Chen foregrounds the vulnerability and the insecurity which both Rétif and Grewe have identified in women writing (about) men. Moreover, although Yuan does betray Sassa, as the letters reveal, it is actually Sassa who ultimately abandons Yuan, contrary to the 'Epistolary Woman's' fate as outlined by Jensen.

Examining the epistolary form from another perspective Patricia Spacks asserts that 'by choosing the epistolary form, novelists implicitly state their concern for individuals, the nuances of their personal voice, awareness of themselves and other people, as well as their place in the world' (2006: 104–105). The epistolary form provides us with a level of intimacy and private introspection which might be seen as lacking in shorter contemporary forms of communication such as Email, texts (SMS) or messaging services (WhatsApp, Facebook messenger). The poise of writing, the thought behind every word, is of paramount importance as Yuan and Sassa pen their letters. Yuan's reflections on his home and his host country are profound even as the epistolary is also a form involving a delay in communication since events continue to unfold as the letters travel to reach their destination. As Irene Oore suggests in her analysis of this text, 'l'intervalle spatio-temporel est d'autant plus important que les lettres sont expédiées par la poste et mettent au moins une semaine (sinon plus) pour parvenir à leur destinataire' (2004b: 3). As with any first-person writing, the distinct choices imbricated in the letter writing process are significant here as the narrative 'je' may also construct and elide what is included in the text. The letter writer is also free to demonstrate their ability to harness the aesthetic powers of poetry and other forms of writing. In response to Sassa calling him her 'soleil' in the previous letter, a sustained metaphor featuring the moon, dawn, dusk and burning suns is employed to convince her to join him 'plus tôt' (1993: 15).

Yet Yuan's letters are counterbalanced by Da Li's letters to Sassa subtly that Yuan and herself are growing close and that Yuan attempts to have sexual intercourse with her: 'il m'a pris les mains et m'a conduite vers le lit' (1993: 112). For Oore, 'de par sa nature monologuale, la lettre est un instrument parfaitement adapté à la révélation ainsi qu'à la dissimulation' (2004b: 5). Here the three-way exchange of letters unveils silences and secrets. While Yuan waxes poetic about his feelings for Sassa, he omits his own implied reprehensible behaviour towards Da Li, who is depicted as 'traditionnelle' (1993: 112), since she asks if he loves her before agreeing to sexual intercourse. Although at first the equal exchanges between Sassa and Yuan read as letters between lovers who miss each other, the inclusion of Da Li's correspondences with Sassa leads to the interrogation of Yuan's behaviour. The balance then shifts towards the women and their friendship.[12] I see the subtlety with which Da Li reveals the truth to Sassa, without divulging the fact that it is her fiancé whom she is falling in love with, as a means of explaining the reason behind Sassa's sudden distance in her letters. This would also partly elucidate the matter of Sassa's own silence about her illness and her refusal to let Yuan return to her side as her health slowly degrades towards the end of the narrative. She then demands that Da Li should not reveal the extent of her ill-health: 'Ne dis rien à Yuan à propos de ma santé: jure-le!' (1993: 66) and 'Quand tu rencontres Yuan, ne parle pas de ma santé. Je ne veux pas le bouleverser' (1993: 127). She does not want Da Li to inform Yuan of her critical health issues but she still maintains her close and intimate relationship with her friend, to whom the details are freely given.

Through Sassa, Chen blames her male protagonist's sudden change on the act of migrating itself. Mobility is seen as generating a loss of bearing, but also a loss of self, as I discussed with Yuan in the second chapter. This loss is also feared by Sassa herself who does not wish to migrate. As Eileen Sivert has argued, 'Just as she is torn between ties to cultural tradition and family on the one hand and a sense of rootlessness on the other, Sassa seems continually caught between a desire for, and a fear of, losing her identity, losing herself' (2001: 221). The epistolary exchange permits an understanding of the inner workings of Yuan's mind, and Da Li's too. The

---

[12] This narrative was first published as a four-way exchange, with extra letters written to Yuan's father. As Oore explains the intensity is heightened in the second version where only one letter to the father remains (2004b: 6). The finalized version sees the exclusion of the father completely, thereby allowing the love triangle to be at the centre of the narrative. See also Oore (2004a).

text is replete with irony as Da Li reproaches Yuan of being 'trop chinois' in love, prior to the recognition that she, herself, 'ne l'étai[t] pas moins que lui' (1993: 112). Moreover, according to Michael Kimmel, 'masculinity and femininity are relational constructs... One cannot exist without the other' (1987: 12). If the construction of masculinity is destabilized and probed, what happens to its relational opposite, femininity? As Yuan doubts himself and loses his bearings, Sassa also succumbs to pessimism, while Da Li decides to leave for France. The letters not only dwindle but are reduced to a mere few lines at the end of the narrative with Sassa stating emphatically she does not like 'idiots' (1993: 140). The significance of 'speaking with', as delineated by Spivak, is underlined here as the exchange of letters permits both characters to progress naturally towards the end of their relationship. In breaking off her engagement with him, Sassa gains an emotional and spiritual autonomy, which is unprecedented. From this perspective, I contend that Chen highlights the fact that immigration in Québec in this case changes both the migrant man and the woman he leaves back home. The epistolary form unveils this as the shift is created simultaneously in the protagonists, as Da Li, too, leaves for Paris.

Furthermore, speaking *as* Yuan, Chen becomes the man who migrates and adopts his points of view, sees how he perceives his fiancée, and understands that his nostalgia for the past leads him to conceal his present in Montréal.[13] Far from blaming Yuan for his behaviour, writing *as* Yuan, Chen expresses his love both for Sassa and by association, his home country, and for the North American life along with the liberal values which surround him in Québec. In her letter to her son, *Lenteur*, Chen writes two decades later that 'ayant vécu de très longues années en Chine puis au Canada, je trouve que ces deux cultures sont beaucoup moins différentes qu'on ne le croit' (2014: 10). Ostensibly, the passage of time has altered Chen's own perception of the two cultures as mutually exclusive and at odds with each other. When Yuan expresses his loss, his inability to reconcile the two, Chen speaks her own initial feeling of loss between cultures which has since been alleviated, as seen in *Lenteur*.

In *Lettres chinoises*, Chen describes Yuan's vulnerability in a sensitive way rather than reproaching him for his actions. Ending the exchange abruptly between Sassa and Yuan, she does, however, give Sassa the last word as the latter curtly finishes with a sharp and unequivocal 'Adieu, Yuan' (1993: 140). This could be interpreted as the reversal of the

---

[13] See Yun (2007, 2013). See Bernier (1999).

'Epistolary Woman' trope that Jensen theorized insofar as Yuan is the one who is ultimately abandoned. The absence of a response to Sassa can also be construed as a feminist ending to the novel, with Yuan unable to speak/ write back, but Chen is equally foregrounding the silence of the suffering man who has lost both women for whom he has feelings and cannot express his loss. If for Spivak, 'speaking with' generates a dialogue between those who suffer and those who see the suffering or cause the suffering, here Chen speaking as and with Yuan exposes the distress of the migrant man who loses his past even as he is unable to anchor himself in the present. In inhabiting the character of Yuan and underlining his weaknesses as well as his emotional loss, Chen enables the reader to empathize with Yuan even as his actions merit pause for thought. In nuancing Yuan and his situation, Chen employs the epistolary novel as a means of providing a commentary on social issues surrounding (im)migration.

Chen uses the same form to write her essay, *Lenteur*, addressing questions of immigration, language and the difficulties of being an immigrant Chinese mother with a son born in Canada. While it takes the form of a letter, it is a long monologue. As the last generation 'qui écrit des lettres' (2014: 28), Chen insists on expressing herself in the form she is most comfortable with. While Chen speaks to and as a man in *Lettres chinoises*, which is a fiction she can control with characters she can inhabit in turn, *Lenteur* is a heartfelt letter-essay underlining the questions she asks herself as a mother and as someone living at the crossroads of cultures. Thus, there is no conversation, no 'speaking with' her son since he is a teenager and is only just beginning to ask questions of her. Her acknowledgement that her son wishes that he were not born to Chinese parents and did not look oriental is poignant (2014: 26). For Egle Kačkutė, 'Chen's guilt is primarily associated with race' (2019: 7), which is instantiated when the writer states: 'Cette douleur en toi vient de ton amour pour ta mère, de ta honte et de ton regret parfois d'être né tel que tu es' (Chen 2014: 11–12). Gabrielle Parker suggests that Chen's purpose is to 'to impress upon her son the relativity of difference' (2016: 169). *Lenteur* is a project that Kačkutė aligns with 'the traditional Chinese practices of talk story' (2018: 66), inasmuch as it is constructed as a series of little stories written to teach her son about the realities of life in the society in which they live.

In her meandering letters, Chen underscores the importance of understanding that Canada itself is a settler land: 'la plupart des Canadiens viennent d'ailleurs. Quand la poussière du temps finit par recouvrir les traces de leur passage, ils n'ont d'autres choix que de se considérer comme apatrides' (2014: 35). Chen's words to her son are evocative of her own quest for a home and ultimate realization that most people in Canada do not truly 'belong'. Thus, in her quest to answer her son's queries, she interrogates her own notion of belonging,[14] identifying what Julie Rodgers sees as 'an openness to the world as opposed to defining identity along more rigid and restrictive parameters' (2019: 106). As her sons grow up, she is cognizant of their reality as non-white Canadians. The racism they experience, the lack of support from the government when 'la jeune population chinoise représente près de la moitié des enfants, sinon plus' in Vancouver schools where her children are educated are overtly underlined (2014: 37). Much as Miano decried with her own daughter and as I examined in Chap. 3, Chen expresses her frustration at herself and her sons being pushed together into the 'ghetto' of a 'communauté inexistente' (2014: 40). Chen reveals that living in Vancouver was an important choice so that 'notre famille passe complètement inaperçue' as 'la population asiatiques est importante ici' (2014: 40). Even if the word 'race' is 'démodé' and has been replaced by 'culture', where diversity is privileged, she can feel a 'sérénité relative en vivant à Vancouver' (2014: 41). The different parts of the letter enable us to understand Chen as a mother who wishes to leave a strong message of love and solidarity to the silent 'tu', her son whom she evokes throughout.

The letter-essay is not in itself a response, but an enjoinder to the son to read, to understand what is written and to celebrate the power of the written word: 'je n'ai pas de réponse à ta question, mon enfant, mais je te recommande les poèmes de Rilke' (2014: 125). Rilke's poetry and his ability to rejoice even in death is the legacy that Chen wishes to leave to her son.[15] Above all, *Lenteur* remains a love letter to her son and a message of hope: 'mon désir d'assurer ton bonheur et mon espoir en l'avenir de l'humanité' (2014: 119). The silence from the young man's side is significant as there are no responses to her thoughts, and it is when he is an adult that he will be able to understand and 'speak with' her in reality. The deferral of the message to a future when the son will read her long letter invokes the passage of time which must occur before he can eventually understand what she means and appreciate what she has sought to clarify for him.

---

[14] See also Silvester (2020).
[15] See Rilke (1934).

Both the texts that I analysed in this segment demonstrate the ultimate impossibility of completely 'speaking with' through letters, due to the spatial and temporal lag separating the moment of writing, the moment of reading and the eventual response. The temporal disjuncture plays a significant role as emotions and feelings cannot always be communicated with immediacy and lose their impact by the time the recipient reads the letter. Similarly, the response arrives long after the expression of feelings, which may since have changed. This temporal lag is alleviated by the use of a more immediate form of communication: the telephone, which plays a central role in the relationship between Salie and her brother, Madické as they maintain their relationship between France, where Salie lives and has her own telephone, and Niodior in Senegal, and its single telephone exchange booth.

The Art of Equal Conversation

> Conversation not only captures the unusual openness and generosity of both participants but also enacts a rare and precious possibility, namely that together black women and men can create and inhabit an ideal space of free and equal conversation.
>
> —Gilroy, *Uncut Funk*

Paul Gilroy's 'Foreword' to hooks's and Hall's (posthumous) oeuvre highlights the value of bringing together both men and women in conversation to ensure that the complexity of gendered Black relationships and narratives are fully encompassed. For Gilroy, conversing, speaking with one another, is a crucial means by which Black individuals, irrespective of their gender, can hope to come to comprehend their positioning, vis-à-vis each other and in the society in which they live.[16] 'Speaking with' one another fosters the appropriate environment to reassess issues from different angles as Black masculinities and femininities are experienced in multifarious ways. Through sharing thoughts, ideas and feelings they are able to come to a mutual understanding and respect for their different needs.

---

[16] Of course this does perpetuate gender binaries, whereas Miano, as I examined in Chap. 2, and again in the next section, opts for a genderless approach, privileging blurred boundaries and pre-colonial queer notions of identity.

At this juncture, I return to Spivak to note that the theorist was criticized for reiterating the idea that women do not have agency and cannot speak.[17] She responds to this criticism in *The Spivak Reader* (1996) where she underlines the fact that there is a difference between talking and speaking insofar as speaking is active and interpersonal, whereas one can talk to oneself. 'Speaking with' someone allows for an interactive and constructive approach to problem-solving while giving equal agency to participants in such conversations.[18] It is precisely in this fashion that Gilroy conceives of the conversations between hooks and Hall as a productive space enabling them to create an open narrative on Black lives irrespective of gender. I draw on Spivak's, hooks's and Hall's theories of 'speaking with' and conversing to explore the ways in which Salie and Madické come to terms with their own situation as a Sub-Saharan man and woman, legitimate and illegitimate, static in Senegal and immigrant in France, through the medium of the telephone conversation. In considering the implications for gendered relationships, I investigate the ways in which Diome creates equality through the sharing of not just information and thoughts, but also of feelings between men and women, through conversations.

In the initial stages of the conversations taking place between Hall and hooks, the former qualifies what a conversation means to him thus:

> [...]one of the nice things about conversation [...] is, of course, its fluidity. It can move from the trivial to the profound, in and out, across boundaries of sexualities and genders, boundaries of experience. It gives you a sense of the dialogic, of conversation as exchange. (2018: 5)

The fact that Hall underlines the possibility of moving beyond gender boundaries while attending to a range of topics is significant to my reading of Diome's text here. Their conversations focus on a number of themes, including the conversation as a mode of communication granting those involved the ability to explore ideas fluidly. For the theorists, of course, conversation is not constraining, it is potentially edifying and allows the dialogue to take any shape. hooks's preface elucidates this further: 'there is a tenderness, a sweetness to our conversation, a moment of private and

---

[17] For instance, Maggio contends that 'Spivak's landmark essay provides an example of the limits of the ability of Western discourse, even postcolonial discourse, to interact with disparate cultures' (2007: 420).

[18] Nonetheless, as Cox demonstrates in *Girl Talk* (2017), talking can also involve a measure of exchange of ideas and active participation from writer to reader through advice.

public revelation that adds new dimensions to our talking to one another and our work' (2018: xv). The dichotomy of private and public involved in the conversation fosters an atmosphere where they can consider several subjects with great sensitivity, including the notions of home, masculinity, and the need to engage with difficult topics. The conversation is understood as an empowering tool offering a form of freedom to those who partake in it. However, the questions arising within the context of Diome's text are whether a conversation is always equal and whether it can ever be one-sided, especially when from the outset men are regarded as superior to women in the society depicted by the writer.

As I discuss earlier, Salie allows us to delve into the gendered social dynamics at play in the community of Niodior. Diome's text opens not on Salie's life as a student or immigrant in France, but as a sister who is avidly watching a football match on television in order to recount it to her younger brother who cannot watch it in Niodior since the only television in the village is out of order. The narrator claims: 'dévouée je suis sa messagère', and while they do not have the same father, he is her only sibling: 'Madické et moi avons la même mère; ceux qui savent aimer à cinquante pour cent vous diront que c'est mon demi-frère, mais pour moi c'est mon petit frère tout simplement' (2003: 18). Thus, the narrator accentuates the importance of her relationship with her brother and the role it plays in her life even after emigrating to France. In *Ventre*, Salie's sole mode of communication with Madické, and indeed with the family in Niodior, remains a single telephone in the village. Positioned in the centre of the village, the telephone functions as the only means of communication to the outside world for the inhabitants: 'le *télécentre*: une petite pièce où le téléphone, que se partagent tous les habitants du quartier repose sur son autel' (2003: 35). The religious imagery of the 'autel' reinforces the central place occupied by this telephone in keeping the bonds intact between the villagers and their kin who are abroad. Yet, for Salie, the number she dials also represents a financial drain: '0221… ce n'est pas un numéro, c'est la partie de ma gorge où France Telecom pose la lame impitoyable de son couteau' (2003: 36). According to Hamid Naficy, the telephone has a preternatural element associated to it in the diasporic setting. Naficy understands the telephone as entailing a form of 'concomitant immediacy, intimacy and intensity' (2001: 117). He ontologizes the telephone as emblematic of the diaspora's unique connection with its different branches. Rooted in a need to connect and the fear of not being able to do so, the telephone becomes an instrument of torture, even as it alleviates the pain of not knowing what others are experiencing. In Diome's text, for those who have emigrated, the telephone remains the only way to keep in touch with the family, be it good or bad news: 'seule une nostalgie foudroyante, la supplique irrésistible d'une mère inquiète ou d'un frère impatient me poussent à composer le 0221' (2003: 38).

Discussing telephone calls in her important work *In the Wake: On Blackness and Being* (2016), Christina Sharpe charts the ways in which the telephone can be a connection as well as a harbinger of death, while foregrounding her own personal experiences of receiving a telephone call announcing her brother's unexpected demise. In her discussion of Sharpe's text, Emma Wilson notes that Sharpe 'registers the phone call as alarm signal and shows the telephone as an imaginary wire that still, at certain limit moments, connects the dispersed members of her family' (2019: 13). Developing the notion of intimacy underpinning telephone calls further, Wilson argues that 'the scenario of listening, hearing and responding takes us back to primal moments of need and connection' (2019: 15). Salie's affective experience of being a Senegalese immigrant woman in France leads to an intensified need for a connection to those she has left behind. Nonetheless, Madické's calls to his sister are unashamedly selfish in purport as he merely wishes to discuss football matches. While Sharpe introduces the notion of familial bonding bolstered through it, and Salie, too, adheres to this principle, Madické's discordant reaction is highlighted. Diome underscores the gendered differences between the two interlocutors as they negotiate their relationship through a medium which connects as much as it disconnects individuals due to the motivations behind the call.

In his foreword to hooks's and Hall's text, Gilroy underscores the need for 'free equal communication' between individuals, irrespective of gender, as I quoted earlier. While equality in thought and status may be sought in the diaspora, and the education level of both parties, as is the case with the theorists, it is not always the case in societies where men occupy a superior to women. Indubitably, there is an inequality between Salie and Madické as reporting football matches is the condition that she has to meet to receive news regarding the rest of the family, news which more often than not, he does not relay to her. Football becomes a bargaining chip, a means of connecting with the family back home for Salie since no one else will call her in France nor come to the telephone centre to converse with her. hooks stresses there is a 'relationship between conversation and power' which is ineluctable (2018: 9). For hooks, often if the conversation is taking place with someone one considers to be superior or inferior, one's demeanour or posture might change. In the text, Madické dictates what Salie can know and what she is denied. The text reads as a critique of how men are brought up in their society, and the position offered to women, aptly underlined in one single word: 'soumission' (2003: 41). In her habitual tongue-in-cheek manner, the narrator contrasts those who claim and assert their masculinity back home and the transgender individuals of Bois de Boulogne who 's'arrachent' 'les testicules', 'pour parader leur torse poilu sur des talons aiguilles' (2003: 41). Men in her native community represent a rigid masculinity which is unlikely to change whereas there is fluid masculinity, and even rejection of masculinity, at times in France as she perceives it.

Conversations between siblings become a means of thinking through cultural differences as well as permitting a reconsideration of prior judgments and preconceptions. For instance, one of the short conversations which occurs between the siblings is a trigger for reflections on the misconceptions harboured by those back home who assume that anyone who lives in France is '[repu], prenant ses aises à la cour de Louis XIV' (2003: 44). Such discourses unveil the inability of families in Senegal (and according to Salie, on the African continent at large) to recognize that immigrants in France are not necessarily rich nor successful and that they suffer 'la solitude de l'exil, [le] combat pour la survie' (2003: 44). This conversation also sheds light on the 'obligation d'assistance' which is 'le plus gros fardeau que traînent les émigrés' (2003: 45).[19] However, since Madické is the only link she has with the family back home, Salie perceives the command to not forget 'de regarder la finale du 2 juillet' as a 'mission sacrée' (2003: 45), thereby highlighting Salie's quasi-religious adoration of her brother.[20]

Salie's frustration is palpable in the narrative as conversations revolve around Madické and his life plans and very little is proffered regarding the family. Yet, lest the reader feel that Salie is under her brother's control, Salie interpellates the reader and threatens to 'vous couper la langue' if the reader forms a negative opinion of Madické. Salie justifies Madické's behaviour as his passion for football (2003: 81). The direct address to the reader is significant here as Salie's role of narrator might be construed as

---

[19] See Zadi (2010).

[20] There are similarities here between Salie and Malika in *Mes hommes*, whose love for her younger brother is all-forgiving, as I explored in Chap. 3.

biased. For Isabelle Hutcheson-Lovett, 'Diome's depiction of football-mania on the island of Niodior acts as a gateway to a wider discussion on migration and the mirage of Europe' (2018: n.p.).[21] Indeed, if there is any blame or accusation levelled in the text, it is directed towards the prevalent discourse that France is superior and living there as the dream to be achieved. Although Madické is a fan of Paolo Maldini, an Italian player, whose last name he adopts when he plays football, France remains his desired destination (2003: 82), since it is the focus of the narrative held by those who believe in the power of France to help them in achieving their goals. However, to accomplish this, financial help and sponsorship are crucial.

The telephone conversations embody another level of hierarchical structure when Madické asks Salie for financial assistance to come to France (2003: 140). According to Christopher Hogarth, the fact that Salie is the woman who can provide financial help to her family is significant here as it reverses the traditional stereotypes wherein it is the man who migrates and sends money home. For Hogarth, 'she suggests that traditional gender roles could be re-imagined' since she is the main bread winner for the family in Niodior (2016: 58). In this text, the reversal is also noteworthy as Madické requesting financial aid undercuts the position of superiority that he has always occupied as a man in the telephone conversations (and indeed as per his society's values), as opposed to the equality that conversations imply according to hooks and Hall. Madické presumes that, since she is in France, his sister can further his career and aid him in 'trouver un club', but as Salie explains: 'ce n'est pas que je ne veuille pas, je ne peux pas' (2003: 140). Football and the dream of reaching Europe, including the wealth and recognition it represents, is depicted as a 'colonization mentale' in the novel (2003: 53). Since his sister cannot afford such an expense, for Madické the solution is to consult witch doctors since 'au moins ils ont toujours une solution' (2003: 140). Here Diome criticizes witch doctors, who prey on desperate individuals. Often exploiting their clients, taking their money, and failing to produce results, witch doctors remain an important aspect of their society.[22] Salie's lack of faith in such practices is perceived by Madické as her being 'occidentalisée'

---

[21] See also Thomas's (2006) examination of football in this text.

[22] As Bello (2018) argues, though there is a strong Islamic presence on the African continent, this coexists peacefully with the ancestral belief systems, including witch doctors and so on.

(2003: 141), and therefore selfish. However, Salie's reticence holds a more profound meaning, as reinforced by her self-interrogations: 'raconter ou pas raconter? Comment raconter?' (2003: 141). The disclosure of a well-kept secret involving a witch doctor asking that she masturbate him for someone else's benefit as she becomes 'un sacrifice fait aux esprits' (2003: 156) is reserved for the reader, while the grandmother relates the story to Madické behind the scenes. The context is explicated as we receive Salie's innermost feelings on learning that sexual abuse on a young girl is acceptable to her tutor, and the latter's daughter, as long as they attain their objective.

Revealing her experience is a difficult process, which should be dealt with delicately and with compassion. However, Madické's reaction is simply 'et alors? Dieu seul jugera. Tous les marabouts ne sont pas comme celui-là' (2003: 158). In diminishing his sister's experience and trauma since he does not see beyond his own motivations, Madické exposes his narrow-mindedness and selfishness. Nevertheless, Salie does not react with shock or disappointment at her brother's words. Instead, she attributes the responsibility to their culture and how it fashions the individual living in it: 'très enraciné dans sa culture, il gardait une foi inébranlable dans les pratiques ancestrales' (2003: 158). In not chastizing her brother and in refusing to judge him, Salie allows the reader to understand that she can place her brother's reaction in the context within which he was born and raised. The text asks us not to perceive such reactions through our own particular experiences and values but through the lens of their community's values and belief system. While Spivak argues for the possibilities afforded by speaking with the 'subaltern', and understanding their position, in this case there is a measure of distress which is sublimated by the explanations provided by the narrator, a justification for a nuanced perception.

Spivak is equally salient in this text as the former 'subaltern' woman, having been educated, returns to educate others so that they do not suffer the fate of Black migrants in France.[23] Salie returns to Niodior as she attempts to dissuade the boys from coming to France through heated debates and conversations. Entering the *huis clos* of the boys, a world which is only open to her since she is educated and lives in France, Salie is able to voice her opinion. Salie's exceptionality is reinforced in the text with anaphoric repetition: 'chaque cahier rempli, chaque livre lu, chaque

---

[23] See Thomas's (2007) analysis of Black migrants in France.

dictionnaire consulté est une brique supplémentaire sur le mur qui se dresse entre elles et moi' (2003: 171). Education may have generated the opportunities for her to experience a different trajectory, but it is also what unequivocally segregates her from the rest of the women. While Salie addresses the boys as naïve victims whom she must help out of the hegemonic machinery of the colonial vision of France as the ultimate destination, she does not converse with the women. Indeed, no attempt is made to 'speak with' the other 'subalterns': the women whose role is to cook and bear children. The widening gap between Salie and the women is exacerbated here as she blurs the gender boundaries through emigration and education and is given the right to address the men as an equal. However, in so doing, she simultaneously loses the ability to 'speak with' the women who do not have access to the education nor the tools to partake in such conversations.

In her attempt at deterring the boys from emigrating, a rift is created between Madické and Salie. Yet, such vicissitudes in relationships cannot last long as 'la distance, paradoxalement, [les] eût rapprochés' (2003: 209). Rather than their emotional bond, Salie attributes this *rapprochement* to the cost of phone calls. The economic repercussions of telephone calls nullifies the need to deny Salie the right to speak her mind here as Madické still relies on her for football news. Nonetheless, his dream of coming to France continues to be a problem as Salie exclaims: 'mais savait-il comment il m'imposait davantage?' (2003: 210). Madické's obsession with emigrating leads to interrogations as to how she can provide him with an alternative solution (2003: 211). The sister's sacrifices, such as 'renoncer au superflu occidental' (2003: 211), isolating herself, so that 'le téléphone était le cordon ombilical qui [la] reliait au reste du monde' (2003: 212), are silenced as she does not share the burden she shoulders with her brother, thereby fuelling his beliefs that earning money in France is facile. But Salie's agenda differs from her brother as her aim is to finance 'un projet viable sur l'île [...] de quoi ouvrir une boutique sur l'île' (2003: 212). The reiteration of 'sur l'île' shifts the focus on the necessity to adapt to life on the island, fortifying her injunction against leaving the African continent to fester in poverty in France, when they could create a new sustainable economy in their country.

Calling his sister to have a conversation about his options, and not to discuss football, finally represents a change in Madické's demeanour. Nonetheless Madické is not ready for a complete transformation in his perception of what a pragmatic situation might be. The narrator's announcement that she has money for him on the condition that he opens a business on the island itself is seen as a form of hypocrisy since he does not understand why she would impede his departure when she herself chooses to live in France. Salie's plea that he should ask their grandmother the reasons behind her choice to live away from their society comes as a final act of unveiling her personal history and allowing him to comprehend her difficult position. As Hogarth aptly states, '[i]t seems that Salie prefers her life in France to the meagre possibilities offered to her as a female illegitimate child in Senegal' (2016: 57). Ultimately, Salie's past and her many negative experiences in Senegal are valid reasons for her not to return to a society which marginalizes her and refuses to acknowledge her as one of their own.

Madické's silence after this phone call and the feeling of rupture it causes, prompt long passages on the narrator's status as an exile and the nostalgia she experiences. Diome's narrator spends some time reflecting on the reasons behind her attempts at dissuading her brethren: 'il ne s'agit pas de dégoûter les nôtres de l'Occident, mais de leur révéler le dessous des cartes' (2003: 247). According to hooks 'conversation is a place of potential pedagogy' (2018: 5). For Salie, it is important to teach others and change their perception about the dominant discourse which privileges emigration as the only solution to poverty in different parts of Africa. Conversation allows for the exchange of ideas but also enables those who can transmit knowledge to do so in a spirit of equality and understanding. Salie does not impose her views inasmuch as she seeks to address a lacuna in their perception of migration and of France in particular. To comprehend this thought process, I turn to Sarah Buekens's recent interview with Diome, wherein the latter underlines her purpose in writing:

> Pour moi, la littérature est simplement un moyen de participer aux débats de mon époque, une façon de dire que je ne suis pas indifférente, je me sens concernée. N'ayant ni le pouvoir de signer des décrets ni celui de changer une loi, il me reste la liberté d'expression pour dénoncer tout ce que je déplore. (in Buekens 2019: 156)

Through this narrative, Diome engages with the problematics of emigration and the mythologization of France as a veritable paradise which will permit dreams to become reality.[24] In penning Salie's story she speaks to all the brothers whose minds have been colonized by thoughts of plenty in Europe. She also carefully lays bare the fragility of the brother-sister relationship when the sister effectively has the power to alter the situation.

Nevertheless, Madické's prickly behaviour, his failure to grasp her circumstances and offer kind words to his sister is attributed to the society's values once again: 'nul n'a appris aux hommes de chez nous que la tendresse n'ôte de virilité à personne, qu'elle donne un supplément d'âme au plus affirmé des caractères' (2003: 250). Once again I return to hooks here as she aptly discusses her own choice of topics as including masculinity: 'that was my other choice of focus for these beginning conversations: masculinity, because that is where there has been the least reworking' (2018: 25). For hooks and Hall, there have not been enough conversations between Black men and women, and they have left their struggles as separate. hooks indicates that while Black women have generated numerous conversations with their sisters on Black femininities, the same cannot be said with regard to masculinities, nor for gender relations (or indeed non-binary individuals). Within the literary world, Diome's text enables the reader to grapple with the singular and contextual experiences of men who do not realize that they are allowed to feel, due to their social context. It further explores the role of women in creating the safe spaces for conversations and dialogues to take place in order for both masculinities and femininities to evolve in an empowering way. According to Salie,

> Madické était devenu ce qu'il souhaitait, un homme, et les jérémiades de nanas il n'aime pas trop ça; celles que font les mecs non plus, me disait-il. Je savais que mon ton au téléphone ne ferait qu'empirer les choses, sauf si, pour une fois, il acceptait une discussion entre égaux. (2003: 250)

Similar to hooks, Diome also focuses on equality and understanding masculinity and reshaping it in her novel, by creating two-way conversations between Salie and Madické. The former is now in the superior position as she has the money, while the latter, despite being a man, and therefore automatically superior in the society he hails from, finds himself in the inferior, asking position. This role reversal is not lived well by Madické but Salie does not exploit her position. The adjective 'égaux' reinforces the

---

[24] See also Bates's (2019) deployment of the trope of the 'miroir aux alouettes' to compare the fascination with France and football in the novel.

fact that she wishes to eschew a hierarchy which would subvert Madické's notion of masculinity and its role in male-female kinship.

Madické's acceptance of her offer is a welcome surprise to Salie. His statement that emigrating to France, 'ça ne [l]'intéresse plus' (2003: 251), unburdens Salie who has been suffering from disconnection through Madické's silence, causing a form of anxiety, as I outlined through Naficy's theory earlier. Ultimately, 'speaking with' him rather than from a position of superiority has proven to be fruitful, as per Spivak's theory. Madické's enumeration of the range of things that take up his time and what he has been able to do since setting up the shop leads to Salie's sense of relief at having created an opportunity for him in the village itself. His suggestion that she should return is experienced as a touching moment for Salie as 'l'amour chez [eux], on ne l'avoue pas ouvertement. [...] Il faut donc le deviner au détour d'une phrase' (2003: 252). Gratitude is expressed in the announcement that the shop is prospering, while his statement that her grandmother wishes to see her is explained as his yearning for her presence. Changes occurring in Madické are visible, but he cannot be honest about his feelings. This is emblematic of years of being told to be stoic that must be changed here. His suggestion that she should return since 'là-bas, tu le sais bien, ce ne sera jamais chez toi' becomes the evidence of his love in Salie's mind, and a hope that she will be a part of their family again (2003: 253). Nevertheless, Salie will not be able to return as she is an outsider to this community as I discussed earlier in this chapter. As hooks, speaking from her personal experience, asserts 'we have to reinvent the notion of home. As long as home is that nostalgic return to the patriarchal household then it can never allow feminism to come through the window or the door' (2018: 23). Thus the very notion of home as a patriarchal space, regulated by disparaging rules and hierarchies, must be dismantled for any potential return to occur for immigrant women who have experienced life in a comparatively more equitable society.[25] In Diome's case a return could only take place if the inhabitants of Niodior are prepared to accept people who do not conform to the norm, such as Salie whose father is from a different genealogical line. While individuals might be prevailed upon to change due to their own personal circumstances, a shift in a whole community's perception might not be easy nor possible.

---

[25] Although critics such as Achin (2016) would argue that although France passed a gender parity law, this has not proven to be favourable for women at all times. In the case of politics, for instance, the law has been deployed to actually reinforce conservative male-centric order.

The love Salie harbours for her brother empowers her to weather the many storms on their way to a conversation between equals. It is her faith in her love for him, in the kinship that links them that enables her to forge ahead and hope to change his perception about remaining in Niodior. In their conversation, hooks and Hall assert that 'love is many things. It is also a conversation, the right conversation' (2018: 120). In speaking her truth, and in encouraging Madické to understand that she wishes to be an equal and enabling him to spread his wings in Niodior itself, away from the quotidian horrors of racism in France, Diome's narrator 'speaks with' her brother in the sense that Spivak intends it, in order to finally understand that 'love' is 'recognition', here, the recognition of equality (2018: 125).

Much as with the father figures in the first section of this chapter, the women who are writing to men in this section do not create tension but defuse it, and in fact, more often than not, reconceptualize communication as the means through which men and women, brothers and sisters, fathers and daughters, and mothers and sons can achieve a form of love which eludes power relationships. Nevertheless, not everyone is able to speak with the other and silence can play a substantial role in the transformation of identities in the host society.

THE UNSPEAKABLE AND THE UNSPOKEN: SILENCES AND MASCULINITIES

Puissance du langage: avec mon langage je puis tout faire: même et surtout ne rien dire.
—Barthes, *Fragments d'un discours amoureux*

Roland Barthes's claims about the power of language to simultaneously say everything and reveal nothing is crucial insofar as silence plays a significant role in the texts examined in the present study. The solitude of the lover delineated by Barthes is significant since the discourse of love is not entertained or sustained by many. What an individual feels impelled to keep silent is as revelatory as that which they expand upon. While coming to writing, and especially, writing about men, immigrant women writers often foreground silences which have either been imposed upon them by patriarchal society, or foisted upon men by their community. Writing about such silences becomes a means of interrogating the choice not to speak as well as highlighting the pressures experienced by both men and women under patriarchy.

In *Writing Not Writing: Poetry, Crisis, Responsibility* (2017), Thomas Fisher discusses the act of not writing itself as a form of political and personal message:

> We cannot count all the poets who stopped writing—or never started—or all the poems not written. These are silences, elisions, absences that cannot be traced, tracked, or measured, but which, perhaps, demand some form of recognition that might trouble the complacency of the written and the readable. (2017: x)

Fisher underscores the space of writing as conducive to the poet or writer exploring and creating through their imagination. The power of writing resides in its 'possibility': 'Writing—and poetry especially perhaps—takes place in the conditional tense of a contingent and precarious possibility', writes Fisher (2017: x). In a similar vein to Cixous and Spivak, Fisher argues that some may not be able to write (or speak), and that writing (or speaking) is a mark of privilege: 'any consideration of silence and writing must include the recognition of those who—even as we are unable to name them—have been silenced before they even begin to "speak"; those, that is, who are denied that privilege speech requires' (2017: 95).[26] Those who are subdued by the lack of opportunity to write do not have access to a medium to break their silence. Others cannot speak nor write since they are denied the freedom to reveal their experiences for the shame or publicity it would bring their family.

Similarly, in *Articulate Silences: Hisaye Yamamoto, Maxine Hong Kingston and Joy Kogewa* (2018), King-Kok Cheung examines three Asian American immigrant women's writing and the silences that pervade their prose. Identifying these silences as often being linked to a double gaze, Cheung perceives these writers' marginalization as resulting from their identity as immigrants, and therefore a minority, in America. For the critic, they need to be aware of their reception as women writing within the Asian American community: 'As minority women these writers are subject not only to the white gaze of the larger society but also to a communal gaze' (2018: 16). They are subject to censure and are expected to uphold traditional values. Nonetheless, such expectations are also extended to

---

[26] This is also the case for Devi, in the previous chapter.

men and children, and they, too, suffer from societal pressures. In this section, I interrogate the male child's experience of sexual abuse and the extent to which silence threatens his psyche in *Crépuscule 2*. In the second part, I consider the treatment of suicide attempts and the secrecy surrounding them in Djebar's *Nulle part*, and how these silences affect the narrator's relationship with men. In the final segment, I contend that the trauma of war takes its toll on men in Thúy's *Ru*. I explore the different ways in which the text break the silences surrounding the difficult decisions men were compelled to make and the repercussions on themselves and their families.

Silencing Masculine Sexual Abuse

Amok garda le silence.

—Miano, *Crépuscule 2*

Miano's *Crépuscule 2* is the final segment in the trilogy which also includes *Tels* and *Crépuscule du tourment 1*. While the latter focuses on the women in Amok's life and, as a polyphonic narrative, offers multiple perspectives on Amok, *Crépuscule 2* is told by a third-person heterodiegetic narrator.[27] The text has an additional subtitle, 'heritage', which testifies to the significance ascribed to legacy in this narrative. The omniscient narrator provides an overarching perspective on Amok's life as it is unveiled on the African continent, where he has elected to return after beginning a relationship with Ixora, Shrapnel's former lover. The relationship is one of convenience, where Amok maintains a platonic friendship with Ixora, who becomes his confidante, and Kabral, Shrapnel's son, can now have a father. Amok thereby alleviates his own 'peur-panique de l'engendrement, son refus de donner une descendance à la lignée des Musesedi' (2017b: 15), which stems from his reluctance to acknowledge his war collaborator grandfather and violent father. The return is conducive to an understanding of his father and his own masculinity. Concomitantly it also leads to a descent into memories of childhood sexual abuse and interrogations about his repressed sexuality and his ensuing silence.

The choice of returning to Amok's family home is justified as a form of protection for Kabral lest he face constant racism as a young Black man in

---

[27] See Genette (1980).

France. That Amok has chosen to go home, when home was such a challenging space for him, is crucial as it highlights the extent to which racism in France would pose more problems for Kabral than it would for Amok to face his past. It speaks to Miano's claims in *Marianne* (Miano 2017a) that Black men suffer the most in France as examined in the previous chapter.[28] The proximity in publication dates (both were published in 2017) suggests that *Crépuscule 2* distils in fiction, what Miano argues in her non-fiction. The text also calls into question the feasibility of a return to the country of origin, to a home which was once reneged, when France has not become the new home. At this point, I return to Ahmed's *Queer Phenomenology* where she explores the feeling of disorientation experienced by the queer individual who returns: 'Now living a queer life, the act of going home, or going back to the place I was brought up, has a certain disorienting effect' (2006: 11). Amok is only just coming to terms with his own sexuality and it is only when he is back home that he fully understands the ramifications of his sexual orientation as I explored in Chap. 2. His 'disorientation' is however not a positive one at first. Far from positing the positivity of this return as a given, Miano begins the narrative after the newly formed family has arrived and settled in the country and is facing obstacles. The onslaught of feelings which overpower Amok from the opening pages are in keeping with a longstanding need to not surrender to what he deems to be his legacy: propensity to violence. Nonetheless, the novel begins with Amok having assaulted Ixora for the first time, leading to a spiral of emotions which he had heretofore controlled: 'au cours des années, il avait appris à se maîtriser, à dominer ses émotions' (2017b: 19).[29] Despite the fact that the repression of emotions was lived as necessary for Amok, due to his being a man, it was also detrimental to his mental health. Thus, Miano foregrounds the psychological effects of masculine repression in this text, while associating it with colonialism and its aftereffects.

Writing with reference to Algeria, Frantz Fanon argues in *Les damnés de la terre* (1961, rep. 2002) that decolonization is by definition 'un phénomène violent' (2002: 39). Violence was vital to wrench the country away from the colonizers and create 'une nouvelle humanité' (2002: 40).[30] Responding to Fanon's claims forty years later in *Le* trauma *colonial,*

---

[28] Kinouani (2021) observes that stop checks generates 'trauma symptoms' in Black individuals as they are regularly targeted.

[29] See Viveros Vigoya (2018).

[30] See Gagiano's (2018) exploration of humanism in Fanon's works.

Karima Lazali exposes the enduring effects of colonization on subsequent generations after decolonization, to the extent that these patients 'sont pris dans une histoire qu'ils n'ont pas connue et qui, le plus souvent leur a été transmise dans un épais silence' (2018: 8). Fanon's quasi-quixotic vision of decolonization as engendering a new form of humanity in spite of the violence that the colonized have undergone, during and in the aftermath of colonization, is debunked by Lazali as the violence associated with colonization leaves its indelible mark decades later and affects subsequent generations. Along the same lines, Guilaine Kinouani, who examines intergenerational wounds caused by colonization in the particular case of Black individuals, notes that 'in the colonial context, many of us have been told about the mundane acts of humiliation and banal degradation our parents and grandparents had to endure' and such 'stories' live on in the children as 'trauma knows no time boundary' (2021: 41–42). In *Crépuscule 2*, for the men who were born during the colonial era, psychological dislocation is depicted as a recurrent malady conducive to domestic violence: 'la génération de leurs parents souffrait de maladie mentale. Chez les hommes, cela se traduisait par de nombreux désordres parmi lesquels une violence conjugale aveugle' (2017b: 47). Memories of his father beating his mother haunt Amok and he envisions this as a legacy which should not be passed on from one generation to the next. Managing his emotions so that history is not repeated, Amok refuses to have children to ensure that the legacy of violence ends with him, leading to Kabral being 'le fils qu'il s'était choisi' (2017b: 38). Since Shrapnel was an absent father and Amok is successful in curbing his violent urges, Kabral does not have the vestige of this 'maladie mentale' passed on to him. Thus, Amok's assault on Ixora and the ensuing realization that he has not escaped this legacy of the past is traumatic for him. Coming to terms with his repressed memories and feelings involves a voyage into the country to speak to his father and a journey to his own mental depths.

The novel explores the past which Amok has silenced, beginning with the reflection that 'le silence ne protégerait personne, n'innocenterait personne. Le silence faisait peser, sur lui seul' as he recalls the story of the young girl who killed herself after the boys he admired abused her (2017b: 99). The narrative sets Ixora up as the confidante, even as she is the trigger for the emotional barrage which overwhelms Amok. In response to her innocent questions about his first sexual experience, he recounts his traumatic memories, which have been immured for decades. The absence of intercourse between the two creates the appropriate setting for Amok to unburden himself, which he could not accomplish with Amandla in *Tels*, where his erectile dysfunction was seen as a flaw. Nevertheless, the revelation of the abuse itself is executed subtly and with euphemisms as he refuses to name his abuser. Referred to simply as the 'parente' (2017b: 104), Amok's sexual abuser 'était innommable' (2017b: 105), or simply 'la dame du Pacifique' (2017b: 112). His father's relative begins initiating Amok to oral sex at the age of eight as a form of revenge against his mother, whom she considers to be of inferior birth, and whose confidence she resents. According to Marjolaine Unter Ecker, 'l'identité sexuelle d'Amok est imprégnée des viols que lui a fait subir sa tante paternelle' (2019: 136). The shock of an adult visiting him at night and forcing him to perform oral sex on her is recalled with guilt and shame: 'Bien sûr, il n'en parlerait à personne. Bien sûr, il ne se permettrait pas de répéter ces gestes avec une fille' (2017b: 115). The anaphora, 'bien sûr', brings to bear the realization that such an act is reprehensible and that he could never reveal this shame to anyone. The enormity of sexual abuse is not lost on the little boy as he resolves that no girl should be subjected to the same actions.

In her work on silence, Cheung states that 'undesirable silences—the speechlessness induced by shame and guilt, the oppressive or protective withholding of words in the family' are significant in immigrant women writers' narratives (2018: 20). In this instance, while it is a woman writing, it is a little boy's shame which is foregrounded as he is equally subjugated:

> C'était sa première fois. C'est ainsi qu'il l'exprimait, en dépit de la répulsion, de la honte. Il n'avait rien dit. Les enfants savent, quand ils peuvent parler. Dans la grande maison il n'y aurait eu personne pour recueillir sa détresse. (2017b: 116)

The absence of an avenue to speak of abuse is decried here as the child is not authorized to accuse his abuser. The culpability of the culture and community in which he lives is stressed and criticized as it does not foster a suitable environment for a child to feel safe. In a similar vein, for Fisher, it is 'political and communal silence that makes audible the wordlessness of others' (2017: 97). Fisher draws on Rancière and the political denial of speech to those who play no part in community. In this case, Amok as a young child is devoid of a voice and agency. I contend that the impossibility of speech is here directly related to the community's lack of support for children and their experiences. Amok is denied a voice because he does not exist in the power play between adult family members. In the space of the text, Miano permits such intimate stories of vulnerability to be exposed and weighed on the scales of literary justice. As Amok unveils his secret, a bond is created between Miano's readers, the little boy and the scarred man he has become, thereby permitting a re-evaluation of the protagonist's decisions and actions.

As Cheung asserts, 'silence can be a direct consequence of prohibition. But it also carries other functions and meanings that vary with individuals and cultures' (2018: 3). In Amok's case, the impossibility of divulging this nightly visit is also due to his wish to protect his mother from the repercussions of the aunt's actions. Children, too, seek to protect their parents from knowledge which threatens to rend the fabric of the family. Equally, his mother's 'impure' blood, due to the fact that she is descended from a slave, is internalized to the point that Amok does not feel he deserves to be treated better. In *Les damnés de la terre*, Fanon posits the dichotomy between colonizer and colonized, master and slave as exacerbated through the use of 'langage zoologique' to refer to the colonized or slave (2002: 45). While Fanon was referring to the white colonizer and the colonized person of colour, here a Sub-Saharan African woman, who perceives herself as superior, treats a little boy from her own family like an animal: 'qu'est-ce que tu me broutes bien, petit mouton', 'comme un chien' (2017b: 117). Animalizing the young boy is a strategy to dehumanize him, much as white individuals did to Fanon in reducing him to his skin colour.[31] The paternal aunt devolves him from his close status as her nephew, to a slave's grandson and ultimately to the state of animal. Miano demonstrates the cruelty of those who live on the African continent and who are no better than the colonial powers who equated slaves and colonized individuals to animals. In so doing, Miano reminds her readers that Sub-Saharan Africans also had kingdoms and slaves and that slavery was not solely a European construct. Thus the words, *'tu sais qui est le maître, tu sais que ce n'est pas toi'* (2017b: 117), are evocative of a deeply entrenched prejudice which is denounced.

Moreover, Miano's text debunks different types of misconceptions as an older adult, and especially a grandmotherly figure, abuses a young boy. That a woman is the sexual predator and expresses her feminine sexuality

---

[31] See also Adams and Donovan (1995) and Dunayer (1995) who examine the role of language in reducing women to the state of animals in patriarchal society. Miano is also reversing this trope here.

to perpetrate such a crime is rendered more shocking as she is depicted as 'une femme sans visage fredonnant une comptine' (2017b: 125). The significance of this situation is not lost on us: that she is humming a lullaby while she is forcing him to perform a sexual act on her is unconscionable, grotesque, incommensurable. Miano demonstrates that inhumanity is also shared by those who can justify it, be they white or Black, man or woman. In her lack of moral rectitude, her lack of respect for the boy and for the kinship that links them, the aunt is as condemnable as the white colonizers she herself criticizes earlier in the novel. Amok's reaction to this repeated trauma is to forget: 'il avait été un temps amnésique des gestes de la tante' (2017b: 119). For critics such as Cheung, who write about the absence of a voice for women who are also doubly disadvantaged due to racial difference, 'voicelessness is induced not only by gender but also by culture and race' (2018: 5). Miano demonstrates that an intersectional approach is needed for both women who suffer from voicelessness and the vulnerable young boys of colour who have no means of expressing their emotions, no outlet for their fears and trauma, and can only have recourse to silence to protect themselves.

In a society where men beat their wives to alleviate their own feelings of inadequacy, opening up about abuse brands the young boy as weak. If for Jean-Paul Sartre, '[…] se taire ce n'est pas être muet, c'est refuser de parler, donc parler encore' (1948: 32), Amok's silence would not be an absence of voice but an eloquent silence, a voluntary choice, an action in inaction. Nonetheless, it is inaction due to the circumstances surrounding abuse as an eight-year-old child in his particular culture. It is only after speaking about these events, as an adult capable of processing these memories, that Amok gains the confidence to actually term her 'son agresseuse' (2017b: 118). Nonetheless, this initiation to sexual acts is recognized as constitutive of his sexual development. Eventually, Amok acknowledges this and can finally 'ne plus souffrir de tant aimer pratiquer les actes auxquels il [a] été contraint enfant. Accepter que cela lui ait laissé des désirs peu communs' (2017b: 269). Ultimately it also permits Amok to unveil other silences, beginning with the multiple masculinities at play in a precolonial Africa, where: 'On pouvait être homme à moitié aux trois quarts ou pas On y avait sa place (*sic*)' (2017b: 158). The suppression of divergent sexual practices by European colonial powers is here deplored. The interior voyage permits a recalibration and a rediscovery of ancestral practices, where 'jadis les garçons s'aimaient en toute liberté' (2017b: 173), and where Amok can find a new home if he so wishes.

Crépuscule 2 also explains the silences in *Tels*. Amok divulges the reason behind his erectile dysfunction in the first narrative. His subpar sexual performance with Amandla is linked to his fear of fatherhood and filiation, as well as his attraction to transgender individuals. In so doing, this text permits the reader to better understand the protagonist and his choices. In revealing his sexual abuse, Miano enables the reader to establish a connection with Amok and his emotions. With his confession regarding his sexual preference for Mabel, Miano creates a different paradigm for Amok and other men who do not identify with heteronormative sexual practices, as articulated in Chap. 2. Amok's silence and repression of his own sexual orientation is another source of angst that could very well be avoided if society were to recognize that love takes many forms. In breaking his long silence the protagonist acquires an alternative mode of living and understanding which leads to his ultimate peace in the text.

Amok's newfound stability in his renegotiation of identity is thus contingent upon a recognition that he can be who he wishes to be, without fear of others' recrimination. Miano's fiction allows for the creation of new spaces where masculine identities may be reshaped after trauma. Nonetheless, such comprehension and peace are not immediately available to women writers penning autobiographical narratives as their content is not fictitious. Coming to terms with acts and consequences in real life may not be as straightforward as writing fiction, and the burden of what is revealed remains on the shoulders of the women writers.

Navigating Non-dits: Poetics of Confession

The not-written leaves no trace, challenging our customary strategies of reading that presume presence, hereness, letters, and legibility; it remains decisively outside our critical grasp, irretrievable and unrecoverable. (Fisher 2017: x)

According to Fisher, the act of not writing is as critical as the act of writing itself insofar as what is not written provides a different perspective which remains outside of our grasp, precisely because it is left unsaid, or here, unwritten. For Djebar, the experience of writing about an aspect of her life she has never revealed before is cathartic. Acquiring liberty from under the yoke of patriarchy enables an interrogation of what silence has wrought upon her. While as Fisher says, the 'not-written' is crucial by its very absence which mocks us and always eschews us, the finally written takes on a different role in *Nulle part*.

In her analysis of Djebar's text, Gabriela Seccardini notes that 'autobiography, is in itself an act of rebellion and a break with a tradition that points to the primacy of the community over the individual' (2013: 120). She explains that: 'Novel and autobiography, in the Arab Islamic world, until a short time ago were considered taboo, practices to avoid and condemn as spaces where intimacy is laid bare' (2013: 120).[32] For the critic, writing about one's individual experiences undermines the spirit of community, the unanimity represented by the collective. In writing about themselves, and their feelings, writers risk disclosing too much of their own individuality, thus undermining the collective project of Islamic identity. If writing itself is taboo, the fact that a woman writes is doubly problematic as it calls into question the role of the woman as belonging to the domestic realm, as seen with Bourdieu elsewhere in this study. Revealing her intimate thoughts and feelings is tantamount to betraying her faith and her brethren.

According to Djebar herself in *Ces Voix*, 'Dès les premiers temps de l'islam, on a peu à peu expulsé les femmes de l'écriture comme pouvoir' (1999: 75–76). Being excluded from power implied that their voice was silenced by men whose authority was undermined by the words of women. I discussed the father as an empowering figure for Djebar earlier in this chapter, since he has enabled her to harness the power of writing. Nonetheless writing takes on different valences in Djebar's text. In a letter, Djebar expresses her desire to write as a legacy which will continue to exist after her death: 'Pourquoi écrire? J'écris contre la mort, j'écris contre l'oubli … J'écris dans l'espoir (dérisoire) de laisser une trace, une ombre, une griffure sur un sable mouvant, dans la poussière qui vole, dans le Sahara qui remonte' (in Chikhi 2006: 1). Thus, while Cixous writes so that the other who has died is resurrected within her imagination and the text that she creates, Djebar also writes to prevent her own absolute death and disappearance.

Nulle part takes the shape of a memoir of Fatima's father,[33] and her reminiscences of her relationship with him, but it is also to break the silence around an 'acte' (2007: 377). This 'acte', which she only mentions

---

[32] See also Mohammed Ali (2008), Mortimer (2013) and Rouabhia (2017) for other discussions of this text as autobiography or autofiction.

[33] See Murray (2009).

after more than three hundred pages of writing, takes courage to broach, and is what Peter Kuon calls a 'tabou' (2017: 139). Through allusions, she employs several deferral techniques to delay the revelation. She uses repetition and enumeration of adjectives in tricolon for emphasis: 'l' "acte" ... quel acte? L'acte fou, irraisonné, imprévisible' (2007: 377). She questions how she is able to live after this act, without mentioning it. Poetic imagery pervades her writing as she deploys the imagery of embers and obscurity devouring her: 'cette braise inentamée me dévorant en dedans, non plutôt cette obscurité tournoyante qui a persisté des décennies durant' (2007: 377). Revealing that this act, has 'certes causé du tort qu'à [elle]-même' serves only to whet the reader's appetite (2007: 378). This is followed by recourse to Greek, as a mode of distantiation from the act: '"*gnôti seauton*" ... Connais-toi toi-même' (2007: 378). As she builds up to the moment which has been silenced, she feels a form of disconnection and disarticulation as she sees herself from outside her body moments before the act (2007: 379). Her memory remains clear as she recalls minute details about the surroundings, the disfigurement of Tarik, the man she knows and loves as he shouts at her to find Mounira, her momentary rival in love, apologize to her and ensure that she comes back, after Fatima has chased her away. The narrator's refusal to bend to his whim, to his injunction to change her attitude towards her rival is seen as audacious and she perceives herself as a vulnerable creature in the face of the 'fauve qui montre ses crocs' (2007: 382).

Here masculinity is seen as domineering and acquires bestial traits, much akin to Raewyn Connell's hegemonic masculinity, which seeks to subjugate.[34] Tarik's overbearing masculinity is toxic and manipulative as the narrator, writing after many years, sees the man acting as the master of the woman: 'l'homme, disons le maître [...] ce mâle gonflé de quel illusoire pouvoir?' (2007: 382). The deployment of rhetorical questions emphasizes the surprise evoked by such behaviour. Indeed, Guendouzi sees Tarik as a 'massive and stifling presence' in the narrator's life (2017: 207). Yet, whilst Tarik displays the traits of a controlling patriarchal man seeking to impose his will on her 's'installant dans un rôle convenu, presque avec confort' (2007: 388), the narrator has only one recurrent thought: 'Si mon père l'apprend je me tue' (2007: 384). Since her meetings with Tarik, their kiss which she sees as the great 'péché' (2007: 390),

---

[34] See also Donaldson (1993) and Demetriou (2001).

the narrator is overwhelmed with guilt and shame, only assuaged by the fact that Tarik is seemingly a good man, who reads poetry in Arabic, and speaks to the language lover in her. His anger and transformation at her dismissing Mounira leads to her regretting her intimacy with him. This betrayal is compounded with the disloyalty felt towards her father, and especially her 'vœu de fidélité à [s]on père' (2007: 414).

The realization that she forsook her father for someone who wishes to control her leads to a form of momentary madness:[35] 'j'ai éclaté d'un rire de malade, saisie de honte pour lui, mais surtout d'un remords incommensurable contre moi-même' (2007: 389). The 'rire de malade' is followed by a frenetic run towards the sea.[36] The double betrayal of the father and of herself leads to an incipient implosion as she lies down on the rail tracks and attempts to commit suicide (2007: 396). The testimony of the train driver: 'elle s'est jetée ... c'est elle qui s'est jetée' (2007: 397), with his incredulous repetition of her actions, is evidence of the solidification of her resolve, which is exacerbated by the questioning of whether the driver would be there to save her 'la prochaine fois' (2007: 398). If Islamic patriarchy does not allow people to write about their individual experiences, then writing about a suicide attempt is more than reprehensible, as the following exclamatory sentence accentuates: 'Le suicide est interdit en islam!' (2007: 411). Daring to write is a derogation; having the audacity to kill oneself defies the edicts of the religion, and therefore, speaking about one's suicide attempt is also an impossibility: 'à partir de ce matin-là je me suis tue devant les miens' (2007: 399). As I read her words 'je me suis tue', I am struck by their proximity to 'je me suis tué(e)'. While her attempt to take her own life was ineffectual, her ensuing silence is also a means of killing a part of herself.

While the narrator's silence had centred around her clandestine meetings with Tarik before this act, now 'un nouveau et durable silence [l]'envahit' (2007: 399–400). The lexical field associated with madness is significant here as the suicide attempt is depicted as 'un acte de folie solitaire' (2007: 400) and 'ce délire qui [l]'avait saisi' (2007: 400). This 'délire' is akin to the madness which Cixous herself has described and which takes control over her as she writes.[37] That the narrator aligns her

---

[35] It is also to eschew such masculine control that Malika refuses to stay with Jamil, as I underscored with Mokeddem's text in Chap. 3.

[36] This is reminiscent of Cixous's *Le rire de la Méduse* (1972).

[37] See also Chessler's (2006) examination of women and madness.

behaviour to a form of madness relegates it to the inexplicable, what was not controlled on that occasion, and that which she cannot bear to address. Nonetheless, Fatima, writing decades later, is now prepared to probe her silence, and especially what this act reveals about her and what she has hidden from the world: 'désormais, si longtemps après, sur ce silence, je me force à réfléchir: combler, habiter ce blanc comme si une exigence me contraignait à scruter un visage muet—mon visage' (2007: 401). Silence is seen as 'un long enfermement' (2007: 401), a prison from which only time and the will to know herself can liberate her.

In the final segment of the text, entitled 'Le Silence ou les années-tombeaux', the narrator identifies the 'besoin soudain—quoique tardif—de m'expliquer à moi-même—moi ici personnage et auteur à la fois–, le sens d'un geste auto-meurtrier' (2007: 419). For her, it is necessary to comprehend the impetus leading to the decision to commit suicide; keeping it a secret is not conducive to sanity: 'je commence à comprendre que le plus grave fut mon silence—mon silence sur cette pulsion qui, malgré moi et en moi, se préparait' (2007: 414). In speaking of her act, she unburdens herself fully, which is intensified with the use of anaphora: 'Enfin le silence. Enfin toi seule et ta mémoire ouverte. Et tu te purifies par des mots de poussière et de braises' (2007: 441). The recognition that the fear, the impulse and the act were due to her feelings towards her father is cathartic, as is the act of writing about it. The new silence that welcomes her is the silence in her mind after she has delivered the words on paper and it is only now that she can be at peace.[38] According to Lisa Block de Behar:

> While linguistic observations have neglected the priority of language as an instrument of communication, diminishing the excluding validity of the utterance, of what is said, these observations have increased the value of what is not said: allusions, insinuations, ellipses, understatements, presuppositions. (1995: 165)

Uncovering Fatima's secret, her ambivalence towards her father, her sense of loyalty and betrayal are important to the reader. The fact that the narrator is finally at peace, and this harmony is also a form of silence, is quite telling insofar as it allows us to weigh the silences in the text in various

---

[38] It is from this perspective that de Medeiros (2012) calls this text 'writing as wounding and healing'.

ways. While keeping quiet can exhaust and burden, it can also involve an absence of mental anguish. Thus, as the narrator reveals her secret, she accomplishes the dangerous task of speaking about a taboo subject in her culture and her religion. The writer and the implied reader create a new relationship where not speaking become a means of acceding to another level of consciousness. The men who have caused grief and led—willingly or unwittingly—to the suicide attempt, are removed from the equation so that the woman writer can find herself and her reason for being.

Djebar's narrative thus prompts us to rethink what circumstances might lead women to take their own lives in a context where they are educated and creating their own paths in a conservative society. The role played by traditional masculinities in exacerbating the disarticulation and mental anguish experienced by such women is underlined here. Fatima's profound pain and anxiety at revealing her emotions and actions, even after a number of years, remains intense. Conversely, where grieving is not allowed as it is not considered to be culturally appropriate nor masculine, Thúy speaks of those whose lives and choices have been silenced by History and war.

The Silences of War and Men

Garder le silence, c'est ce que à notre insu nous voulons tous, écrivant.
—Blanchot, *L'Ecriture du désastre*

In his text, Maurice Blanchot speaks of the horrors of war and the inability to write about disasters. In claiming that 'quand écrire, ne pas écrire, c'est sans importance, alors l'écriture change—qu'elle ait lieu ou non; c'est l'écriture du désastre' (1980: 25), he calls into question the possibility of writing to make a difference in the face of life-changing circumstances such as war. Yet writing is also the only means of coming to terms with such situations as the writer grapples with modes of expressing reality. In a direct address to a putative writer, Blanchot exhorts: 'écris pour ne pas seulement détruire, pour ne pas seulement conserver, pour ne pas transmettre, écris sous l'attrait de l'impossible réel, cette part du désastre où sombre, sauve et intacte, toute réalité' (1980: 65). Examining Blanchot's concept of disaster writing as part of his thoughts on not writing, Fisher underlines the fact that 'our very capacity to make articulate the terms of

disaster withdraws into the unthinkable and the unrepresentable'
(2017: 115).

Writing about disaster is contradictory to an extent as war silences those
who have experienced it. Elaborating on this notion in an online article on
Blanchot, Eric Hoppenot asserts that:

> Le désastre ne se réduit pas à envisager l'événement comme cataclysme de
> l'Histoire, mais à faire de l'écriture elle-même un lieu où le désastre se mani-
> feste comme tel. Plus qu'une écriture de survivant, le désastre est le lieu
> d'énonciation du revenant. Langue fantomatique qui a incorporé la voix des
> disparus. Le désastre est l'écriture où s'enfouissent comme dans une crypte
> les cendres de ceux qui restent sans sépulture. Littérature testimoniale et
> testamentaire, testamentaire parce que testimoniale. (2014)

Thus, while writing cannot fully encompass the enormity of disaster, it can
become disaster itself by speaking of the silences and the incompleteness
of History. I contend that Thúy's *Ru* is a re-inscription of several silences
which are in turn ruptured in the text. *Ru* is the writer's début novel and
won the Prix du Gouverneur Général in Québec in 2010. Described as a
'lightly fictionalised' account of the writer's own life,[39] the text has been
translated into several languages. Written in the form of vignettes or
anecdotes,[40] using what Jenny James has called a form of 'bricolage'
(2016), it recounts the fall of Saigon in 1975 and the narrator's family's
struggle for survival. The principal narrator, Nguyen An Tinh, unveils a
deeply moving story of war, exile and traumatic childhood in Saigon, during the Communist invasion and the fall of Saigon in 1975.[41] She underlines the dire circumstances in the Malaysian refugee camps and the
horrifying journey towards freedom after the family flees the former capi-
tal. Enmeshed in the narrative of innocence in the days prior to war are the
tales of those whose losses have marked the narrator, and her own family's
stories.

According to Helen Buss, the form of the anecdote or vignette enables
Thúy to tap into a mode of expression which has long been part of human
society. Buss also underlines the fact that the word 'vignette' 'has a special
use in theories of psychology to describe involuntary memories. The short
anecdotal style of the book imitates the suddenness and quick movement

---

[39] Nurse (2018).
[40] See Sing (2016) and Buss (2018).
[41] For more on the Vietnam wars see Gilman (2006).

of involuntary memory, which can stem from traumatic experiences' (2018: 607). Of course, trauma is often part of refugee experiences such as that of the tens of thousands who escaped Vietnam by boat.[42] Often in Thúy's text, the present will give way to flashbacks of events that occurred either in the distant past (when the narrator was a child) or in a more recent past (when the narrator has become a mother). The inception of the book remains framed in the historic moment of the narrator's birth, the fall of Saigon and the disruption that it caused, leading to An Tinh and her family escaping by boat. Yet, as the narrator begins her narrative, she moves between those anecdotal accounts of her birth to her current predicament as the mother of a child who is autistic. His autism becomes the trigger for a series of other anecdotal recollections that build the bigger picture of refugee experiences both personal and collective.

'Mon fils Henri était emprisonné dans son monde [...] il est de ces enfants qui ne nous parlent pas, même s'ils ne sont ni sourds ni muets' writes Thúy's narrator (2010: 20). Henri is immured in silence since he is autistic. The author does not portray his autism as a form of disability but as a catalyst for rethinking silences and the ways in which they punctuate the narrator's life. Henri's unexplained silence permits the narrator to assess the different silences which have impacted her and those around her. From the beginning of the narration, the mother's despair at the fact that 'il ne m'appellera probablement jamais "maman" avec amour' is poignant (2010: 20). Her son's incapacity to express emotions is a source of deep anguish.[43] Her declaration—that 'je ne cesserai jamais de livrer combat contre l'autisme, même si d'avance je le sais invincible' reaffirms her intent to understand the causes of silence in her own life and, thus, to comprehend Henri's silence (2010: 21).

In her presentation on her work, 'There's no place like home: Migrant children in World cinema', Stephanie Hemelryk Donald stresses the fact that 'stories matter [...] stories give us clues to what else we are, who else we might possibly become'.[44] She asserts that 'stories explore what we are frightened of and what we want most'. Although she examines films, and world cinema in particular, Hemelryk Donald's work focuses on migrant journeys and trauma which parallel the texts examined in this section.

---

[42] I elaborate on this in my forthcoming book *Refugee Afterlives* (2022).

[43] See also my discussion of trauma and silence in this text (Kistnareddy 2020).

[44] The presentation is online on YouTube, see Hemelryk Donald (2014: n.p.). This was later reworked into her book *There's no place like* home (2018).

Thúy's narration begins with the narrator's birth but quickly shifts to the disruptive and traumatic experience of war: 'nous étions engourdis [...]. Nous étions paralysés' (2010: 16). The collective paralysis which is at stake here mirrors Henri's own inability to comprehend and speak in the way that the world expects him to. However, while Henri lives in his own mind and understands things in his own way, the children who lived through the traumatic experience of war could not comprehend the events surrounding them and the collapse of society as they knew it, as Thúy demonstrates.

Psychologist Laura Brown explains that trauma ranges from:

> catastrophic events that happen to people in socially dominant positions to "insidious trauma," [...] the traumatogenic effects of oppression that are not necessarily overtly violent or threatening to bodily well-being at the given moment but that do violence to the soul and spirit. (2008: 107)

In *Ru*, during the war in Vietnam, children are caught in crossfires, hastily bundled onto boats by their parents in an attempt to escape Communist camps, and often separated from their families. Many die during the journey to refugee camps or are victims of rape perpetrated by pirates who terrorize the people who are trying to survive on the boats. I argue that Thúy's narration is a means of bringing back to life '[l]es autres qui avaient coulé pendant la traversée, [et qui] n'avaient pas de nom', since '[i]ls sont morts anonymes' (2010: 33). While the Vietnam war is a well-known period of history,[45] the lives of those who were lost on a daily basis are not always spoken of. Their erasure is underlined by Thúy in this text and in bringing them to the forefront of the narrative, Thúy's narrator engages with a part of history which has been suppressed and which needs to be recollected. Nevertheless, she does so by grounding them in her own reality.

Thus, Thúy's narrator draws parallels between Henri's autism and her own life in the shadows as a child: 'Je parlais très peu, parfois pas du tout' (2010: 38). Later, the difficulties she experiences in understanding French when she eventually arrives in Granby, in Québec, as a refugee, are depicted as a bond she shares with Henri: 'j'étais comme mon fils Henri: je ne pouvais pas parler ni écouter, même si je n'étais ni sourde ni muette' (2010: 23). However, the impossibility of speech predates her arrival in Québec

---

[45] See Gilman (2006), Engel et al. (2014) and Opper (2020).

and plays a prominent role in her life both prior to and after the war. The child narrator lives in her cousin Sao Mai's shadow and suffers from acute shyness. Depicting herself as the opposite of Sao Mai, she highlights their difference through the lexical fields of light and darkness: 'son visage était du côté clair et le mien du côté de l'obscur, de l'ombre, du silence' (2010: 38). Silence remains the child narrator's way of coping with life and the demands of her mother that she learn to express herself. Here, her incapacity to speak is perceived as psychological.

According to Jeannette den Toonder, the narrator experiences a form of 'interior exile' during her childhood in Vietnam (2016: 41). For den Toonder, 'she erases herself through her silence' (2016: 41). Sao Mai's confidence overshadows the narrator so much that she loses her own sense of selfhood. Since Sao Mai's family does not leave Vietnam, the narrator gradually gains the confidence to speak when she arrives in an environment where friendships become more egalitarian. Thus, her first friend, Joanne is portrayed as an angel who helps her feel at home in Granby. Joanne takes her out and invites her into her family home 'sans qu'[elle] comprenne les paroles, ni sa conversation avec ses parents' (2010: 46). The genuine camaraderie displayed by Joanne empowers her to understand that it is feasible to have her own identity and her own likes and dislikes. Thúy's narrator highlights the debt of gratitude towards her first friend. Joanne demonstrates that friendships can be equal relationships whilst she was often mocked by Sao Mai.

Silence as affect is evident in Granby, where the refugees begin their new life with the help of the legions who provide them with food, shelter, clothes and other necessities. For Thúy's narrator, the absence of language, of the ability to adequately convey their gratitude is not detrimental to the close relationship they develop with the families who welcome them to their homes for lunch as primary schoolers: 'nous pouvions ni leur parler ni les écouter. Mais l'essentiel y était' (2010: 43).[46] Gestures, acts of kindness and body language convey what words fail to transmit to their hosts. In fact, the narrator even wonders: 'si les mots n'auraient pas entaché ces moments de grâce. Et si parfois ces sentiments ne sont pas mieux compris dans le silence' (2010: 44). The notion that feelings are sometimes best conveyed in keeping quiet is important in this text where words fail to express what refugees have endured, and where the son cannot express emotions. Equally, silence can also permit love to blossom as in the

---

[46] See Nguyen's examination of the text as 'refugee gratitude' (2013).

case of the couple who fall in love without speaking each other's language. Indeed, although 'leurs premiers moments furent sans paroles' (2010: 44), their protracted alliance and subsequent marriage attest to the durability of feelings even in the absence of language. The ability of feelings to transcend what can be said and what is uncommunicable is crucial here as the power of love to rise above linguistic barriers is celebrated in the text.

Similarly, Thúy creates a space where multiple voices and actors break the silences that are entwined in the fabric of the narrative. As such, there are quiet heroes and antiheroes who live in a moral continuum in her memory. The first instance of this equivocal moral aspect is the revelation that the narrator's father would have killed her and her brothers rather than allow them to be imprisoned: 'Mon père avait prévu, si notre famille était capturée par des communistes ou des pirates, de nous endormir pour toujours, comme la Belle au bois dormant, avec des pilules de cyanure' (2010: 18). The simile deployed linking her story to Sleeping Beauty adds to the poignancy of the situation as the child is aware of her father's intentions. Unlike Sleeping Beauty, there would, however, be no prince to awaken her. In the face of the certainty of death in that situation, the narrator questions her father's decision. Her meeting with Mr Vinh in Québec leads to her recognition that fathers have had to make extremely difficult decisions to protect their children during the war, since Mr Vinh 'espérait sauver un, peut-être deux de ses enfants en les lançant à la mer' (2010: 19). For Alexandra Kurmann and Tess Do, 'Monsieur Vinh in fact saves all five of his children by placing them in separate boats, an act that stands in contrast to his failure to safeguard the fatherland in the face of the communist invasion' (2018: 224). The notion that the children might be saved by drowning brings to bear the enormity of what the alternative might be for them. While the critics see it as a failure to protect them from the Communist invasion, it is difficult to single-handedly fight against a power which has defeated the USA and its allied forces in the Vietnam war. In both cases, fathers are depicted as preferring to end their children's lives themselves rather than see them suffer at the hands of others.[47] Here writing becomes testimonial, as delineated by Hoppenot. It enables us to

---

[47] A comparison can be drawn between the slaves who chose to kill themselves and their offspring rather than be captured by their former masters. For instance, Morrison's *Beloved* (1987) tells the story of Sethe, who kills her daughter as she fears her former slave master is about to recapture her. The subsequent haunting she experiences is a direct impact of her actions. Thúy herself draws comparisons between the slaves in the plantations and the women who work in the rice paddy fields in her text.

live through those decisions and their repercussions on the protagonists. It also creates the space for the refugee child to engage with such painful episodes of personal history and share it with a wider readership who might not understand the decisions that parents have made in harrowing situations. In focusing on these vulnerable fathers who have had to make such difficult judgments, Thúy permits a re-evaluation of masculinities and the burdens placed on them as heads of families.

Similarly, their enemies, the Communists, are nuanced as their backgrounds and stories are provided, allowing us to understand their position. For instance, Thúy's depiction of the arrival of the young inspector in her house and their subsequent need to share their family home with the enemy is accomplished with sensitivity and recognition that he is as much a victim of the disastrous situation as they are:

> Ce jeune inspecteur, il avait marché dans la jungle depuis l'âge de douze ans, pour aller libérer le sud du Vietnam des mains "poilues" des Américains. Il avait dormi dans les tunnels souterrains, passé des journées entières dans des étangs sous un nénuphar, vu les corps des camarades sacrifiés pour empêcher le glissement des canons, vécu des nuits de malaria. (2010: 58)

Recounting the days of adjusting to the presence of these strangers, the narrator focuses on the human aspects of the hostile occupation of Saigon. While the Communist police do impose upon them, they also become close, bonding through music, leading the narrator to comment that her father corrupts them. Through the use of rhetorical questions ('Qu'était-il advenu de lui?'(2010: 59), 'Que sont devenus ces soldats?' (2010: 62)), Thúy also interrogates the silences surrounding those other victims of war, including the Communist soldiers who lived with them and who, despite being their enemies, shared their lives. Thúy reinforces the fact that there are victims on both sides and that the silence of history dissimulates both their realities. In posing these questions, Thúy's narrator makes the reader wonder whether they survived or whether they too became casualties, as with the many Southern Vietnamese who perished during the war. From the countless fathers and sons who disappeared in Communist re-education camps (2010: 66), who died as martyrs and are remembered only by those they left behind, to the thousands who died in the war on both sides, Thúy's text unveils a part of history which is absent from history books.

Personal history is also at the forefront of the narrative as former heroes become antiheroes. For instance, her Uncle Two,[48] whom she idolizes as a child, denounces his own children prior to their escape to refugee camps. For the narrator there can only be two reasons for this betrayal of his own kin: 'leur père, mon oncle, leur roi, les avait dénoncés ... était-ce par peur de les perdre en mer ou par peur de représailles contre lui, en tant que père?' (2010: 98). In the accumulation of nouns outlining the roles uncle has played is an emphatic and undeniable sentiment of disappointment at his action. Her attempts at justifying his denunciation, through the questions she asks, read as a last effort to understand his motivations. Yet in the face of the other fathers who did their best to save their children, including her own father, her uncle is irredeemable. He is also set up as a contrast to Anh Phi, the boy-hero who assisted them in regaining the gold they threw out so the Communist police would not recover it prior to their escape (2010: 140). Anh Phi's own destitution and precarious position does not impede him from aiding the family in their escape, despite not being a family member, thereby further casting doubts on Uncle Two's choice.

The narrator compels us to weigh the actions undertaken by the men she meets within the context they are taken. Nonetheless, she recognizes that some men are more adaptable than others, as in her father's case:

> Mon père, lui, n'a pas eu à se réinventer. Il est de ceux qui ne vivent que dans l'instant, sans attachement au passé. Il savoure chaque moment de son présent comme s'il était toujours le meilleur et le seul, sans le comparer, sans le mesurer. (2010: 107)

The contrast between her father's status before the war and the menial labour he accomplishes in Québec is understated, even as the reader appreciates the fall from wealth to material precarity at stake:[49] 'C'est pourquoi il inspirait toujours le plus grand, le plus beau bonheur, qu'il fût sur les marches d'un hôtel avec une serpillère dans les mains, ou assis dans une limousine en réunion stratégique avec son ministre' (2010: 107). Her father's resilience is perceived as exemplary as he focuses on his children and their future, rather than the past. Nonetheless, the narrator is not privy to her father's anguish since he only smiles in front of his family and

---

[48] In Vietnamese families uncles and aunts are referred to by the order of their birth, beginning with the number two.

[49] See also Thai's (2012) examination of low-waged labour among Vietnamese male immigrants and its relationship to masculinity.

does not demonstrate his negative affect. For a generation of men who were taught to remain stoic as the heads of the family, he too silenced his own suffering, as many have done and continue to do, thereby leading to inner distress.

Likewise, other silent refugee men influence Thúy's narrator in different ways, for instance, Monsieur An, the autistic man whom she had thought 'muet pendant longtemps' (2010: 135). His ability to cry when he falls, and his unbridled emotions are a source of surprise to the narrator who repeats 'il pleurait. Il ne cessait de pleurer' (2010: 136), particularly when he had been laughing about his fall seconds earlier. Unlike her father, Monsieur An displays an inability to deal with a barrage of emotions. Despite his idiosyncrasies, Monsieur An's credentials are impressive: he was a 'juge, professeur, diplômé d'une université américaine, père et prisonnier' (2010: 136). The narrator reinforces his social standing prior to the war and his incarceration in a 'camp de rééducation' (2010: 137). Although the actual experiences within the confines of the camp are not revealed, the text implies that Monsieur An was fortunate enough to escape a senseless death unlike countless others due to a malfunctioning gun pointed at his head. The incident's impact is understated since the narrator cannot imagine the emotions going through the man's mind at that instant. Through these stories, the narrator inscribes the vulnerable masculine subjectivities at play during the war. The narrative is a reminder that it is the men who are sent to the camps, who are expected to fight in the war, regardless of whether they are able or disable. In so doing, Thúy underlines the repercussions of these experiences on men both physically and mentally. Writing about the horrors of such events restores agency to those who were denied their own individuality in the camps. In breaking such silences and writing about such disasters, as outlined by Blanchot, Thúy does not allow their stories to be muted.

Moreover, the narrator's interactions with the male survivors of camps serve different purposes. While 'Monsieur An [lui] a appris les nuances, Monsieur Minh [lui] a donné le désir d'écrire' (2010: 138). Monsieur Minh is a graduate of the Sorbonne, who studied literature. While his psychopathologies are underscored through his obsession with one way streets, particular addresses and people to avoid, his passion for writing becomes a way out of suffering in the camps:

> Il avait écrit plusieurs livres pendant ses années au camp de rééducation, et
> ce, toujours sur le seul et unique bout de papier qu'il possédait, une page

par-dessus l'autre, un chapitre après l'autre, une histoire sans suite. Sans l'écriture, il n'aurait pas entendu aujourd'hui la neige fondre, les feuilles pousser et les nuages se promener. Il n'aurait pas non plus vu le cul-de-sac d'une pensée, la dépouille d'une étoile ou la texture d'une virgule. (2010: 139)

The poetic depiction of Mr Minh's experience of writing in the camp, his obsessive compulsive behaviour resulting from the trauma of his camp days, mirror his own way of perceiving life and his new space in Québec. As with Blanchot's notion of disaster writing as a means of making sense of overwhelming events, Monsieur Minh's writing is itself as form of *tabula rasa*, the constant re-inscription enabling a renewed understanding of the beauty of life and nature in spite of the reality of war. Thúy's portrayal of Monsieur Minh and his behaviour demonstrates a tenderness towards men and their own ways of dealing with stress and trauma. While she unveils their truths and their experiences, she does not judge nor invite readers to judge these men as they learn to navigate their new lives while carrying the burden of their past.

Towards the end of the narration, Thúy's narrator claims: 'mes enfants m'ont donné le pouvoir [...] de comprendre les mots non prononcés' (2010: 175). In understanding Henri's silences, in reliving her own memories of silences that have burdened her or shown her that life is also a set of choices to be made, Thúy's narrator allows the text to take the form of a revelation. Her unveiling of events and disruption of silences lead to an interrogation of who is allowed to speak and whose lives (cannot) remain forgotten by the silences of history.

Understanding Masculinities

This chapter began with the notion that 'speaking with' the other allows for a reconfiguration of identities insofar as women writers give the space to men in their narratives to speak and share their feelings as they negotiate life in a host society. Each section has given us pause to think through what it means to be an immigrant woman writer writing about men or writing as men. In reading and eventually writing down their personal histories, both Fatima and Salie bear witness to men who were forward thinking and, in many ways, feminists, insofar as they promulgated equality and pushed them beyond the limits of the possible. Djebar and Diome demonstrate that men are not always the source of pressure and violence for women.[50] In writing about Tahar and Ndétare, their relationships with the daughter or daughter figure, they re-inscribe love and vulnerability into masculinities which otherwise are seen to oppress and imprison women in those particular societies.

Diome and Chen foreground the importance of equal communication between men and women in their texts, or 'speaking with', as outlined by Spivak. This can take place in the form of the author herself inhabiting her different characters through the letters the protagonists write to each other, using the epistolary form to convey first-person feelings and vulnerabilities. The male protagonist in Chen's text is the one whose suffering is central as his loss is unsurmountable. In writing as a man and writing to a man, Chen allows both protagonists to play out the transformation which migration brings to both sides, without judging Yuan for the decisions he makes. His punishment, so to speak, comes in the form of his fiancée leaving him and breaking his heart. His suffering is sensitively handled without judgement and in presenting such a careful treatment of changing masculinities, Chen permits a crucial shift in the readers' perspective of masculine identities.

Similarly, while the reader might be frustrated with Madické, the narrator goes to the extreme of threatening us to manage our feelings towards him. For, in not knowing the culture, the stoicism imposed on boys, the pressure to be 'manly' and to expect adoration from women, we have no right to judge Madické. As with Chen, Diome's protagonist reverses the hierarchy between men and women, but equalizes their relationship by giving Madické a choice. The importance of conversation, and in particular, the telephone conversation, in allowing for this egalitarian and understanding between the siblings to occur is foregrounded here. Love is seen in subtlety rather than overt measures.

Lastly, Miano, Djebar and Thúy all foreground the theme of silence and its impact on individuals. If for Amok, silence is protection against shame and guilt and the need to maintain the familial status quo, for Djebar, silence preserves her relationship with her father. Both are afraid of the community's gaze, as delineated by Cheung. In placing Amok in the position of victim, Miano underlines the fact that boys are equally subjugated by patriarchy. Djebar nuances this notion by alternatively shifting the

---

[50] Rice (2012) uses the notion of the witness stand to discuss the autobiographical narratives of Cixous, Djebar and so on, drawing on Derrida's understanding of the concept of testimony in *Demeure: Maurice Blanchot* (1998).

blame onto herself, drawing on the form of the confession, her lover and ultimately the patriarchal Islamic community's values which cause Tarik's transformation, and which deny her the possibility of breaking this silence until decades after her suicide attempt. Similarly, silence plays a crucial role in Thúy's narratives as the Vietnamese propensity to speak through actions or inaction allows Thúy to explore a range of masculinities and their ambivalent roles during the war and in its aftermath. In breaking silences, using the form of anecdotes, and foregrounding men in their complex humanity, Thúy enables us to understand a community which is destroyed by war and needs to rebuild itself anew.

In the works I explore, whether through writing texts, writing letters or having conversations, immigrant women writers create a fruitful space in which women and men can speak equally and in which powerful exchanges can occur. In also including the silences that endure, and breaking these silences, they foster a compelling environment to reshape masculinities. Ultimately all the women writers whose texts I examine in this chapter demonstrate a sensitive approach to masculinities as mutable. In this mutability, their vulnerability is accentuated. Such masculinities, rather than being problematic, testify to the complex variables at stake for women writers in understanding men and their sense of identity as they attempt to negotiate life at the crossroads of cultures and values.

REFERENCES

PRIMARY TEXTS

Chen, Ying. 1993. *Les lettres chinoises*. Paris: Babel.
———. 2014. *La Lenteur des montagnes*. Montréal: Boréal.
Diome, Fatou. 2003. *Le Ventre de l'Atlantique*. Paris: Anne Carrière.
Djebar, Assia. 1985. *L'Amour la fantasia*. Paris: Poche.
———. 1999. *Ces voix qui m'assiègent*. Paris: Albin Michel.
———. 2003. *La disparition de la langue française*. Paris: Poche.
———. 2007. *Nulle part dans la maison de mon père*. Paris: Babel.
Miano, Leonora. 2017a. *Marianne et le garçon noir*. Paris: Pauvert.
———. 2017b. *Crépuscule du tourment 2: Héritage*. Paris: Grasset.
Thúy, Kim. 2010. *Ru*. Montréal: Liana Levi.

SECONDARY MATERIAL

Achin, Catherine. 2016. The French Parity Law: A Successful Gender Equality Measure or a "Conservative Revolution"? In *Gender and Family in European Economic Policy: Developments in the New Millennium*, ed. D. Auth, J. Hergenhan, and B. Holland-Cunz, 179–197. Cham: Palgrave Macmillan.

Adams, Carol, and Josephine Donovan. 1995. *Animals and Women: Feminist Theoretical Explorations*. Durham: Duke University Press.

Ahmed, Sara. 2006. *Queer Phenomenology*. Durham: Duke University Press.

———. 2017. *Living a Feminist Life*. Durham: Duke University Press.

Barthes, Roland. 1977. *Fragments d'un discours amoureux*. Paris: Seuil.

Bates, Séverine. 2019. Un miroir aux alouettes? Des matchs de foot télévisés à la migration africaine en Europe: *Le Ventre de l'Atlantique* de Fatou Diome. *Nouvelles Études Francophones* 34 (2): 138–153.

Bello, Abdulmajeed Hassan. 2018. Islam and Cultural Changes in Africa. *Arts and Humanities Open Access Journal* 2 (1): 25–32.

Bernier, Sylvie. 1999. Ying Chen: S'exiler de soi. *Francofonia: Studi e ricerche sulle letterature di lingua francese* 37: 115–131.

Bhabha, Homi. 1994. *The Location of Culture*. London: Routledge.

Blanchot, Maurice. 1980. *L'Ecriture du désastre*. Paris: Gallimard.

Block de Behar, Lisa. 1995. *A Rhetoric of Silence and Other Selected Writings*. Berlin: Mouton de Gruyter.

Braidotti, Rosi. 1994. *Nomadic Subjects: Embodiment and Sexual Difference in Feminist Theory*. New York: Columbia University Press.

Brisley, Lucy. 2016. "Auto-analyse" and the Ethics of Memory in Assia Djebar's *Nulle part dans la maison de mon père* (2007). *Nottingham French Studies* 55 (3): 328–342.

Brown, Laura S. 2008. *Cultural Competence in Trauma Therapy: Beyond the Flashback*. Washington: American Psychological Association.

Brown, Marissa. 2017. Writing Hybridized Identities in Fatou Diome's *Le ventre de l'Atlantique*. *Odysseys/Odyssées*, 198–209.

Buekens, Sarah. 2019. Marianne et l'identité française. *Fixxion* 19: 156–161.

Buss, Helen. 2018. Kim Thúy's Ru and the Art of the Anecdote. *a/b:Auto/Biography Studies* 33: 605–612.

Calle-Gruber, Mireille. 2001. *Assia Djebar: La résistance de l'écriture*. Paris: Maisonneuve & Larose.

Campbell, Elizabeth. 1995. Re-Visions, Re-Flections, Re-Creations: Epistolarity in Novels by Contemporary Women. *Twentieth Century Literature* 41 (3): 332–348.

Chessler, Phyllis. 2006. *Women and Madness*. Basingstoke: Palgrave Macmillan.

Cheung, King-Kok. 2018. *Articulate Silences: Hisaye Yamamoto, Maxine Hong Kingston and Joy Kogewa*. Ithaca: Cornell University Press.

Chikhi, Beida. 2006. *Assia Djebar: Histoires et fantaisies*. Paris: PUPS.

Connell, Lisa. 2013. Movement, Education, and Empowerment in Assia Djebar's *L'Amour la Fantasia* and *Nulle part dans la maison de mon père*. *Journal of Contemporary Women's Writing* 79 (3): 291–308.

Cox, Lizzie. 2017. *Girl Talk: Growing Up*. London: QED Publishing.

De Medeiros, Ana. 2012. Writing as Wounding and Healing in Djebar's *Nulle part dans la maison de mon père*. *International Journal of Francophone Studies* 15 (2): 277–296.

Demetriou, Demetrakis. 2001. Connell's Concept of Hegemonic Masculinity: A Critique. *Theory & Society* 30 (3): 337–361.

Den Toonder, Jeannette. 2016. Migrant Writing in Quebec: Female Mobility in Kim Thúy's *Ru*. In *Exiles, Travellers and Vagabonds: Rethinking Mobility in Francophone Women's Writing*, ed. Kate Averis and Isabelle Hollis-Touré, 33–53. Cardiff: University of Wales Press.

Derrida, Jacques. 1998. *Demeure: Maurice Blanchot*. Paris: Galilée.

Diouf, Mbaye. 2010. Ecriture de l'immigration et traversée des discours dans Le Ventre de l'Atlantique de Fatou Diome. *Francofonia* 58: 55–66.

Doka, Kenneth J., and Terry Martin. 1998. Masculine Responses to Loss: Clinical Implications. *Journal of Family Studies* 4 (2): 143–158.

Donaldson, Michael. 1993. What is Hegemonic Masculinity? *Theory & Society* 22: 643–657.

Dunayer, Joan. 1995. Sexist Words: Speciest Roots. In *Animals and Women: Feminist Theoretical Explorations*, ed. Carol Adams and Josephine Donovan, 11–32. Durham: Duke University Press.

El Guabli, Brahim. 2019. Writing Against Mourning: Assia Djebar's *Francographie*. *Cambridge Journal of Postcolonial Inquiry* 6 (1): 14–29.

Engel, Jeffrey, Mark Atwood Lawrence et al. 2014. *America in the World: A History in Documents from the War with Spain to the War on Terror*. Princeton: Princeton University Press.

Eubanks, Abdeleid. 2015. Fatou Diome's *Le Ventre de l'Atlantique*: From Island Girl to Atlantic Woman. *FLS* 40: 122–134.

Fanon, Frantz. [1961] 2002. *Les Damnés de la terre*. Paris: La Découverte.

Fisher, Thomas. 2017. *Writing Not Writing: Poetry, Crisis, and Responsibility*. Iowa City: Iowa University Press.

Gagiano, Annie. 2018. Frantz Fanon: toward a revolutionary humanism. *Journal of Postcolonial Writing* 54 (1): 130–131.

Genette, Gérard. 1980. *Narrative Discourse: An Essay in Method*. Translated by Jane Lewin. Ithaca: Cornell University Press.

Gilman, Owen. 2006. Vietnam War. In Wilson *The New Encyclopedia of Southern Culture: Volume 3*, ed. Charles Regan. Chapel Hill: University of North Carolina Press.

Gilroy, Paul. 2018. Foreword. In *hooks, bell and Stuart Hall, Uncut Funk: A Contemplative dialogue*, ix–xiii. London & New York: Routledge.

Goldblatt, Cullen. 2019. Setting Readers at Sea: Fatou Diome's *Ventre de l'Atlantique*. *Tydskrif vir Letterkunde* 56 (1): 89–101.

Grewe, Andrea. 2016. Ni animal domestique ni animal sauvage': Les representations du masculin dans l'oeuvre de Yasmina Reza. In *Le Masculin dans les oeuvres d'écrivaines françaises*, ed. Françoise Rétif, 223–248. Paris: Classiques Garnier.

Gronemann, Claudia. 2010. Fictions de la relation père/fille: La dé/construction des mythes paternels dans Assia Djebar: *Nulle part dans la maison de mon père*. In *Repenser le Maghreb: Hybridations, Métissages, Diasporisation*, ed. Alfonso de Toro, Khalid Zekri, Réda Bensemaia, and Hafid Gafaiti, 233–247. Paris: L'Harmattan.

Guendouzi, Amar. 2017. Assia Djebar and the legacy of French colonialism in Algeria: mimicry and subalternity in Nowhere in my Father's House. *The Journal of North African Studies* 22 (2): 205–219.

Harrison, Nicholas. 2009. Assia Djebar: Fiction as a Way of "Thinking". In *Postcolonial Thought in the French Speaking World*, ed. Charles Forsdick and David Murphy, 65–76. Liverpool: Liverpool University Press.

Hemelryk Donald, Stephanie. 2014. There's No Place like Home: Migrant Children and World Cinema. Accessed 10 December 2019. https://www.youtube.com/watch?v=ckx-g33u9mE.

———. 2018. *There is No Place like Home: The Migrant Child in World Cinema*. London: I.B. Tauris.

Hiddleston, Jane. 2017. *Writing after Postcolonialism: Francophone North African Literature in Transition*. London: Bloomsbury Academic.

hooks, bell, and S. Hall. 2018. *Uncut Funk: A Contemplative Dialogue*. London and New York: Routledge.

Hoppenot, Eric. 2014. L'écriture du désastre. Accessed 11 May 2019. https://journals.openedition.org/temoigner/1263.

Hutcheson-Lovett, Isadora. 2018. Football and Migrant Crises: Fatou Diome's *Le Ventre de l'Atlantique*'. Accessed 20 January 2020. http://mulosige.soas.ac.uk/football-migrant-crises/.

James, Jenny. 2016. Frayed Ends: Refugee Memory and Bricolage Practices of Repair in Dionne Brand's *What We All Long For* and Kim Thúy's *Ru*. *MELUS* 41 (3): 42–67.

Jensen, Katharine Ann. 1995. *Writing Love: Letters, Women, and the Novel in France, (1605–1776)*. Carbondale, IL: Southern Illinois University Press.

Juncker, Clara. 1988. Writing (With) Cixous. *College English* 50 (4): 424.

Kačkutė, Egle. 2018. Mothering across Languages and Cultures in Ying Chen's Letters to Her Children. *Women: A Cultural Review* 29 (1): 59–74.

———. 2019. Relational Aspects of Migrant Mothering in Nathacha *Appanah's La Noce d'Anna* and Ying Chen's *La Lenteur des montagnes*. *Crossways Journal* 3 (1): 1–13.

Kane, Cheikh Amidou. 1961. *L'Aventure ambigue*. Paris: Julliard.

Kimmel, Michael. 1987. *Changing Men: New Directions in Research on Men and Masculinity*. Newbury Park, CA: Sage.

Kinouani, Guilaine. 2021. *Living While Black: The Essential Guide to Overcoming Trauma*. London: Ebury Press.

Kistnareddy, Ashwiny O. 2015. *Locating Hybridity: Creole, Identities and Body Politics in the Novels of Ananda Devi*. Bern: Peter Lang.

———. 2020. Dire l'indicible: Children, Trauma and Post-war Silences in Kim Thúy's *Ru* and Grace Ly's *Jeune fille modèle*. *International Journal of Francophone Studies* 23 (1&2): 99–117.

———. 2022, forthcoming. *Refugee Afterlives*. Liverpool: Liverpool University Press.

Kotowska, Katarzyna. 2017. La (re)construction du père chez Annie Ernaux (*La Place*) et Assia Djebar (*Nulle part dans la maison de mon père*). *Romanica Silesiana* 12: 205–216.

Kuon, Peter. 2017. Écrire 'sous le poids des tabous': *L'amour, la fantasia* et *Nulle part dans la maison de mon père* d'Assia Djebar. In *L'inconvenance*, ed. Béatrice Laville, Élisabeth Magne, and Florence Plet, 139–149. Pessar: Presses Universitaires de Bordeaux.

Kurmann, Alexanda, and Tess Do. 2018. Children on the Boat: The Recuperative Work of Postmemory in Short Fiction of the Vietnamese Diaspora. *Comparative Literature* 70 (2): 218–234.

Lazali, Karima. 2018. *Le Trauma colonial: Une enquête sur les effets psychiques et politiques contemporains de l'oppression coloniale en Algérie*. Paris: La Découverte.

Lionnet, Françoise. 1998. Questions de méthodes: Itinéraires ourlés de l'autoportrait et de la critique. In *Postcolonialisme & Autobiographie*, ed. Alfred Hornung and Ernstpeter Ruhe, 5–20. Amsterdam: Rodopi.

Maggio, Jay. 2007. "Can the Subaltern Be Heard?": Political Theory, Translation, Representation, and Gayatri Chakravorty Spivak. *Alternatives: Global, Local, Political* 32 (4): 419–443.

Marteau, Delphine J. 2013. *L'Expatriation au féminin*. Paris: L'Harmattan.

Matu, Florina. 2015. Oser la métamorphose, arracher le voile dans *Nulle part dans la maison de mon père*. *Etudes Francophones* 28 (1–2): 73–86.

Mehra, Nishta J. 2017. *Sara Ahmed: Notes from a Feminist Killjoy*. Accessed 12 August 2019. https://www.guernicamag.com/sara-ahmed-the-personal-is-institutional/.

Miraglia, Anne Marie. 2016. Cet amour de père, gardien du gynécée. *Études françaises* 52 (1): 35–53.

Mohammed Ali, Dar. 2008. Autobiographie et auto-analyse dans *Nulle part dans la maison de mon père* d'Assia Djebar. *Limag* [online, http unavailable, Google search gives a link to the PDF directly].

Morrison, Toni. 1987. *Beloved*. London: Pan/Chatto and Windus.

Mortimer, Mildred. 2013. Writing the Personal: The Evolution of Assia Djebar's Autobiographical Project *from L'amour, la fantasia* to *Nulle part dans la maison de mon père*. *Journal of Women's History* 25 (2): 111–129.

Murray, Jenny. 2009. "La mort inachevée": Writing, Remembering and Forgetting in Assia Djebar's *Le Blanc de l'Algérie, La disparition de la langue française* and *Nulle part dans la maison de mon père*. In *Anamnesia: Private and Public Memory in Modern French Culture*, ed. Peter Collier, 71–83. Oxford: Peter Lang.

Naficy, Hamid. 2001. *An Accented Cinema: Exilic and Diasporic Film-making*. Princeton: Princeton University Press.

Nguyen, Vinh. 2013. Refugee Gratitude: Narrating Success and Intersubjectivity in Kim Thúy's *Ru*. *Canadian Literature* 219: 17–36.

Nurse, Donna Bailey. 2018. Kim Thúy and the Burdens of the Past. Accessed 20 January 2020. https://reviewcanada.ca/magazine/2018/04/kim-thuy-and-the-burdens-of-the-past/.

Oore, Irène. 2004a. Les lettres chinoises de Ying Chen: le mobile et l'immobile. *Studies in Canadian Literature/Études En littérature Canadienne* 29 (1). Accessed 19 March 2019. https://journals.lib.unb.ca/index.php/SCL/article/view/12762.

———. 2004b. *Les lettres chinoises* de Ying Chen: un roman épistolaire. *Voix plurielles* 1 (1): 2–7.

Opper, Marc. 2020. *People's Wars in China, Malaya and Vietnam*. Ann Arbor: University of Michigan Press.

Parker, Gabrielle. 2016. Ying Chen: Biography. Accessed 25 April 2019. https://modernlanguages.sas.ac.uk/researchcentres/centre-study-contemporary-womens-writing/languages/french/yingchen.

Rétif, Françoise. 2016. *Le Masculin dans les oeuvres d'écrivaines françaises*. Paris: Classiques Garnier.

Rice, Alison. 2012. *Polygraphies: Francophone Women Writing Algeria*. Charlottesville: University of Virginia Press.

Rilke, Rainer M. 1934, rep. 1993. *Letters to a Young Poet*. London: W.W. Norton & Company.

Rodgers, Julie. 2019. The Emergent Posthuman Landscape in Ying Chen's *La rive est loin*. *Quebec Studies* 68 (1): 101–120.

Rouabhia, Sarra. 2017. L'autofiction entre deux mondes: Le cas de *Nulle part dans la maison de mon père* d'Assia Djebar. *Cahiers d'Études sur la Représentation* 2: 53–65.

Sartre, Jean-Paul. 1948. *Qu'est-ce que la littérature?* Paris: Gallimard.

Sawadogo, Boukary. 2016. Cross-Atlantic Mobility: The Experience of Two Shores in Fatou Diome's *Le Ventre de l'Atlantique*. In *Exiles, Travellers and Vagabonds*, ed. Kate Averis and Isabelle Hollis Touré, 153–168. Cardiff: University of Wales Press.

Seccardini, Gabriela. 2013. Exile in the French Language: Assia Djebar and Malika Mokeddem. In *Languages of Exile*, ed. Axel Englund and Anders Olsson, 119–140. Oxford: Peter Lang.

Sharpe, Christina. 2016. *In the Wake: Blackness and Being*. Durham: Duke University Press.

Silvester, Rosalind. 2020. *Ying Chen's Fiction: An Aesthetics of Non-Belonging*. Oxford: Legenda.

Sing, Pamela. 2016. Kim Thúy: A Gentle Power. In *Ten Canadian riters in Context*, ed. Marie Carrière, 179–193. Alberta: University of Alberta Press.

Sivert, Eileen. 2001. Ying Chen's *Les Lettres chinoises* and Epistolary Identity. In *Doing Gender: Franco-Canadian Women Writers of the 1990s*, ed. Paula Ruth Gilbert and Roseanne Dufault, 217–234. Madison and London: Fairleigh Dickinson University Press.

Spacks, Patricia Meyer. 2006. *Novel Beginnings: Experiments in Eighteenth-Century English Fiction*. New Haven: Yale University Press.

Spivak, Gayatri. 1988. Can the Subaltern Speak?. In Patrick Williams and Laura Chrisman (Eds), *Colonial Discourse and Postcolonial Theory: A Reader*, 66–111. New York: Harvester Wheatsheaf.

Thai, Huang Cam. 2012. Low-wage Vietnamese Immigrants, Social Class and Masculinity in the Homeland. In *Men and Masculinities in Southeast Asia*, ed. M. Ford and L. Lyons, 56–67. Oxford: Routledge.

Thomas, Dominic. 2006. African Youth in the Global Economy: Fatou Diome's *Le ventre de l'Atlantique*. *Comparative Studies of South Asia, Africa and the Middle East* 26 (2): 243–259.

———. 2007. *Black France: Colonialism, Immigration and Transnationalism*. Bloomington: Indiana University Press.

Unter Ecker, Marjolaine. 2019. Léonora Miano et Virginie Despentes: Lectures croisées des masculinités "désaxées". *Études littéraires africaines* 47: 131–146.

Viveros Vigoya, Mara. 2018. *Les couleurs de la masculinité: Expériences intersectionnelles et pratiques de pouvoir en Amérique latine*. Paris: La Découverte.

Wilson, Emma. 2019. Telephone Calls in Gianfranco Rosi's *Fire at Sea* (Fuocoammare, 2016). *Alphaville* 17: 12–23.

Yun, Chul-Ki. 2007. Aspects spatio-temporels de la migration dans *Les Lettres Chinoises* de Ying Chen. *Etudes québécoises: Revue internationale de l'ACEQ* 1: 137–141.

———. 2013. Migrance, sensorium et translocalité chez Ying Chen et Kim Thúy. *International Journal of Francophone Studies* 16 (3): 281–301.

Zadi, Samuel. 2010. La "Solidarité africaine" dans *Le Ventre de l'Atlantique* de Fatou Diome. *Nouvelles Études Francophones* 25 (1): 171–188.

CHAPTER 5

Conclusion: Towards a Poetics of Migrant Masculinities

Globalization changes masculinities—reshaping the arena in which national and local masculinities are articulated and transforming the shape of men's lives. Globalization disrupts and reconfigures traditional, neo-colonial, or other national, regional, or local, economic, political, and cultural arrangements. In so doing, globalization transforms both domestic and public patriarchy.
—Kimmel, *Misframing Men*

Michael Kimmel's observation testifies to the importance of finding new modes of rethinking masculinities in the diaspora. When I first embarked upon this project, the first questions that were posed to me were: 'Why women writing about men? Why not focus on men talking about themselves?' My answer was simple: 'We are always reading about men and their accounts of their circumstances. I want to examine what it means to be an immigrant woman writing about men and how she understands and perceives the changes in her male counterparts as she gains a new voice and status in the migratory space'. In this study, I have attempted to highlight the different ways in which immigrant women have employed their newfound voices and positions in their host societies in France and

A. O. Kistnareddy, *Migrant Masculinities in Women's Writing*, Global Masculinities, https://doi.org/10.1007/978-3-030-82576-8_5

233

Canada,[1] to depict the concomitant transformations which can be observed in masculinities. My purpose has not been to identify and reconstruct these masculinities through the texts I have explored, nor has it been to reify the concept of masculinities itself. Rather, I have sought to demonstrate that migration allows for a reshaping of masculinities, and underlines their mutability. The capacity for change, in turn, permits an understanding that men and their suffering too must be treated sensitively. My contribution to the conversations around masculinities that has been growing in the past two decades has been through close readings of immigrant women who write about men through autobiographical narratives, short stories, essays, an epistolary novel, a novel written in anecdotal form, leading to what I would call a form of poetics of masculinities.

In her introduction to *Postcolonial Poetics*, Elleke Boehmer articulates the notion of literature as 'a mode through which we understand the world and ourselves in it' (2018: 2). Processes of writing and of reading influence the ways in which the world is perceived. Considering what, in her case 'postcolonial writing' can '*do*' (2018: 3), she encourages us to think of the 'literary object' itself as a source of understanding and rethinking concepts. Calling for a form of 'score for reading' (2018: 7), Boehmer promulgates a return to the text as a means of inferring meaning and the textual connotations across time, space and migratory processes. Adopting her understanding of 'reading as doing', I charted the ways in which the 'truth' of the 'conditions from which the writing springs' 'to gather in the intensified knowledge or awareness that it (the writing) offers' regarding 'inhabiting a new nation, or a periphery, or an outsider condition' (2018: 10). In this book, it is more precisely the poetics of migrant masculinities that I have offered. A way of reading immigrant

---

[1] Of course, this does not imply that other migratory spaces are necessarily different. Paul Gilroy, for instance, in *Postcolonial Melancholia* (2005), reminds us that in the UK, too, immigrants from former colonies have experienced racism and major interrogations of their belonging, even as the UK society itself grapples with its colonial past. Similarly, in the case of the USA, Silva E. Bonilla has examined the lingering effects of racism and racial inequality in the USA in *Racism Without Racists: Color-blind Racism and the Persistence of Racial Inequality in the United States* (2017). As I demonstrated in my discussion of George Floyd's death and the subsequent ramifications nationally and internationally, racism and discrimination remain pervasive. Nonetheless, my study does bring in some nuances as I look at a range of geographical spaces from a Francophone world and address wider issues simultaneously.

women's writing as a means of understanding masculinities through the experiences that migration have generated.

In the three main chapters of this study, I have mapped the ways masculinities are affected by migration, through questions of hospitality, through an interrogation of belonging and community and via the experiences of the immigrant women who seek to foster a space for dialogue and egalitarian perceptions in their writing. In the first instance, this analysis has drawn on Derrida (1997) to articulate the notion of 'inhospitality' as host countries, such as France, can create a hostile environment for Black male (im)migrants, or as in the case of Canada, welcome immigrants and yet might not be the home which was hoped for. The impossibility of regrounding oneself, as outlined by Ahmed, or constructing a new home, while one yearns for a past home, was foregrounded as one of the reasons behind male migrants' inability to thrive in France and Canada. I examined the linguistic inhospitality foregrounded by each text, while offering close readings of the texts as they articulate the dislocation undergone by the protagonists. Every text examined offers different possibilities for their protagonists to come to terms with their new sense of identity in their new societies.

Nonetheless, as underscored in the second chapter, traditional communities might reject such incumbent (im)migrant masculinities as they threaten the fabric of a society which prides itself in its (white) history, as I explore with Miano's short story, her novels and her essays, juxtaposing fiction and non-fiction, while highlighting the message that the writer delivers through both modes of writing. Nancy provides a different means of conceptualizing community through the notion of 'interruption of myth', even as race and skin colour inhibit the negotiation of a French identity for Afropeans in the first section. With Malika's autobiographical emancipatory dissident voice in Mokeddem's text, I underline the possibility of subjectivation while allowing for a recognition of the nefarious impacts of patriarchal communities on men and women. Similarly, with Devi's autobiographical narrative, this study has demonstrated that the edicts of patriarchy and toxic hegemonic masculinities impede the mutual respect and love of men and women, mothers, and sons. In her attempts at negotiating her own affected fragile identity, which I read through a discussion of the genre of autofiction, and through her intertextual practices, Devi creates an ungendered community of writing, as outlined by Nancy, which allows her to be who she wants to be and whose demands are purely aesthetic.

I end this book on the notion that women writing men, in the texts I examine, present interesting paradigms insofar as the mode of 'speaking with', whether it be with a father (figure) instructing a daughter (figure), a trio of lovers and friends writing letters to each other, a mother writing to her son, or a sister's telephone conversations with her brother back home, permit an egalitarian exchange. Through a discussion of the forms of the confession with Djebar, the epistolary with Chen, the telephone conversation with Diome, anecdotes with Thúy, and the return narrative with Miano, I have demonstrated the range of ways in which immigrant women writers reconsider masculinities in their texts. In writing men, writing to men, and, at times, writing as men, women writers see different angles and perceptions which were heretofore inaccessible to them. This new positioning and conceptualization of masculinities reshape the literary landscape where men traditionally wrote about women without the opposite movement occurring. Thus, women writing men enables a decentring of literary subjectivities as well as a recognition that women, too, can grasp the many subtleties at play in the world and translate it into their texts. Writing from a new mode of seeing and speaking permits a subversion of accepted notions of masculinities and femininities, leading to a plurality of possibilities for writing as an ungendered space and a home for those who remain homeless in their (im)migrant condition.

As the book draws to a close, the final segment foregrounds the silences which pervade the narratives, with difficult subjects such as sexual abuse, suicide and war. Traumatic events alter relationships between men and women in ways that are incommensurable and, at times, unfathomable. The sexual abuse experienced by Amok at the hands of an older female relative brings to bear horrific lack of respect and absence of acknowledgement of the male child as a human being by a motherly figure. Similarly, the shock of Fatima's admission of having attempted suicide unveils not only the pressures on women to conform, but also the capacity of men to eschew the fetters of patriarchal society. Her inability to convey her feelings to her father also attests to the limits of openness between fathers and daughters in traditional societies. Finally, the silences of the men in Thúy's narrative call into question the impossibility of transcending war when trauma persists. The narrative space permits an opening up of what has been silenced during such atrocities. My discussion of Blanchot's disaster writing invites an interrogation of what it means to write in the aftermath of such life-changing events.

Indubitably a single section of a chapter will not suffice to explore the intricacies of silence and the act of writing in the wake of wars. It is from this perspective that this project has led to my thinking through what the next step would be after the discussions that this study has elicited. In endeavouring to comprehend the ways that silence plays a prominent role in the texts Thúy writes, I wonder who writes, and who is allowed to write about such experiences. If, as in the case of Thúy herself, war narratives are written by those who have been through such radically traumatic experiences in their childhood, then it would be interesting and important to understand why and how they translate such experiences to the space of writing. The potential of such narratives to shift host societies' understanding of refugee children and adults in their lived experience is immense. From this viewpoint, my next projects, *Refugee Afterlives* and *Refuge* are intended as ways of thinking through the place of children in war and force displacement, and especially how to envisage them as active participants in shifting dominant discourses around refugees. Moreover, another possible avenue for research would be the different modes of writing and interpreting gender. Since the texts I shortlisted mostly deal with heteronormative masculinities, a potential project for scholars could be to examine Queer migrant masculinities hailing from former colonies and written by women. Such an analysis might throw up other aspects of masculinities and gender that my own study has not.

In writing this analysis I have sought to draw attention to an aspect of (im)migration which is not often examined nor evaluated. I wanted to bring visibility to the many women across different geographical terrains who write about (im)migration and the impact on men even as women, too, acquire a different position in the new society. In so doing, I have underscored the potential possibilities for looking at migration as giving rise to new paradigms, and especially, for understanding immigrant women's writing as a means of changing perceptions, of discrediting accepted ideas. Ultimately, I sign off with the hope that as new scholarship acquires traction and emergent perspectives are examined through the work of immigrant writers, further literary studies foregrounding the putative exchanges between host societies and diasporic voices will permit new re-conceptualizations of gender and affect. Immigrant women writers create characters who defy accepted notions of virility and gender norms in order to generate and map new alternative visions of masculinities. The wider implications of this are significant as my reading permits a rethinking of the opportunities afforded by not only comparing masculinities from a wide range of geographical spaces, but also understanding that one does not need to vilify one gender to reclaim the other. The recuperation of masculinities as vulnerable hinges upon the recognition that masculinities also alter, and thus, there should be no need to pit one gender against the other. Immigrant women writers debunk myths of masculinities in the texts and as they engage with the problematic nature of phallocentric masculinities back 'home' and in the new spaces of creation provided by their writing and their imaginary, we can only hope that readers in France, Canada, Vietnam, Africa, China and indeed, across the world, in a form of Glissantian 'Tout-Monde' (1997), will re-examine their own notions of masculinities and eventually challenge them.

References

Boehmer, Elleke. 2018. *Postcolonial Poetics: 21st Century Critical Readings*. Basingstoke: Palgrave Macmillan.

Bonilla, Silva E. 2017. *Racism Without Racists: Color-blind Racism and the Persistence of Racial Inequality in the United States*. Lanham: Rowman & Littlefield.

Derrida, Jacques. 1997. *De L'hospitalité*. Paris: Calmann-Lévy.

Gilroy, Paul. 2005. *Postcolonial Melancholia*. New York: Columbia University Press.

Glissant, Edouard. 1997. *Traité du Tout Monde*. Paris: Gallimard.

Kimmel, Michael. 2010. *Misframing Men: The Politics of Contemporary Masculinities*. New Brunswick, NJ: Rutgers University Press.

INDEX[1]

---

[1] Note: Page numbers followed by 'n' refer to notes.

CPSIA information can be obtained
at www.ICGtesting.com
Printed in the USA
LVHW081339240922
729069LV00011BA/330